HONOUR TO THE AIRBORNE

PART 1 1939–48

First published by Elmdon Publishing
Elmdon Books, 117 Valley Road, Solihull,
West Midlands, B92 9AX. Great Britain.
1985

© 1985 & 1993 David Buxton
Second Revised Edition published by Liverpool Medal Company
42 Bury Business Centre, Kay Street,
Bury, Lancashire, BL9 6BU.

ISBN 1 899422 00 5

HONOUR TO THE AIRBORNE

PART 1 1939-48

FROM LITTLE ACORNS . . .

Contents

(i) Foreword

I decided to write this book, when I experienced some difficulty to find some information concerning a medal to the Parachute Regiment, one of the Airborne units I had decided to collect to. Unfortunately the Airborne Forces Museum could not help, since they do not hold nominal rolls of their personnel nor lists of awards won. This too, was apparent with several other museums that I had approached for similar information.

So, in January, 1979, I decided to start on the groundwork of this reference, thinking that it would be fairly simple to obtain information, and that I would soon be finished. Of course, as I delved deeper into the project, I soon found out how wrong I had been. From May I began a concerted effort, and by late 1980 had amassed a wealth of information. I then thought that I would put in the book a history and list of units that were connected within the Airborne ideal. I had come across units of the Arms & Services, which supported the Airborne Infantry soldiers, whilst reading various works on the Airborne warfare by established authors and experts.

This led to another facet of collecting the insignia of the Airborne Forces, and also to more correspondence with ex-members of the Airborne, and their respective museums.

In 1981, on showing a portion of my research work to some Airborne friends at a Services' Club, they suggested that I might try and get the work published. I took their advice, but found it difficult to achieve, and interest waned. Then in 1984, I decided to redo various portions, and try and add more awards, since several members of the Birmingham Medal Society to which I belong, expressed an interest in my work. Thus I decided to produce it myself, and hope that the fruits of my research have been worthwhile. I apologise to any who may have been left out and would welcome any additional items, be it new names or Battalion information against existing ones, which could be added, if a reprint is feasible in the future.

I hope that it will be of benefit to those with an Airborne interest, whether as ex-members; serving members; or collectors, and that the gallantry of all those mentioned is now on a permanent record.

Dave Buxton, May, 1985.

(ii) Foreword to the 2nd Edition

Following the success of the limited edition of Part 1 of "Honour To The Airborne" in 1985, it was put to me following the 50th Anniversary of the Parachute Regiment in 1990, that I should think of a reprint.

It had crossed my mind that I should like to produce a worthwhile new edition, but at the time finances would not permit this. However, I began to try and locate some of the information on new awards, which had been missed in the first edition, as well as new information on insignia variants.

Then in the middle of 1993, I received a letter from the Airborne Forces Museum stating that they had been asked to compile a list of awards to the Airborne and had thought this a daunting task until they came across my book, and had I any additional information! Also at the same time I had the opportunity for this to be republished.

Here then is the new edition, with this time, a narrative of the events and additional information, which I hope will be of benefit to those with an Airborne interest.

Dave Buxton, 1993.

(iii) Abbreviations

1. **RANKS**

A.	–	Acting Rank
A.D.M.S.	–	Assistant Director, Medical Services
Brig.	–	Brigadier
C.	–	Commander, Army Units
Capt.	–	Captain
C.F.	–	Chaplain To The Forces
C.O.	–	Commanding Officer
Col.	–	Colonel
Col. Sgt.	–	Colour Sergeant
Cpl.	–	Corporal
C.Q.M.S.	–	Company Qr-Mr Sgt
C.S.M.	–	Company Sgt-Major (WOII)
Genl.	–	General
G.S.O.I.	–	General Staff Officer 1
L/Cpl.	–	Lance Corporal
L/Sgt.	–	Lance Sargeant
Lieut.	–	Lieutenant (also Lt.)
Lt-Col.	–	Lieutenant-Colonel
O.C.	–	Officer Commanding
Pte.	–	Private
Qr-Mr.	–	Quarter-Master
R.M.O.	–	Regimental Medical Officer
R.S.M.	–	Regimental Sgt-Major (WOI)
2/I.C.	–	Second In Command
Sgt.	–	Sergeant
S/Sgt.	–	Staff Sergeant
T.	–	Temporary Rank
Tpr.	–	Trooper
W.O.	–	Warrant Officer I (one) or II (two)

2. **REGIMENTS or CORPS**

A.A.C.	–	Army Air Corps
Abn.	–	Airborne
A/Lng.	–	Air-Landing
A.F.A.	–	A/Lng. Field Ambulance
A/Tk.	–	Anti-Tank Artillery
Bde.	–	Brigade
Bn.	–	Battalion
Coy.	–	Company

Div.	– Division
D.L.I.	– Durham Light Infantry
G.G.	– Grenadier Guards
H.L.I.	– Highland Light Infantry
Lt. Bty.	– Light Battery, R. Arty.
Lt. Regt.	– Light Regiment, R. Arty.
Para.	– Parachute
P.F.A.	– Parachute Field Ambulance
R.A., R. Arty.	– Royal Regiment of Artillery
R.E., R. Engrs.	– Corps of Royal Engineers
R.E.M.E.	– Royal Electrical & Mechanical Engrs.
R. Sigs.	– Royal Corps of Signals
Recce.	– Reconnaissance
R.A.Ch.D.	– Royal Army Chaplains Department
R.A.M.C.	– Royal Army Medical Corps
R.A.O.C.	– Royal Army Ordnance Corps
Regt.	– Regiment
Sqn.	– Squadron
Y.&L.	– York & Lancaster Regiment

3   **OTHERS**

K.I.A.	– Killed In Action
P.O.W.	– Prisoner of War
Surg. Tm.	– Surgical Team
W.D.	– Wounded

4   **AWARDS**

The majority of awards listed, have the recipient's unit as Army Air Corps, so I have left this out, and substituted where possible the Brigade/Battalion/Company where known e.g:

Major (temp) Roy Smith   123456   "B" 3rd Bn.

So we know that Major Smith served with "B" Company, 3rd Battalion.

Infantry and Corps units' awards are self explanatory.

With regard to the British Orders, I have not used their full titles, which I list below in the order of priority of wearing:

V.C.	– Victoria Cross
G.C.	– George Cross

The Most Honourable Order Of The Bath (Military Division)

G.C.B.	–	Knight Grand Cross
K.C.B.	–	Knight Commander
C.B.	–	Companion

The Most Excellent Order Of The British Empire (Military Division)

G.B.E.	–	Knight Grand Cross (before D.S.O.)
K.B.E.	–	Knight Commander (before D.S.O.)
C.B.E.	–	Commander (before D.S.O.)
O.B.E.	–	Officer (after D.S.O., before M.C.)
M.B.E.	–	Member (after D.S.O., before M.C.)
B.E.M.	–	British Empire Medal
D.S.O.	–	Distinguished Service Order (Officers only)
M.C.	–	Military Cross (Officers and W.O.'s only)
D.F.C.	–	Distinguished Flying Cross (Officers and W.O.'s only)
A.F.C.	–	Air Force Cross (Officers and W.O.'s only)
D.C.M.	–	Distinguished Conduct Medal (N.C.O.'s & men)
C.G.M.	–	Conspicuous Gallantry Medal (N.C.O.'s & men)
G.M.	–	George Medal (Officers & men)
M.M.	–	Military Medal (N.C.O.'s & men)
D.F.M.	–	Distinguished Flying Medal (N.C.O.'s & men)
A.F.M.	–	Air Force Medal (N.C.O.'s & men)

M.I.D.   –   Mentioned In Despatches—single bronze Oak Leaf worn on ribbon of War Medal, only one is worn, no matter how many times the recipient has been mentioned. For Java and Palestine, the emblem is worn on the General Service Medal ribbon.

Foreign Awards may only be worn by recipients, when the Monarch's permission has been given, and they are worn at the end of all British medals, in order of date of award.

Dates below award and against name are the London Gazette dates, and not the date of the action for which the award was given.

5   SERVICE MEDALS

Worn in order of service, quite a number of men had pre-World War Two service, and these medals were worn first, behind any Awards. For W.W.2 service un-named medals were awarded, these are also worn behind Awards, and any pre-war service medals. Long Service and Good Conduct medals are worn after service medals.

1939-45 Star
Africa Star (with 1st or 8th Army bars, if qualified)
Italy Star
France & Germany Star
Defence Medal (if qualified)
War Medal

There were also stars given for Atlantic; Burma; Pacific; and Air Crew Europe service.

For the campaigns in Java and Sumatra, a bar was granted "S. E. ASIA 1945-46" and for Palestine, "PALESTINE 1945-48". These were worn on the **General Service Medal 3rd Issue, King George VI**, in the majority of cases, the medal did not swivel. The medal is worn after the War Medal, unless pre-war bars have been awarded, in which case it is worn before the 1939-45 Star.

The G.S.M. is named with number, rank, name and unit.

Most G.S.M.'s to the 6th Airborne Division, are named "A.A.C."— "Army Air Corps", with support and infantry units bearing their own disignations. Some maybe found named "PARA", "PARA R.", "PARA REGT", these are late claimed medals— "PARA" being the current style of naming.

Some soldiers who were pre-war Territorial soldiers also qualified for the **Efficiency Medal bar** "TERRITORIAL", and it too is named with number, rank, name and unit. Members of the Parachute Regiment have usually "PARA", but I have seen on the 1st type King George VI, i.e. motto ends "INDIAE IMP"—"PARACHUTE R, A.A.C." In 1948, the Army Air Corps ceased, and the Regiment became Infantry of the Line, thus the 2nd Type King George VI "FID DEF" has only "PARA".

Those who qualified for the **Army Long Service & Good Conduct Medals** had their medals named "A.A.C." (pre 1948) or "PARA" (post 1948).

The qualifying period for the **T.E.M.** is twelve years, but war service counts double; for the **L.S.G.C.** it was eighteen years, but in the late 1970s it changed to fifteen years.

PART I 1939-45

FROM LITTLE ACORNS . . .

(iv) Introduction

Today, the mention of Airborne Divisions still stir the imagination. Nearly all the world's countries nowadays have an Airborne/Special Forces element of some kind.

Ancient Mythology; 16th Century artists; and some scholars first brought about the idea of armies from the air. Following the use of the balloon in civilian areas, some military minds thought of its use as a weapon. In the Franco-Prussian War of 1870-71, artists created scenes of aerial conflict using balloon supported winged infantry. With the advent of the aeroplane, parachutes started to be used, but early pilots thought their reliability suspect.

However, their tactical use in later years, added a new dimension to military thinking. Though in the 1920's, this was not the case, and to land troops from the skies was unheard of. The British and Americans had airlifted troops onto battlefields during exercises, and in 1923 in Kurdistan, the 1/11th Sikhs were airlifted into action.

It was to be the Russians that led the way of the parachute being used in military affairs, as parachuting in the 1930's was a national sport. They were the first country to have organised parachute troops, though their use in the Second World War was limited, in that they generally fought in a ground role, except for the partisan-aid jumps behind the German lines. In these, small combat groups were dropped, whereas the British and Germans often jumped at Divisional strength.

The Italians, closely followed by the Germans, soon perfected the use of the silken canopy, and had formed Parachute Battalions, and later whole Divisions. The Germans were also using glider-borne troops, and in 1940 after crushing Poland, German paratroops landed in Norway, whilst gliders captured the Belgian fort of Eben-Emael.

Winston Churchill, the British Prime Minister, stated the need for a Corps of Paratroops and work began. By mid-1942, after a couple of successful raids, and much training, the 1st Parachute Brigade consisting of three Parachute Battalions had been formed shortly to be followed by a 2nd. It was then that a return to Mythology was made, when all ranks received the Divisional flash, designed by Major Edward Seago, and destined to be worn by all Airborne soldiers—Bellerophon mounted on the winged horse Pegasus, who in Greek Mythology, swooped down from the heavens, and with his spear, killed the Chimaera—a three-headed fire breathing monster, (presumably representing Germany, Italy and Japan).

Chapter 1

THE EARLY BEGINNINGS 1940-42

DUE to the excellent results of the German use of airborne troops in both glider and parachute roles, the British finally decided that it was time to get organised, and form their own Airborne Arm.

Major J. F. Rock, Royal Engineers was detailed by the War Office to take charge of forming such a force, in June 1940. An Airborne School was set up at Ringway Airport, Manchester and became known as the Central Landing School—its purpose—to investigate all aspects of Airborne organisation from training the troops in parachuting and glider elements; to how all types of equipment could be carried. Major Rock had been working with Sqn. Leader L. A. Strange, D.S.O., M.C., D.F.C., who was responsible for the aerial side of the training. Initially, Ringway had to make do with six Whitley bombers for parachute training, but later in 1941, recruits were trained from balloons, which is still the practice today.

The first recruits were from No. 2 (Army) Commando: another war-raised unit. The Director of Combined Operations—Admiral Sir Roger Keyes had agreed in the need for an airborne commando unit, and the first training jumps were in July, 1940. Instruction at that time was done mainly by a mixture of R.A.F. Instructors from Henlow—where pilots were taught emergency baling out techniques, and Army instructors from the Army Physical Training Corps. All being under the command of Flt-Lt. (afterwards Wing Commander) J. C. Kilkenny, O.B.E. However, by the end of 1941, the parachute training had been passed to the R.A.F. as a whole, and the Central Landing Establishment, (the School's title after August, 1940), had become known as the No.1 P.T.S. (Parachute Training School.)

In November, 1940, the five hundred or so recruits, now qualified

1

parachutists, were formed into the **11th Special Air Service Battalion**, (no connection with the S.A.S. formed in the following year in the Middle East). The Battalion was to have a Parachute Wing and a Glider Wing, the Commanding Officer was Lt-Colonel C. I. A. Jackson of the Royal Tank Regiment.

Towards the end of 1940, an uneasiness had crept into the ranks, due to the non-activity, apart from exercises for the hierarchy of the Staff and Government officials. Men began to request that they be "R.T.U."—Returned To Unit—an expression usually reserved for the unsuitable or troublesome soldier. Then rumours, via the Orderly Room started, to the effect that an operation was being planned. In January, 1941, the Battalion was paraded before the Commanding Officer, who explained that this was indeed true, and called for volunteers for a dangerous operation behind the lines, although the arrangements for the removal of survivors could not be guaranteed. Every Officer and Other Rank took a pace forward.

The operation was code-named "COLOSSUS" and its object—to destroy a main aqueduct that carried the water supply for many of the larger towns in the district of Campania in Southern Italy. The aqueduct also supplied Taranto and Brindisi, and the raid, afterwards, took the name of the stream for its title—The TRAGINO AQUEDUCT RAID.

The force of 38 men, known as "X" Troop for the operation, assembled in Malta on 8th February, 1941, and on the 10th February, they were carried to Italy in six Whitley bombers, with two additional bombers, who were to bomb the railway yards at Foggia as a diversion. An aerial reconnaissance the previous day had shown that there were two, and not one, aqueducts, one larger than the other—the group decided to go for the larger one.

In the full moon, the first Whitley arrived over the D.Z., among those in the party—Lieutenant A. J. Deane-Drummond, Royal Corps of Signals, it was twelve minutes late. Following; the four Whitleys, which carried the covering party under the command of Captain C. G. Lea, Lancashire Fusiliers, and some of the engineers. Casualties during the drop were light, amounting to several sprains and bruises. However, the group became short of arms and explosives, due to two of the aircraft failing, through technical faults, to drop their supply containers. A sixth Whitley that carried the main demolition party, with the senior Royal Engineers Officer, Captain G. F. K. Daly, lost its way and dropped them in the next valley, two miles from their objective.

2

In the absence of the senior engineer officer, 2nd Lieutenant A. Paterson, R.E. assumed command of the demolition, and sufficient explosives were found to destroy a main Aqueduct pier. It had been found to be composed of reinforced concrete, and not brick, as had been originally thought. Also they blew up a bridge over the nearby River Ginestra—a tributary of the Tragino. By 3am the following morning, an effective breach had been made and the group split up into three parties to attempt to make the rendezvous with HM Submarine "Triumph" waiting in the mouth of the River Sele. Unknown to them, however, the submarine had not sailed, as one of the bombers sent to bomb Foggia, had made a forced landing on the same beach, where the parachutists were to be picked up.

All three parties, plus Captain Daly's party were all eventually captured. One of the interpreters—an Italian called Fortunato Picchi, was shot as a traitor by the Fascists. They were first sent to Naples, and then to Sulmona P.O.W. Camp.

After two escape attempts had been thwarted, Lieutenant Deane-Drummond finally escaped to Switzerland in June 1942 from the P.O.W. Camp he had been sent to near Florence. From Switzerland he travelled to Marseilles via the French Resistance Movement, and arrived in England in July, 1942. He was the only member of the force to get back and was awarded the M.C. for his exploits. Other awards to stem from the raid, which in itself was a success, was the award of the D.S.O. to the Commanding Officer of "X" Troop—Major T. A. G. Pritchard, who was also Mentioned In Despatches. Also a Military Medal award to L/Cpl. H. Boulter for persistent escape attempts following capture at Tragino, which culminated in a successful attempt in 1944.

It was to be another year before another raid, which was to become famous in its own right was contemplated.

In October, 1941, Lord Louis Mountbatten, G.C.V.O., D.S.O., A.D.C. succeeded Sir Roger Keyes as Director of Combined Operations.

The previous month, the 11th S.A.S. Bn. had been renamed the **1st Parachute Battalion** under the command of Lt-Colonel E. E. Down, who had taken command of the 11th Bn. in the June. It was also in September, 1941, that the **1st Parachute Brigade** was formed, under the command of Brigadier R. N. Gale, O.B.E., M.C. and was to consist of three parachute battalions:

1st Parachute Bn.—Lt-Colonel E. E. Down
2nd Parachute Bn.—Lt-Colonel E. W. C. Flavell, M.C.

3

3rd Parachute Bn.—Lt-Colonel G. W. Lathbury

At that time the 4th Para. Bn. was also forming, under the command of Lt-Colonel M. R. J. Hope-Thompson, M.C., M.B.E. and was destined to be the first battalion of the new 2nd Parachute Brigade, which formed in August, 1942.

Also, in October, 1941, Brigadier F. A. M. Browning, D.S.O., Grenadier Guard was appointed a Major-General "Commander Paratroops and Airborne Troops". Everything seemed to happen at once: orders for a Division to be raised; the formation of an Air-Landing Brigade of glider-borne troops; and the formation of a Regiment of Glider Pilots to fly them—all encompassed in the new ARMY AIR CORPS formed on 21st December, 1941.

Glider Forces

Now a look at another aspect of the airborne to be used for the first time by British in war—the Glider elements.

In 1940, the HOTSPUR Glider was the first British glider, designed and built by General Aircraft Ltd., soon to be superseded by the HORSA Glider, though it was in these that initial training and experimental glider-towing was carried out. It was never used offensively, but over 1,000 were produced.

The HORSA Glider was designed by Air-Speed Ltd. and the Royal Aircraft Establishment, and could carry 29 men, as compared with the Hotspur's 8; or a jeep and 6 Pdr. Anti-Tank gun and crew. It was to be used in every major operation by British, as well as American airborne forces.

The HAMILCAR Glider was the largest glider ever built in Britain, and carried a TETRARCH Light Tank, or a Bren-Gun carrier. It was designed by General Aircraft Ltd. and brought into service in 1943, and used in Europe during 1944-45.

The first R.A.F. station to be used for glider borne operations was Thame, Buckinghamshire, under Sqn-Leader Hervey, with the Army personnel under Major J. Lauder, Royal Corps of Signals, and Major R. P. Cooper, Royal Artillery. In late 1941, volunteers were called for the **Glider Pilot Regiment**, and the 1st Battalion was formed in December 1941 under command of Lt-Colonel Rock—the man, who did so much in the formation of the Parachute Forces. His second-in-command was Major G. J. S. Chatterton, Queen's Regiment, who had served in the R.A.F. in the 1930's, but was discharged through an aeroplane crash, and then served in the Army—B.E.F. in France in 1940. There was still a shade of animosity between the ranks of the R.A.F. and the Army, but through training side by side, a Combined Operational spirit came through. The Regiment retired to a base camp at Tilshead on Salisbury Plain, and the R.A.F. also set up several training schools for various airborne tasks.

In January, 1942, **No. 38 Wing** was formed at R.A.F. Netheravon, under the command of Wing Commander Sir Nigel Norman. It was to co-ordinate the work of the R.A.F. and Army units. Under its control were 296 (Glider Exercise) and 297 (Parachute Exercise) Squadrons. This Wing later in 1943 became a Group, with ten Squadrons responsible for the conveying of glider-borne troops.

A second battalion of the G.P.R. had been formed in 1942, under command of now Lt-Colonel Chatterton, though when Lt-Colonel Rock was killed in a glider crash, he assumed command of the **1st Battalion, GPR.** Major Iain Murray therefore assumed command of the **2nd Battalion,G.P.R.**

As previously stated, October, 1941 saw several events in the forma-tion of the airborne forces. On 10th October, 1941, the 31st Independent Brigade Group, which had returned from India in the summer, was selected to form the **1st Air-Landing Brigade** under the command of Brigadier G. F. Hopkinson, O.B.E., M.C., (who replaced Brigadier H. E. F. Smythe).

The Brigade consisted of the following:
    1st Bn., the Border Regiment
    2nd Bn., the South Staffordshire Regiment
    2nd Bn., the Oxford & Bucks Light Infantry
    1st Bn., the Royal Ulster Rifles
plus its support elements from the Arms and Services.

Bruneval

By 1941, British scientists knew that the Germans had perfected a form of radar, and set up stations along the French coast. In November, 1941 a photograph was being examined of a "Freya" radar station at Bruneval on the northern coast of France, when the scientist noticed an unknown object near the cliff edge. Another low-level reconnaissance flight was organised, and flown by Flt. Lt. (later Sqn.Ldr.) Tony Hill, D.S.O., D.F.C. & Bar, and the results showed a new radar dish and aerial type of arrangement—the "Wurzburg" system. Following this discovery, the Director of Combined Operations—Lord Mountbatten proposed that parachute troops be used to capture the equipment. On January 21st, 1942, the Chiefs of Staff agreed and plans were put forward.

The code-name for this operation was "BITING" and with its success was to give the Parachute Regiment its first Battle Honour.

It was decided that "C" Company, 2nd Parachute Battalion, under the command of Major J. D. Frost, Cameronians, should be the assaulting force. They were to have with them a Radar expert from the R.A.F.— Flight-Sergeant G. W. H. Cox, who spent several weeks on an extensive parachute course. Also with the party, would be seven engineers from the 9th Field Company, (Airborne), R.E. under the command of Lt. D. Vernon.

Finally after much training and cancellations due to weather, the force of 119 men flew out on February 27th, 1942. They were transported in twelve Whitley bombers of No. 51 Squadron, under the command of Wing Commander P. C. Pickard, D.S.O., D.F.C. Soon they were over their objective recognising all the fine points, that had been evident in the training model, (which can be seen at the Airborne Forces' Museum at Aldershot—the Depot of the Parachute Regiment).

There were to be three groups that comprised the raiding force— "DRAKE" —which would drop first, consisted of fifty men, split into two combat groups: one—"JELLICOE" under Lt. Peter Young was to assault the radar station "HENRY", and the sappers and Flt. Sgt. Cox were to dismantle the equipment. The other—"HARDY" under the officer commanding the force—Major John Frost would attack the villa "LONE HOUSE".

"NELSON"—under Lt. Euan Charteris plus forty men were to go down the slope of the cliffs, and secure the beach for the naval landing craft to collect them at the end of the operation.

"RODNEY"—under Lt. John Timothy, plus thirty men were to cover the inland against any German reinforcements from "LA PRESBYTERE" an orchard and farm, and from the village of BRUNEVAL.

The drop only suffered one setback, in that most of "NELSON" and its commander was dropped some two miles from their objective.

With surprise on their side, the DRAKE'S two combat groups successfully assaulted the villa and the radar station, with only two casualties. The dismantling party had got down to work, with bullets flying about them, and removed most of the radar system, more, they later found, than the scientists could have hoped for.

Heavy firing was now coming from the beach defences, as well as

6

from the surrounding area, and Captain John Ross, the second-in-command reported that the beach had not been taken. The reason was that the "NELSON" party were fighting their way around the outskirts of Bruneval, having been dropped in the wrong place. However, they attacked, shouting Scottish war cries, at the same time as Major Frost mounted his attack on the pillboxes and machine-gun posts, and fought their way down to the beach.

The Navy force under Commander F. N. Cook, R.A.N. was late, due to avoiding a German sea patrol of three ships, but shortly after the appointed Very Light signal—as wireless contact could not be made, the six Landing Craft came into view. They were put under an intense fire from the cliff positions, but the ramps came down, and the parachutists and the precious equipment were put on board, under covering fire from a small contingent from the South Wales Borderers and the Royal Fusiliers.

Of the raiding force of 119, two were killed; six were missing—later captured; six wounded; and two German prisoners from the radar station were brought back to England.

It is also interesting to note that the Royal Army Medical Corps Airborne elements took part in their first action, as part of the Seaborne force—a section of the 181st (Airborne) Field Ambulance under the command of Captain A. S. Baker, and comprised 20 N.C.O's and men.

On the 15th May, 1942 members of the airborne and seaborne forces received decorations "in recognition of gallant and distinguished services in successful Combined Operations against the enemy at Bruneval.

Developments To The End Of 1942

In April, 1942, Hardwick Hall near Chesterfield, Derbyshire, became the Depot of the Airborne Forces, and was officially approved as such in December.

In May, 1942 prior to an inspection, by HM King George VI and Queen Elizabeth, of the 1st Parachute Brigade, the emblem designed by Major Edward Seago of Southern Command was being worn by all ranks—the Pegasus badge, but it was to be another year before the beret badge was authorised for wear on the maroon beret.

June, 1942 was to see Brigadier Gale appointed to the War Office to head the Air Directorate, which was in the throes of being established. In his place as O.C. 1st Para. Bde. was Brigadier E. W. C. Flavell, who was to command it, throughout its first campaign in North Africa.

In August, 1942, an order came from the War Office stating that all Parachute Infantry units would belong to a single entity—the **PARA-CHUTE REGIMENT**, which finally appeared in the Army List, under the Army Air Corps.

Also the same month, the **2nd Parachute Brigade** was formed under the command of Brigadier E. E. Down (ex C.O. 1st Para. Bn.) and consisted of:

4th (Wessex) Para. Bn.—Lt-Col. M. R. J. Hope-Thompson, M.C., M.B.E.

5th (Scottish) Para. Bn.—Lt-Col. A. Dunlop

6th (Welch) Para. Bn.—Lt-Col. C. H. V. Pritchard

With America in the war, the two countries formed a close alliance in the exchange of ideas and lending of equipment. The Americans in early 1942 let the British airborne forces use their Douglas C-47 or more commonly known as the "Dakota" aircraft for the dropping of parachutists. These fine aircraft were to be used in all theatres of war, and parachutists found their exits far easier via the side door, than through a hole in the floor as with previous British aircraft.

Soon the day dawned for yet another airborne raid, this time a glider raid was planned. The objective the Norsk Hydro plant at VERMORK in Norway, two miles West of Rjukan, and sixty miles from Oslo. It was here, from intelligence reports, that the Germans were making heavy water—an ingredient in the making of an atomic bomb.

For this task, 34 soldiers were hand-picked from the two Airborne Engineer Companies:

9th Field Company (Airborne), R.E.—Lt. A. C. Allen, R.E.

261st Field Park Coy. (Airborne), R.E.—Lt. D. A. Methuen, R.E.

The operation was code-named "FRESHMAN" and on November 19th, 1942 two Halifax aircraft towing two gliders set off independently towards their target. Only one aircraft was to return, it had released its glider, which had crashed killing 8 of the 17 men; 5 were captured and after interrogation by the Gestapo were shot on January, 18th, 1943; the 4 that were injured were poisoned by a Gestapo doctor. Of the second towplane, it crashed into a mountain after releasing the glider, which also crashed, killing 3 and the rest were shot by the Gestapo, within several hours of capture, due to a directive issued by Hitler. The plant was later destroyed by Norwegian saboteurs. Although the raid had been a failure, it had seen the use of yet another new technical breakthrough: the use of the "Rebecca-Eureka" radio location device. Although on this occasion it had failed to be of assistance, in later combat drops, it proved to be fairly successful, when used by the Pathfinder elements of both Airborne Divisions.

In November, 1942 the British and Americans turned their efforts to North Africa in an attempt to rid that theatre of Rommel and his Afrika Korps, and landed an Anglo-American force in Algeria.

Part of this force, and to be used initially in a ground role, was the 1st PARACHUTE BRIGADE.

Awards for the TRAGINO AQUEDUCT RAID 10.2.41

Distinguished Service Order
25.11.41   49939   Capt. (T/Major) Trevor Allan Gordon Pritchard
(Subsequently awarded O.B.E. (Mil.) whilst P.O.W.)   Ryl. Welch Fus.

2nd Bar to the M.C.
20.6.46   130870   Lieut. George Robert Paterson, M.C.   R. Engrs.
(Awarded M.C. 1.3.45 following escape and joining Italian Partisans.
Awarded Bar 4.10.45 following service with No.1 Special Force (S.O.E.)
and capture in Milan 9/44.)

Bar to the M.C.
20.6.46   71076   Lieut. Anthony John Dean-Drummond, M.C.
(awarded M.C. 29.9.42 following successful escape;   R. Signals
subsequently joined 1st Abn. Div. & M.I.D. for Arnhem.)

Military Cross
20.6.46   73126   T/Capt. Christopher Gerald Lea   Lanc. Fus.
20.6.46   130598   2/Lt. Arthur Geoffrey Jowett   H.L.I.

Military Medal
20.6.46   3952374   WOII Arthur William Albert Lawley   11 S.A.S.,
                                                                 A.A.C.
20.6.46   2564415   Sgt. Percy Priestley Clements   Leics. Regt.
(since commissioned into A.A.C. Awarded D.C.M. 2.3.44 for escaping and
aiding Italian Partisans.)
20.6.46   1881068   Sgt. Edward William Durie   R. Engrs.
14.9.44   5047114   L/Cpl. Harry Boulter   N. Staffs.
(his medals are in the Staffs. Regt. Museum, Lichfield)

Mentioned In Despatches
20.6.46   69066   T/Capt. G.F.K Daly, B.A.   R. Engrs.
20.6.46   1888254   L/Cpl. J. E. Maher   R. Engrs.
20.6.46   1888304   L/Cpl. R. B. Watson, M.M.   R. Engrs.
20.6.46   5340622   Pte. N. Nastri   Oxf. & B.L.I.

Appendix 1/2

Awards for the BRUNEVAL RAID 27.2.42

L.G. 15.05.42
"The King has been graciously pleased to approve the following awards in recognition of gallant and distinguished services in successful Combined Operations against the enemy at Bruneval'

Military Cross
53721	Capt. (T/Major) John Dutton Frost	Cameronians (Sco. Rif.)
		(att'd The Airborne Div.)
174279	2nd Lieut. Euan Basil Cyril Charteris	K.O.S.B.
(K.I.A. 29.11.42 North Africa)		*(att'd The Airborne Div.)*

Military Medal
2748467	Cpl. (A/Sgt.) Gregor McKenzie	Black Watch
		(att'd The Airborne Div.)
2824086	Sgt. David Grieve	Seaforth Highlanders
(K.I.A. 29.11.42 North Africa)		*(att'd The Airborne Div.)*

Mentioned In Despatches
129341	Lieut. P. A. Young	East Surrey Regt.
		(att'd The Airborne Div.)
1871780	Cpl. S. Jones	Corps of Ryl. Engineers
		(att'd The Airborne Div.)

Killed In Action
5347681	Pte. Alan W. Scott	9/R. Berkshire R.
3252284	Rfn. Hugh D. McD. McIntyre	9/Cameronians

Military Medal
955754	Flt. Sgt. Charles William Hall Cox	R.A.F.

Croix De Guerre & Gilt Star
2751640	C.S.M. Gerald Alexander Strachan	Black Watch

Chapter 2

HOT BAPTISM OF THE RED DEVILS

IN this first Anglo-American venture, the American participation was emphasized throughout the landings in Morocco and Algeria, due to the dislike of the British by the Vichy French, who controlled the areas. It was on November 8th, 1942, that the Allies landed on the North African coast in operation "TORCH". Their objective with this "Second Front"—to cut off the Axis forces and link up with the British 8th Army, that was slowly fighting its way from the east. When this was accomplished the way would be clear to invade Europe, via Sicily and Italy.

The first Army, under Lt-General Sir Kenneth Anderson, K.C.B., M.C. of which the 1st Parachute Brigade formed part, (and was to operate as an independent unit), landed east of Algiers, with its objective—the capture of Bizerta and Tunis, 500 miles to the east.

The American landings met with sporadic resistance, however the British landing went relatively smooth, as the O.C. had the help of the French district commander.

The Commander-In-Chief of the operations was relatively unknown to the British, but would later make his mark in history—Lieutenant-General Dwight D. Eisenhower.

On the 9th November, 1942, a day after the landings, Field Marshall Albert Kesselring—Chief of German forces in the Mediterranean sent troops from Sicily and Italy to the airfields of Bizerta and El Aouina, near Tunis and soon the rapid advance of the British 1st Army was slowing down. Both Commanders—Anderson and Kesselring required forward bases, and Kesselring despatched a Parachute Battalion to capture BONE AIRFIELD, but they turned back, as they saw British paratroops already landing.

Due to the shortage of Dakotas, only "B" and "C" Companies of the 3rd Parachute Battalion, could be taken to Gibraltar from Hurn airfield. "A" Company had to travel by sea with the rest of the Brigade.

On the 9/10th November, 1942, the two companies were flown to Maison Blanche airfield in Algeria, where they were instructed on the 11th to make ready for an airborne assault on BONE AIRFIELD on the following morning. Two Dakotas had already been put out of action; one had crashed into the sea, all the men were rescued by an American ship en route to New York, and they rejoined the 3rd Battalion two months later. On board as well as the parachutists, was the section commander of the No. 3 Section 16th Parachute Field Ambulance—Captain J. H. Keesey, and two of his orderlies. The second Dakota had been hit by anti-aircraft fire over Algiers harbour. On the 12th November, 1942, twenty-nine Dakotas carrying 360 Officers and men of the **3rd Parachute Battalion** left the airfield, and flew to their objective—BONE AIRFIELD. However they almost dropped over the wrong target area, as the commander in the lead Dakota—Lt-Colonel Dorset of the 60th Group, 51st Wing, USAAC, had mistaken Bougie for Bone. At that time, the Dakota pilots and navigators were finding it hard to adapt to combat situations, and to navigate in unknown territories—a fact that was to plague them yet again in the Sicilian landings in 1943.

The drop was successful, although there were thirteen casualties, including one killed, it was thought that this was due to the atmospheric conditions, which gave rise to heavier landings. The airfield was deserted, until a horde of Arabs arrived and started to purloin quantities of ammunition and parachute silk. Later in the day, the airfield was attacked by dive-bombers, and soon the Battalion was relieved by No. 6 (Army) Commando, and a squadron of R.A.F. Spitfires landed. The first Parachute operation had been a success, and the First Army had a strategic airfield, and General Anderson had beaten Kesselring to it.

"A" Company of the 3rd Parachute Battalion, disembarked in Algiers harbour on the 13th November, 1942, after waiting for two days under intermittent air attacks. They marched to the village of St. Charles, where they were reunited with the rest of their Battalion on the 19th November. The other component units of the Brigade were based around the Maison Blanche area by the 15th November.

The next Airborne task was allotted to the **1st Parachute Battalion**. They were to seize the airfield at SOUK EL ARBA, and the key road junction of BEJA. The medical support, this time, was to come from No.1

Section, 16th P.F.A. with No.1 Surgical Team.

On the 16th November, the Battalion was dropped on and near SOUK EL ARBA, the attempt the previous day had failed due to low cloud, but this time it was successful. There were two casualties in the drop: a soldier was strangled by a rigging line, and Major W. R. des Voeux, the Brigade liaison officer broke his leg on landing.

Using some commandeered French transport, Lt-Colonel Hill and his Battalion moved to the outskirts of BEJA, which they reached in the evening, during a torrential rain storm. The French commander was eventually won over by a show of British strength, when the Battalion marched through the town in the morning. This was done three times, the men wearing different headgear, and exaggerated reports received by the Germans in Tunis showed that the ruse had worked.

They were some 350 miles from Algiers, and with Lt-Colonel E. D. Raff and his 2nd Battalion of the U.S. 503rd Parachute Infantry Regiment which had landed near YOUK LES BAINS in the south, they were the foremost elements of the Allied forces.

On the 17th November, 1942, Major P. Cleasby-Thompson, M.B.E. and two platoons of "R" Company, with a detachment from the 1st Parachute Sqn., R.E. were sent to the village of SIDI N'SIR. Their orders were to make contact with French Commander, and his battalion of Sengalese, and to make a reconnaissance of the area towards MATEUR. This was accomplished, and on the 18th, an ambush was laid on a German light armoured column of five vehicles. Of these, three were destroyed by the parachutists. The soldiers and wounded, including several Germans were taken back to Beja in the captured vehicles.

Over the next couple of days, the Battalion remained in Beja, and was subjected to more dive-bombing attacks, which also killed over sixty of the civilian population and wounded many more.

Now the forward elements of the First Army had reached the Parachute Battalion's position, (namely the 2nd Lancashire Fusiliers—who on the same day: the 20th, lost their C.O.—Lt. Col. Manly). The rest of the 11th Brigade (78 Division) were involved in the fighting around MEDJEZ EL BAB and on the 24/25th LONGSTOP HILL.

On the 26th November, the Battalion became part of "Blade Force" (title from the 78th Divisional insignia), and moved to MATEUR, where its main duty was that of fighting patrols led by Officers as well as N.C.O's.

Now a look at the **2nd Parachute Battalion**, under Lt-Colonel Frost that was biding its time as Brigade Reserve at Maison Blanche. It had been decided that the Germans must not be able to use the airfields to the South of TUNIS—DEPIENNE and OUDNA.

This then was to be the task of the 2nd Parachute Battalion—the capture of the airfields and destruction of any enemy aircraft found.

At 11.30 hrs on the 29th November, 1942, the 2nd Parachute Battalion took off in 44 Dakotas, at the same time, the 5th Battalion of the Northamptonshire Regiment (11th Brigade) made tentative assaults near DJEDEIDA, (which the Germans had recaptured and were using its airfield for support). At 1445 hrs, the Battalion dropped onto a deserted DEPIENNE, one man was killed and several injured in the drop, but were looked after by the French. Accompanying the Battalion was No. 2 Section, 16th P.F.A. Later at 1700 hrs., a troop from the 56th Recce Regiment reported the existence of a German road block on the Tunis Road, which went through to OUDNA. Lt-Colonel Frost decided to march across country, and reached PRISE DE L'EAU on the 30th November.

After a meal, "A" Company moved towards the airfield at OUDNA, "B" Company was now in reserve, with "C" Company on the flank. The airfield was found to be deserted, but "A" Company had a brief skirmish, but drove off the enemy, who then, supported by tanks, attacked the "C" Company position. It was during this period, that Sgt. D. Grieve, M.M. (won at Bruneval) was killed. Unfortunately, the Battalion did not have any anti-tank guns to defend itself against the German tank force, and they then were strafed by ME109 fighter aircraft.

By the morning of the 1st December, radio contact was finally made with the 1st Army, who told them that they had been halted at DJEDEIDA, and through this, could not link up with the 2nd Battalion, as had been hoped.

They were then subjected to two heavy attacks, and it was then that the C.O. decided to withdraw, leaving his wounded at a farm, with Lt. McGavin—the Medical Officer, Lt. Playford, and the remnants of his defence platoon. The Battalion's casualties were some 150 killed or wounded.

The retreat began towards MASSICAULT, various parties became detached, and surrounded by enemy patrols. Major P. Teichman was killed and many were taken prisoner. Captain R. L. Stark and Lt. D. E. Crawley, who had been temporarily blinded, both of "B" Company managed to escape, as did Lt-Colonel Frost, Major J. G. Ross and most of

15

"A" Company, with small parties arriving at EL FEDJA. On the 2nd December, the Battalion lost its Intelligence Officer: Lt. E. B. C. Charteris, M.C. (won at Bruneval) who, with a small party tried to get to FURNA, where, it was hoped, were the forward units of the 1st Army. The Battalion was now surrounded, but holding its fire as ordered, they made for the ridge of the DJEBEL EL MENGOUB in the early morning of the 2/3rd December. Near there, they came across a farm, where they were all given a welcome meal. They then at daybreak moved on, and marched into MEDJEZ-EL-BAB, which was in Allied hands at 1700 hrs. Of the 460 that started the mission, 16 Officers and 250 other ranks were missing; either wounded, killed or taken prisoner. So ended the remarkable retreat from Oudna. However the remnants had to stand their ground with the rest of the Allied forces during the heavy German counter-attacks against Medjez and the surrounding area, until the 12th December, when the Battalion was sent to SOUK EL KHEMIS for a well earned rest.

The **1st Parachute Brigade** now came under the control of the 78th Infantry Divisional area.

The **3rd Parachute Battalion** that had been at St. Charles had had several proposed airborne drops cancelled, and were then sent to BEJA. From here they were sent to a rocky position known as HUNTS GAP, where they conducted several fighting patrols, including one by Lt. Livesey and three men from the **1st Parachute Sqn, R.E.**

Unfortunately due to the sudden change in the weather, the 1st Army and the Americans became bogged down in the thick mud, that had evolved from the hard earth. The Germans counter-attacked in strength, which had culminated in a brilliant tank strategy, and the capture of LONGSTOP HILL near Medjez. In the New Year, the 1st Army started to be equipped with the new American Sherman tank with its 75mm gun, which was on a par with the German Panzer IV, and certainly brought the strength of the British Armoured Divisions up to scratch. They beforehand had been equipped mainly with 2 Pdr. and 37mm guns.

The **3rd Para Battalion** had been moved to the Northern sector to attack GREEN HILL near MATEUR on the 4/5th January, 1943, "A" Company captured the crest, though were shelled by British guns, after they had negotiated the wire entanglements and booby traps. "B" Company captured the second crest, but were forced off.

The Battalion was then withdrawn to St. Charles, where on the 7/8th January, with the **1st Para. Battalion**, they were moved to Algiers by rail, for a projected operation that never evolved, under 1st Army control. Then they were returned to the control of the Allied Forces Headquarters, and thence to 5th Corps on 25th January, 1943.

Prior to this, the **2nd Parachute Battalion** in the BEJA area, had been moved to SIDI N' SIR following a draft of 200 men, which swelled their ranks once again. It was also here, that the war cry "WAHO MAHAMMED" was adopted from some local Arabs, who scolded their donkeys in a similar fashion, and soon it was taken up by the Brigade. The Battalion was then moved to the right flank and fought through to the 7th February.

On the 8th February, it returned to the Brigade, now in the BOU ARADA sector, and under the 6th Armoured Division, which had a week earlier, fought off German attacks, in which the Tiger tank had made its first appearance.

It was decided by the 5th Corps Commander to capture the heights of DJEBEL MANSOUR and EL ALLILIGIA to alleviate the German pressure, and this ground role attack was allotted to Lt-Colonel Pearson, (who was to be awarded the D.S.O. after this action and following fighting up to the 5th February), and his **1st Parachute Battalion**. There would also be a battalion from the Grenadier Guards in support on the one flank, plus a company from the French Foreign Legion on the other.

Lieutenant-Colonel M. McEwan, D.F.C., T.D., the O.C. 16th Para. Fld. Amb. made a tentative reconnaissance of the routes to be taken by the Parachute Battalion, and set up C.P.'s (Car Posts), though the hilly terrain necessitated the need of a stretcher-relay service, and this luckily was successful. Eventually, Captain Cassidy, and twenty volunteers went onto the swept ridge of the DJEBEL MANSOUR itself on the 5th February. Between the 3/5th February, the 16th Para. Fld. Amb. treated over 200 casualties. During the action, No.1 Section, now under Captain Wright, was with the Battalion, and No. 4 Section under Captain Percival was at the base of the Djebel.

On the 3rd February, the assault began at 0500 hrs., with "R" and "T" Companies of the 1st Parachute Battalion using tapes, laid by Captain H. B. Coxen, for guidance.

The assault companies were soon on the ridge, sweeping into the enemy's position at the bayonet, and by 0630 hrs., both Djebels were under control. However the two companies, now on EL ALLILIGIA were subjected to a fierce counter-attack, and withdrew to reform with the depleted "S" Company on DJEBEL MANSOUR. Lt-Colonel Pearson hoping that the Grenadier Guards' Battalion would take the former objective, but they were later unable to do so, and with the French company also being forced off the ridge, the Parachute Battalion was left high and dry.

At dawn on the 5th February, more heavy shellfire started and by 0915 hrs., the Battalion's mortars had run out of ammunition, and they couldn't receive artillery support. "S" Company was out of ammunition, but stood firm with grenades ready. "R" Company also was soon spent, it was also without officers, as Major J. S .C. R. Conron was killed. "T" Company had more rounds than "R" Company, however orders for withdrawal came, and the Company was led out by Major J. T. Bull. The action had cost the Battalion, 13 Officers killed or wounded, and 169 other ranks killed, wounded or missing.

Following this battle, the entire Brigade regrouped, still in the BOU ARADA area, and most of the fighting through to the end of February was restricted to the usual fighting patrols. In mid-February, the German forces forced through the U.S. 2nd Corps at the battle of KASSERINE PASS, however the Allies had recaptured the area by the end of February. The 6th Armoured Division was sent south to counter Rommel's advance, as he slowly became entangled with the forward elements of the 8th Army, who were beginning to break through the MARETH LINE. This was finally achieved in March, 1943.

By the 26th February, 1943, the enemy had amassed reinforcements along the Brigade's position near ARGOUB and DJEBEL MANSOUR, and were ready to strike, which they did in the morning.

The 3rd Parachute Battalion was savagely attacked, but "A" Company with "B" Company held their ground and beat off the enemy attacks, due to having ranged the ridges and dips the previous day. It was during this engagement, that pamphlets were found, dealing with the best way to fight the "Red Devils". This was the first time, that they had heard about their nickname.

Whilst the 3rd Battalion was being engaged, a similar attack was brought onto the **2nd Parachute Battalion's** position. "B" and "C" Companies were attacked solidly for about nine hours, but held their ground.

Following this action on the 5th March, the Brigade was placed under the command of the 46th (North Midland & West Riding) Infantry Division. Its own 139th Brigade was hard pressed in the SEDJENANE VALLEY, and the Parachute Brigade was put into the line near TAMERA, where they faced the German Parachute Engineers among others. It was this unit that had taken part in the assault on EBEN-EMAEL in Belgium in 1940.

The **1st Parachute Battalion** was in the wooded sector, which it could only patrol, rather than fortify. The **2nd Parachute Battalion** took over from the 6th Bn., Lincolnshire Regiment of 138th Brigade, and both the Parachute Battalions were attacked on the 8th March. Enemy movement was cut short by elements from the 6th Bn., York and Lancaster Regiment, and the 2nd Para.'s machine-gun platoon. The 3rd Parachute Battalion was then ordered in, to try and restore the situation, which they did at a cost of several killed. On the 11th March, the 3rd Battalion was brought into battle once again, by attacking positions in front of the 2nd Battalion. In this action they were supported by Churchill tanks.

The 2/5th Bn., Sherwood Foresters of 139 Brigade attacked east of TAMERA on the 13th March, through the 1st Parachute Battalion's position, in an attempt to take the DJEBEL BEL, but little was gained.

The next enemy attack was on the 17th March, after they had been resupplied most evenings by parachute. They tried to assault the 2/5th Leicester's position, who in the end had to withdraw, as did the 2/5th Sherwood Foresters, who were for a time surrounded by the enemy.

The Parachute Brigade also withdrew—the 2nd Battalion having to withdraw along the TAMERA VALLEY, and across the river OUED EL MEDENE, losing two killed: Cpl J. B. Dee and Pte. C. Wilson, eleven wounded and five missing presumed drowned, whilst under heavy shellfire. They then held positions near the DJEBEL ABIOD, and orders came from 5th Corps, that it would be held at all costs, and that there would be no further withdrawals.

On the 18th March, the **1st Parachute Battalion** retook a rocky position called BOWLER HAT.

There was to be no further action, other than the occasional fighting patrol, until the 27th March, when the 1st and 2nd Battalions which were now both at half strength, were ordered to attack the enemy positions near to SEDJENANE, and an intense artillery barrage was started. The **3rd Battalion** was in reserve on BOWLER HAT.

The Parachutists captured their objectives before dawn. The **1st Parachute Battalion** captured the entire Italian Bersaglieri, who opposed them. Captain Wright and No.1 Section, 16th P.F.A. was attached to the 1st Battalion for this action.

On the Parachutists' right, the 1st Thabor (Goums), which was composed of irregular Moroccan troops commanded by French officers, captured their objective, there were casualties, and these were treated by Captain Young and his No.3 Section, 16th P.F.A.

The **2nd Parachute Battalion** was short of its objective, after having lost part of "B" Company in an undetected minefield. The C.O: Lt-Colonel Frost pulled back some of his men, and almost immediately the Germans counter-attacked at midday. However, the Battalion had been reinforced by a company from the **3rd Parachute Battalion** and held firm.

Finally on the 30th March, SEDJENANE fell to the Allies, and the 1st Parachute Brigade was relieved by the Americans.

The **1st Parachute Brigade** was sent to BOU FARIK, and then to SOUSSE in June. The First and Eighth Armies finally joined in May, and on the 13th May, 1943, the war in North Africa was brought to a close with the capitulation of all Axis forces.

Appendix 2/1

Awards of 1st Para. Bde—N. Africa 1942-43

Distinguished Service Order

22.4.43   Brigadier (temp) Edwin William Conquest Flavell, M.C.
48661   C.O. 1st Bde.

4.5.43 Major (A/Lt-Col.) Alastair Stevenson Pearson
62972   2/I.C./C.O. 1st Bn.

11.2.43   Major (T/Lt-Col.) Stanley James Ledger Hill
56248   *(W.D. 24.11.42)*   C.O. 1st Bn.

11.2.43   Capt. (A/Lt-Col.) John Dutton Frost, M.C.
53721   C.O. 2nd Bn.

15.6.43   Capt. (T/Major) Harold Brian Coxen
73534   "S" 1st Bn.

22.4.43   Capt. (T/Major) David Theodor Dobie
67437   O.C. "B" 3rd Bn.

11.2.43   Capt. (T/Major) John Graham Ross
88111   O.C. "C" 2nd Bn.

Bar to the D.S.O.

18.5.43   Major (T/Lt-Col) Alastair Stevenson Pearson, D.S.O.
62972   C.O. 1st Bn.

Military Cross

23.9.43   Capt. (A/Lt-Col.) Richard Geoffrey Pine-Coffin
40705   (BD90)   (Devon att. A.A.C.) 3rd Bn.

11.2.43   Capt. (T/Major)   Richard Ashford
168721   *(K.I.A. 18.1.43)*   O.C. "A" 2nd Bn.

23.9.43   Capt. (T/Major)   Peter Cleasby-Thompson, MBE
63704   *(L.F. att. A.A.C.)*   O.C. "R" 1st Bn.

18.5.43   Capt. (T/Major)   John Henry Vine Hall
89555   *(K.I.A. 11.3.43)*   O.C. "C" 3rd Bn.

18.5.43   Capt. (T/Major)   Humphrey Lloyd Jones
89372   1st Bn.

23.9.43   Capt. (T/Major)   Alastair Stevenson Pearson, D.S.O.
62972   C.O. 1st Bn.

| 22.3.45 | Capt. Dennis Bossey Rendell | |
| | 180657 | 2nd Bn. |

23.9.43 Lieut. (T/Capt.)(A/Major) Douglas Edward Crawley
108192 *(Loyals att. A.A.C.) (W.D. 1.12.42)* O.C. "B" 2ndBn.

15.6.43 Lieut. (T/Capt.)William Ellery Anderson
148939 1st Bn.

15.6.43 Lieut. (T/Capt.)Herbert David Burwash
251647 3rd Bn.

23.9.43 Lieut. (T/Capt.) Harold Brian Coxen, D.S.O.
73534 "S" 1st Bn.

15.6.43 Lieut. (T/Capt.) Ronald Leslie Stark
167154 "B" 2nd Bn.

11.2.43 Lieut. John Desmond Brayley
183734 2nd Bn.

15.6.43 Lieut. Richard Gwynedd Ellis
187030 3rd Bn.

11.2.43 Lieut. Philip Evert McIlvaine Mellor
130458 *(K.I.A. 3.2.43)* "B" 1st Bn.

23.9.43 Lieut. Christopher Perrin-Brown
121945 "T" 1st Bn.

22.4.43 Lieut. Gerard Lewis William Street
156041 3rd Bn.

1.6.43 Lieut. John Timothy
164821 2nd Bn.

11.2.43 Lieut. Stanley Wandless
145683 1st Bn.

Distinguished Conduct Medal

18.5.43	5722253	W.O.II (C.S.M.) Roy Richards	1st Bn.
18.4.43	3963788	Sgt. Harold Howells	1st Bn.
22.4.43	3447097	Sgt. John McDonnell	3rd Bn.
22.4.43	2928612	Sgt. Robert McDougall	3rd Bn.
11.4.46	2748467	Sgt. Gregor McKenzie	2nd Bn.

Military Medal

23.9.43	2979279	W.O.II Macleod Forsythe	2nd Bn.
23.9.43	5495443	W.O.II Samuel Charles Steadman	"R" 1st Bn.
		(W.D. 16.11.42) (BD23)	
22.4.43	3527354	C.Q.M.S. Joseph Anthony Patrick Donbavand	3rd Bn.
26.8.43	3530918	Sgt. Wilfred Bailey	3rd Bn.
22.4.43	5054670	Sgt. John Branthwaite	3rd Bn.
18.5.43	4975024	Sgt. Albert John Clements	1st Bn.

1.6.43	5771257	Sgt. William Cloves	"H.Q." 2nd Bn.
15.6.43	2617789	Sgt. Leslie Arthur Curtis	1st Bn.
		(K.I.A. Arnhem 20.9.44)	
22.4.43	5617901	Sgt. Cyril Leonard Eveleigh	3rd Bn.
1.6.43	2989834	Sgt. William Fleming	"C" 2nd Bn.
23.9.43	3964747	Sgt. Albert Edward John	"T" 1st Bn.
23.9.43	3132924	Sgt. William Kerr	1st Bn.
23.9.43	3446906	Sgt. John Lawson	"A" 2nd Bn.
15.6.43	1116016	Sgt. Victor Padureano	1st Bn.
		(K.I.A. Sicily 14.7.43)	
11.2.43	5333588	Sgt. Joseph Patrick Ryan	"R" 1st Bn.
15.6.43	5441604	Sgt. Alexis Peter Vedeniapine	3rd Bn.
23.9.43	5779742	L/Sgt . John Percival Copling	3rd Bn.
23.9.43	7901320	L/Sgt . Gordon Thomas Piney Strong	1st. Bn.
23.9.43	5107512	Cpl. James Harry Bennett	1st Bn.
15.6.43	3654679	Cpl. Leslie Bradley	1st Bn.
15.6.43	1695912	Cpl. Thomas David Griffiths	2nd Bn.
23.9.43	2619341	Cpl. William George Alexander Westripp	
11.2.43	550613	L/Cpl. Horace Nathaniel Bainbridge	1st Bn.
		(K.I.A. 3.2.43)	
22.4.43	3317592	L/Cpl. James Sinclair Grabham	3rd Bn.
23.9.43	6463023	L/Cpl. Eugene Noel Larner	1st Bn.
11.2.43	883217	L/Cpl. Roy James Morgan	1st Bn.
22.4.43	7012729	L/Cpl. James Murphy	3rd Bn.
		(K.I.A. 11.3.43)	
22.4.43	4198210	L/Cpl. Ivor Royles	3rd Bn.
23.9.43	4130853	L/Cpl. Walter Westwood	1st Bn.
23.9.43	2984461	Pte. (A/Sgt.)James Colville	1st Bn.
		(K.I.A. 8.3.43)	
23.9.43	6465199	Pte.(A/Cpl.) Donald Frederick Wilson	3rd Bn.
23.9.43	T/73935	Pte. Harry Bartley	1st Bn.
18.5.43	2051490	Pte. Michael Gerard Crowe	"T" 1st Bn.
1.6.43	174774	Pte. Jack Hacking	2nd Bn.
23.9.43	3970674	Pte. Edmund Harris	1st Bn.
15.6.43	324267	Pte. Charles Lamb	1st Bn.
18.5.43	4209536	Pte. Anthony Bertram Lloyd	1st Bn.
		(K.I.A. Arnhem)	
15.6.43	5339257	Pte. Matthew McAllister	2nd Bn.
15.6.43	4752311	Pte. William Ewart McDermott	2nd Bn.
11.2.43	3524913	Pte. James Gladstone Meadows	1st Bn.
11.2.43	5780288	Pte. David Scott Miller	2nd Bn.
15.6.43	4620046	Pte. Harry Frank Williamson Parker	3rd Bn.

15.6.43	6405479	Pte. Raymond Reginald James Weller	3rd Bn.
11.2.43	2885157	Pte. Francis Welsh	2nd Bn.
11.2.43	4543869	Pte. Frederick George Wright	1st Bn.

Bar to the M.M.

| 23.9.43 | 2754054 | Sgt. (A/W.O.II)(C.S.M.) James Low Sharp, M.M. | |
| | | (M.M. 18.10.40 Black Watch, France) | "C" 2nd Bn. |

Mentioned In Despatches—23.9.43

Capt. (A/Major) J. T. Bull	66958	"T" 1st Bn.
Lieut. (T/Capt.) J. D. Brayley, MC	183734	2nd Bn.
Lieut. (T/Capt.) R. L. Stark, MC	167154	"B" 2nd Bn.
Lieut. (T/Capt.) J. R. C. Stewart	92023	1st Bn.
(K.I.A. 20.11.42)		
Lieut. (A/Capt.) G. N. Bromley-Martin	91446	3rd Bn.
(K.I.A. 26.2.43)		
Lieut. W. Blewitt	164767	3rd Bn.
(K.I.A. 6.1.43)		
Lieut. A. B. Clements	130431	
(K.I.A. Rhine Crossing 24.3.45)		att. 3rd Bde.
Lieut. J. H. Elton-Tuckett	193751	3rd Bn.
(K.I.A. 6.1.43)		
Lieut. A. R. H. Kellas	106166	"R" 1st Bn.
(W.D. 16.11.42)		
Lieut. J. A. D. Richey	151648	1st Bn.
4387613 Sgt. J. W. Baynes	*(K.I.A. 17.8.43)*	3rd Bn.
5617901 Sgt. C. L. Eveleigh, M.M.		3rd Bn.
3452476 Sgt. J. P. Hetherington	*(K.I.A. 20.12.42)*	3rd Bn.
2878834 Sgt. J. C. Rainnie		1st Bn.
58782 Sgt. A. Watson		
317636 Cpl.(A/Sgt) F. A. Tucker		
4341886 Cpl.(A/Sgt) J. H. Webb	*(K.I.A. 11.3.43)*	3rd Bn.
5781918 Cpl. L. G. Kidman	*(K.I.A. 8.3.43)*	1st Bn.
3189280 Cpl. J. Newton		
6465423 Pte.(A/Cpl.) M. H. Bromnick		
4804341 Pte.(A/Cpl.) H. Fisher		
4192138 Pte.(A/Cpl.) T. H. Jones		
7012729 L/Cpl. J. Murphy, M.M.	*(K.I.A. 11.3.43)*	3rd Bn.
864817 Pte. D. R. Humphrey		
4122605 Pte. A. Mackie		
2052215 Pte. W. Wain	*(K.I.A. 30.11.42)*	2nd Bn.
6208152 Pte. T. H. Wilkinson		2nd Bn.

Foreign Awards Received
France
Croix De Guerre, with star

Captain Edward O'Brien	1st Bn.
Sgt. Hayhow	'A' 2nd Bn.
Cpl. Wright, F.	'A' 2nd Bn.
L/Cpl. Thirkell	'A' 2nd Bn.

United States of America (15.2.44)
Distinguished Service Cross

3654909 Col.Sgt. Reginald Allen	3rd Bn.
(K.I.A. Arnhem 19.9.44, W.O.II)	

Silver Star

Capt. (T/Major) Eric Charles Yeldham   44202   Hamps. Regt. 3rd Bn.
Capt. Andrew Joseph Hawksley Rutherford 67178   Adjt. 2nd Bn.
4202334 Pte. Mervyn Bower Peters

Awards to 1st Para. Bde. Support Units
for North Africa 1942-43

1st Parachute Squadron, Royal Engineers

Military Cross

23.9.43	106883	Capt. (T/Major) Douglas Campbell Murray,	O.C. Sqn.
22.4.43	220968	Captain Stephen George	
23.9.43	126400	Lt. (T/Capt.) Charles Dennis Harling Vernon	
11.2.43	22702	Lieut. Trevor John Livesey	

Mentioned In Despatches

23.9.43　1919427　L/Cpl. W. L. G. Simpson
(K.I.A. Arnhem 20.9.44)

U.S. Silver Star

15.2.44　1919427　L/Cpl. William Leslie George Simpson

16th Parachute Field Ambulance, R.A.M.C.

Distinguished Service Order

11.11.43　22266　A/Col. Malcolm MacEwan, O.B.E., D.F.C., T.D., M.B.
C.O. P.F.A.
14.6.43　188966　Captain James Watt Logan, M.B.　　O.C. H.Q. Section

Officer Of The British Empire—for gallant and distinguished service

23.9.43　　Major (T/Lt.-Col.) Malcolm MacEwan, D.F.C., T.D.　22266

Bar To The M.C.

23.9.43　94268 Captain Ronald Rodger Gordon, M.C., M.B.
R.M.O. 2nd Bn.

Military Cross

11.2.43　205598　Captain Michael Henry Knox Haggie, M.B.,
R.M.O. 1st Bn.
23.9.43　218952　Captain David Wright, M.B.　　O.C. No.1 Section
11.2.43　230698　Lieut Charles Granville Robb., M.B., F.R.C.S.
O.C. No.1 Surg. Tm

Distinguished Conduct Medal

15.6.43　7373608　S/Sgt.Eric George Stevens　　　No. 3 Sectn.

Military Medal

| 15.6.43 | 7395054 | Cpl. Ernest Hardie | No. 3 Sectn. |
| 15.6.43 | 7380110 | Cpl. James Holt | Att. 2nd Bn. |

Mentioned In Despatches—23.9.43

114828	Capt. J. G. Cassidy	*(K.I.A. 10.3.43)*	Att. 1 Bde. H.Q.
223758	Capt. A. Percival, M.B.		No. 4 Sectn.
7347294	S/Sgt. S. Clegg		No. 1 Sectn.
7358788	S/Sgt.T. G. Anderson		No. 4 Sectn.
7522533	Pte. E. N. Hewitt	*(K.I.A. 17.3.43)*	Att. 1st Bn.

Silver Star (U.S.A.)

15.2.44   7394382   Pte. George Currie Neal

Soldiers Medal (U.S.A.)

15.2.44   7344530 Sgt. Alfred Henry Powell

Awards to 4th Para. Bde. in
Middle East 1942-43

Mentioned In Despatches

13.4.44	6400234	Sgt. T. C. Bentley	10th Bn.
13.4.44	6285440	Sgt. F. H. Chesson	10th Bn.

(Sgt. Frank Herbert Chesson K.I.A. Arnhem 19.9.44)

13.1.44	6400067	Pte (A/Cpl.)W. Garibaldi	10th Bn.

(William GARIBALDI K.I.A. Arnhem 21/22. 9.44)

New Year & Birthday Honours, 1943

Companion of the Bath (1.1.43)
Col. (T/Major-Genl.) Frederick Arthur Montague Browning, D.S.O.

22588   *(Late Gren. Gds.)*   G.O.C., Paratroops & Airborne Troops

Commander Of The British Empire (2.6.43)
Lt.-Col. (T/Brigadier) Ernest Edward Down

23809   K.S.L.I.   C.O. 2nd Para. Bde. 1942-43

Member of the British Empire (2.6.43)
Capt. (T/Major) Peter Cleasby-Thompson   15067   Lanc. Fus. 1st Bn.

British Empire Medal
4037780   A/Cpl. Edward Jones   A.A.C.

George Medal To A Para Jump Instructor

19.11.43   George Medal in recognition of conspicuous gallantry in carrying out hazardous work in a very brave manner.

468922   Sgt. Instructor Alfred Cook   Army Physical Training Corps

Citation

On the 9th August, 1943, Sergeant Instructor Cook was despatching a squad of parachute trainees from a C.47 A/C on a dropping zone in North Africa, when Private Trevor jumped, his parachute failed to open, and he was suspended underneath the aircraft on the end of his static line at approximately 800 feet above the ground.

Sergeant Instructor Cook realising what had happened, stopped the other men from jumping, and attempted to pull Private Trevor back into the aircraft, but failed. Sergeant Instructor Cook thereupon took a parachute off one of the men in the aircraft, put it on and hooked himself up to the aircraft.

He then left, and climbed down the static line of Private Trevor, and gripped him by his feet; whilst holding on to Private Trevor's static line with his right hand, he attempted to release the parachute with his left hand. Whilst doing this, the slipstream of the aircraft began to force his own rigging lines out of the bag, and owing to two bodies swinging around, these lines began to wind around Private Trevor's static line.

Sergeant Instructor Cook realising that his own parachute was becoming fouled, ordered Private Trevor to hold onto him, whilst he dropped in an endeavour to pull Private Trevor free, and enable both bodies to descent on his own parachute.

Sergeant Instructor Cook thereupon released himself, but Private Trevor was unable to retain his grip on the instructor's harness. Seargent Instructor Cook's parachute then developed and he landed safely. On inspecting his parachute, he discovered that five of his rigging lines had been broken during his attempt to free Private Trevor, who was subsequently pulled back safely into the aircraft.

Throughout the action, Sergeant Instructor Cook displayed a complete disregard for his own personal safety, and although unsuccessful, he made an exceptionally courageous effort to release his pupil's parachute.

Sergeant Instructor Cook was later Battery P.T.I. of the 1st Air-Landing Anti-Tank Battery, and fought at Arnhem.

Chapter III

AIRBORNE ATTACK

WITH the war in North Africa over, the Allies now turned to Europe. After much discussion between the Chiefs of Staff, it was decided that SICILY should be the next target, although the Americans had hoped more for an invasion of France, but in the end Operation "HUSKY" was agreed.

Between May and June, 1943, the 2nd Parachute Brigade, 4th Parachute Brigade (less one Battalion), and the 1st Air-Landing Brigade arrived from the U.K. to join the 1st Parachute Brigade—sadly much depleted from its first campaign, and the units now formed the **1st Airborne Division**, based at MASCARA and then, SOUSSE.

The Seaborne assault by the units of the **8th Army** on the east side of the island, and the **US 7th Army** on the west were planned for the 10th July, 1943. Airborne troops—parachutists and glider-borne would be used to capture key bridges in front of the invasion forces.

During June, 1943, the troops of the **1st Air-Landing Brigade** trained for its part in the operation, although there were casualties when a glider carrying elements of the 2nd South Staffords crashed on the 27th June over the Atlas mountains, killing most of those on board.

The Brigade now consisted of:

    1st Bn., Border Regiment—Lt-Col. G. V. Britten (Northants)

    2nd Bn., S. Staffords.—Lt-Col. W. D. H. McCardie

as the other two Infantry Regiments had remained in England, to form the 6th Air-Landing Brigade: part of the newly formed **6th Airborne Division.**

Also the Americans supplied 150 Waco Hadrian gliders, which had to be assembled on the airstrips near ORAN. The British flew out from the U.K.—29 Horsas towed by Halifax bombers; which were the only aircraft capable of towing a glider for the range involved. Each glider, in this operation, codenamed "TURKEY BUZZARD", carried three members, so at any one time, one was resting. The operation was commanded by Wing Commander MacNamara, D.S.O., however there were the inevitable casualties.

Captain A. J. Cooper, with Sgt.'s D. A. Hall and S. Antonopoulos were flying over the Bay of Biscay, when the nylon tow rope snapped, and they crashed into the sea. They were found, after eight hours in their dinghy, by a Royal Navy corvette, and within twenty-four hours, they were flying other gliders to Morocco. Captain Cooper received the Air Force Cross, and the two sergeants—the Air Force Medal. The two sergeants flying their second mission, with Sergeant Conway as third man were attacked by German Condors, and the glider had to cast off. They drifted in their dinghy for eleven days, before being rescued by a Portuguese fishing boat.

In the end only 19 of the 29 Horsa gliders made the trip to North Africa. "FUSTIAN" was the overall code-name for the airborne operations, Operation "LADBROOKE" was to be the capture of the PONTE GRANDE BRIDGE, and a portion of SYRACUSE by the **1st Air-Landing Brigade.** There was to be a drop by the **2nd Parachute Brigade** near AUGUSTA, but this was cancelled due to the speed of the 8th Army, linking up with the **Special Raiding Squadron** at AUGUSTA, which they captured on the 12th July. Operation "MARSTON" was the code-name for an operation, in which the **1st Parachute Brigade** was to drop on the PRIMOSOLE BRIDGE over the SIMETO RIVER on the 13th July.

The landing on the evening of the 9/10th July, 1943 of the Airborne force, was to consist of 127 Waco gliders and 10 Horsas, being towed by No. 295 Squadron (Halifaxes), No. 296 Squadron (Albemarles) and Dakotas of 51st Troop Carrier Wing U.S.A.A.F.

The glider force was commanded by Lt-Colonel G. J .S. Chatterton, who later received the Distinguished Service Order for his part in the operation. His glider carried the Brigade Commander—Brigadier "Pip" Hick who had taken over the Brigade from Brigadier Hopkinson, O.B.E., M.C., who now commanded the 1st Airborne Division as a Major-General.

The gliders and their tugs took off from KAIROUAN and EL DJEM at about 1900 hrs. on the 9th July, and had passed Malta at 2200 hrs. turning then for SICILY. However, rough winds started, and on casting off, about 60% of the gliders crashed into the sea, just short of the shoreline.

The **1st Bn., Border Regiment**, with **No.1 Section, 181st A.F.A.** under Captain Greaves, was to land on the Southern side of the harbour, on the MADDALENA PENINSULA, and with the South Staffords. seize the PONTE GRANDE BRIDGE, cutting off SYRACUSE. This was in readiness for the 17th Brigade (of the 5th Division), commanded by a former officer of the Border Regiment—Brigadier G. W. B. Tarleton, M.C. who was awarded the D.S.O for this operation.

Lt-Colonel Britten and his 2/I.C.—Major T. Haddon, both in different gliders crashed into the sea, but most managed to swim to the shore, under machine-gun fire. Lieutenant W. G. Welch and thirty men, who landed four miles from their objective, made for the bridge, met with members of the South Staffords., who they reinforced, and held the bridge until forced off by shellfire. Lt. Welch escaped with seven men, as the rest of the force of 87 were killed or wounded, and so captured. Later, the bridge was retaken by elements of 17th Brigade. Lt. Welch received the Military Cross, as did the R.M.O. of the Battalion—Captain J. E. Miller.

Of course, most parties were scattered and fought small actions against enemy patrols, which gave rise to exaggerated reports to the Axis High Command, although some 250 men of the battalion were down in the sea.

Brigadier Hicks and his Staff, plus Lt-Colonel Warrack of the 181st A.F.A., in Chatterton's glider, also crashed into the sea. They all managed to swim to the shore at CAPO MURRO DI PORCO, where the assault craft of Lt-Colonel "Paddy" Mayne's Special Raiding Squadron came in.

Of the force of 134 gliders, only 12 landed at their targets and only 2 out of 8 reached the PONTE GRANDE BRIDGE; one piloted by Captain J. N. C. Denholm struck the bank, killing all the occupants, but the second piloted by S/Sgt. D. P. Galpin landed successfully, and he received the D.F.M. Major A. J. Cooper, A.F.C. was killed, when his glider crashed and his tug blew up. Captain W. N. Barrie landed his passengers and jeep, and fought with the infantry; Captain A. F. Boucher-Giles also fought in command of a small party of South Staffords., and both were awarded D.F.C.'s as was Lt. J. A. Dale.

The **2nd Bn., South Staffords.**, with **No.2 Section, 181st A.F.A.** under Captain B. Brownescombe, (who won the George Medal saving the life of a non swimmer orderly, when his glider crashed), also landed in various places, including the sea.

The capture of the PONTE GRANDE BRIDGE was the prime objective of "C" Company under Major G. Ballinger, who was killed on landing. Lieutenant L. Withers and No. 15 Platoon landed near the bridge and held it, until reinforced by men from the Borders, he received the Military Cross. Other members who received awards included—Captain R. S. Foot, who with his two platoons held off Italian counter-attacks on the main SYRACUSE Road; Lieutenant E. Deuchar, who organised a composite force near the bridge; L/Cpl. G. Pratt led one of two sections against the bridge, and he destroyed a lorry load of enemy; Pte. R. Hall covered the withdrawal of a force of ten men with a Bren and a rifle. Medical orderlies, Pte.'s C. F. Weate and R. Eden brought back wounded men and received M.M.'s, as did Ptes. Charlesworth, Tyrer and L/Cpl. Jackson. A Military Cross was won by the R.M.O. of the Battalion— Captain J. E. Miller, R.A.M.C.

Also present at this engagement, and used for the first time were members of the **Naval Bombardment Force**, composed of Royal Artillery Observation Officers, and Naval Telegraphists, all parachute trained. The cruiser "Newfoundland" and the monitor "Erebus" were the supporting warships.

The operational losses had been heavy—over 250 drowned, 61 killed, and 174 wounded or missing. The Glider Pilot Regiment lost 58 killed and numerous wounded. In all about a fifth of the force were casualties, and the operation only marginally successful, a lot of the Seaborne landings had been bogged down by assault craft floundering on unknown sandbars, and more opposition than had been thought. In the end the 17th Infantry Brigade and the rest of 5th Division was soon fighting towards SYRACUSE.

Primosole Bridge

The 1st Parachute Brigade, now with a new Brigadier (G. W. Lathbury) was under the command of the 1st Airborne Division, which itself was under the control of 8th Army. On the 15th July, 1943, this control passed to 15th Army Group H.Q., (the overall command of the 8th Army and 7th U.S. Army), until the September, 1943.

With the heavy fighting still continuing in Sicily, and the German forces starting to co-ordinate their movements, a rapid advance was again called for. 13th Corps (8th Army) was ordered to capture CATANIA, with its 5th Infantry Division pressing northwards across bridges captured by: No.3 Army Commando—LENTINI RIVER, and 1st Parachute Brigade—PRIMOSOLE BRIDGE over the SINETO RIVER. Both occuring during the night of 13/14th July. However, German reinforcements in the shape of the 1st Parachute Division landed at Catania airfield from Italy to reinforce the various units in the front line.

On the 13th July, 1943 at 2230 hrs., No.3 Commando under Lt-Colonel J. Durnford-Slater, D.S.O., (who was to be awarded a Bar to his D.S.O. for this action), landed at AGNONE from HMS "Prince Albert". They were under machine-gun fire from pill-box defences, which were soon silenced, and then fought several short actions across country towards the river.

At the same time, aircraft flew overhead carrying the members of the 1st Parachute Brigade, who were to drop at the next bridge.

The commandos finally got to the LENTINI BRIDGE, which was defended by German paratroops, took and held it, although under mortar fire, and shellfire from a Tiger tank. They waited for the elements of 50th Infantry Division (151st Inf. Bde.) to reach them, but it had been held up just before Lentini itself. As dawn broke, the commandos were forced to retire in small groups. Their losses had been 28 killed, 66 wounded and 59 missing out of the four hundred or so that started out. The enemy also withdrew leaving the bridge unguarded, and later in the day, (14th July), the Sherman tanks of the 4th Armoured Brigade, (from Augusta) rumbled across, as they made their way to the PRIMOSOLE BRIDGE, where the parachutists also waited, under fire.

At 1900 hrs. on 13th July, the first elements of the **1st Parachute Brigade** took off from KAIROUAN airfield—operation "MARSTON" was on. A total of 107 aircraft—Dakotas, plus eleven Albemarles carried the parachutists, and 17 gliders towed by Halifaxes and Albemarles carried the 12 jeep-towed anti-tank guns and crews.

The parachute drop was timed for 2200 hrs. on 13th July, and the glider elements, which took off later, were to land at 0100 hrs. near the bridge. The approach flight ended up as being almost as hazardous, as the landings itself, since many aircraft were fired upon by Allied shipping, who thought the formations were Axis aircraft. In all, 14 aircraft were lost, and 26 aircraft returned to Africa, without dropping anybody, through other problems. One of the downed C47's contained **No. 4 Section, 16th P.F.A.** under Captain A. Percival, and all except for four, managed to swim to the surface, and were rescued by a Greek destroyer, taken first to Malta, and then to Sousse by 15th July.

Out of the total aircraft—their crews still experiencing navigational difficulties—44 aircraft dropped wide, varying from half a mile to twenty miles; 9 dropped nearby the bridge, and 30 dropped onto the Dropping

Zones. The results of this were more apparent, when it was found that only 12 officers and 283 other ranks, out of 1, 856 were present.

Four gliders landed correctly, and seven others further away, but only three anti-tank guns out of twelve came into action, under the command of Sergeants Anderson, Atkinson and Doig, and some glider pilots.

The landing zones had been partially marked by the Eureka radio location device by members of the **21st Independent Parachute Coy.,** although a couple of the landing zones were on fire and were thus more clearly marked. Major J. Lander, the company's C.O. was killed, when his plane crashed, he was only on a reconnaissance mission, to see how his detachment fared on the ground.

The **1st Parachute Battalion** was to seize the southern end of the bridge and the explosive devices if any, would be disposed of, by members of the **1st Parachute Squadron, R.E.** under Major Murray.

The **2nd Parachute Battalion** was to reinforce the 1st Bn., and they both would have parties on the higher ground as well.

The **3rd Parachute Battalion** would land near to the northern end of the bridge. However, there were not enough men for the job now on the ground.

Brigadier Lathbury landed on the high ground, and met his Brigade Major: Major D. Hunter, and a small proportion of his staff, including the S.M.O.: Lt-Colonel Wheatley, who at once set off in search of the two H.Q. R.A.M.C. sticks, under Captain D. H. Ridler, A.D.C. and Major C. J. Longland. An M.D.S. was set up, manned by the men from the H.Q. sticks, and the R.A.P.'s were soon coping with casualties.

Brigadier Lathbury met Lt-Colonel Frost and about fifty of his men heading for the bridge. Captain Rann and fifty men from the **1st Parachute Battalion** stormed the bridge from the north side and took it. As Lathbury and the men from the **2nd Battalion** crossed the bridge, the Brigadier was wounded by a grenade fragment.

Now at 0630 hrs., there were some 120 men of the **1st Battalion**, and two platoons of the **3rd Battalion**, with the three anti-tank guns holding the bridge. Also a platoon under Lt-Colonel Frost were now in position on the higher ground, south of the bridge.

The German parachutists started their counter-attacks against the **2nd Parachute Battalion**, which was out of touch with those on the bridge, due to Germans dropping their reinforcements partially on the wrong side of the bridge, this mistake of course proved fruitful for the Germans.

Brigadier Lathbury, with radio contact finally established with 8th

35

Army, heard that the 4th Armoured Brigade had been held up at LENTINI, but were fighting their way through.

With ammunition running low, contact was made with the cruiser "Newfoundland", which from the fire-directions given by the F.O.O.— Captain Vere Hodge, R.A. brought down a heavy fire onto the enemy positions.

On the high ground, German assaults on "Johnny I" and" Johnny II" were being fended off. With Lt-Colonel Frost, was "A" Company under Major R. T. H. Lonsdale, M.C., (who was awarded the D.S.O. for this action).

Then at 1930 hrs., tanks from the 4th Armoured Brigade (44th R.T.R.) appeared, and with the 9th Bn., Durham Light Infantry from the 151st Inf. Bde. (50th Inf. Div.) attacked the bridge. This attack failed and it was not until the 17th July, that the way was cleared of opposition.

So operation "MARSTON" it could be said was yet another failure though the airborne men who fought there, were a credit to the Brigade. They were again left on their own, without support, which was too far away to have been of use. They were to hold a position of which the enemy strength opposing them, seemed to have not been calculated, with a view to the possibilities of Axis airborne reinforcements and mobile forces. This was to show itself again in a later action during the following September, 1944, at a place called Arnhem.

On the 16th July, 1943 the survivors: there had been 115 casualties out of the 292 at the bridge, were transported back to Syracuse. Then by sea to North Africa via Valetta, Malta on the 17th, and disembarked at Sousse on the 18th July.

CATANIA was held by the Hermann Goring Division and could not be taken. In the end, the Allies used a thrust inland and finally reached MESSINA in mid-August, trying to keep as many Axis troops in Sicily as possible. So on August 17th 1943, the war in Sicily ended.

Appendix 3/1

Awards of 1st Air-Landing Brigade at the Ponte Grande, Sicily—9/10.7.43

The Border Regiment
Military Cross
21.10.43   132473   Lieut. William Gordon Welch

Military Medal
21.10.43   3593710   C.Q.M.S. James Smith
23.12.43   3603310   L/Sgt. Jackson Gardner-Roberts
21.10.43   3597789   Cpl. John Waring

Mentioned In Despatches
23.4.44   3603643   Pte. P. Booth
23.4.44   4339643   Pte. J. L. Sheldon

South Staffordshire Regiment
Military Cross
23.12.43   94068   Lt. (T/Capt.) Henry Trevor Fairclough
21.10.43   138194   Lt. (T/Capt.) Reginald Sydney Foot   *(W.D.)*
21.10.43   240289   Lieut. Ernest Deuchar
21.10.43   189385   Lieut. George Willie James Goodman
21.10.43   190738   Lieut. Jack Reynolds   Ryl. Regt. of Arty.
                                                               att. S/Staffords.
4.11.43   142742   Lieut. Sidney Stoy   *(K.I.A. Sicily)*
21.10.43   174423   Lieut. Lennard Withers   Northamptons.
                                                               att. S/Staffords.
21.1.0.43 267242   2/Lt. John Badger   *(W.D.)*   *(K.I.A. Arnhem)*

Military Medal
21.10.43   4925795   L/Cpl. George Pratt
21.10.43   4916533   Pte. William Henry Charlesworth
21.10.43   6104442   Pte. Rodney Alfred Hall
21.10.43   4913373   Pte. Bernard Jackson
21.10.43   4460071   Pte. Reginald Tyrer
21.10.43   4914495   Pte. Charles Frederick Weate

Mentioned In Despatches
23.4.44   Capt. (T/Major) J. C. Commings   58146
23.4.44   Capt. (T/Major) H. Shirlaw   52317

9th Field Company (Airborne), R.E.
Military Cross
243580   Lieut. Eric Charles O'Callaghan

Mentioned In Despatches
23.3.44   Capt. (T/Major) Basil Saunders Beazley   126365
          (K.I.A. 10.7.43)

181st Air-Landing Field Ambulance, R.A.M.C.
Military Cross
21.10.43   163133   Capt. Joseph Esmond Miller   R.M.O., 2/S. Staffs.
23.12.43   216228   Capt. Guy Rigby-Jones, M.B.   O.C. No. 1 Surg. Tm

George Medal
30.11.43   246170   Lieut. Brian Brownscombe   No. 2 Sectn.
(Awarded for saving the life of a non-swimmer soldier, when glider crashed into the sea near objective.)   (K.I.A. Arnhem 24.9.44 R.A.M.C. att. 2/S. Staffs.)

Military Medal
21.10.43   7364542   Pte. Harold James Eden   att. 2/S. Staffs.

1st Air-Landing Bde. H.Q.
Distinguished Service Order
21.10.43   946   A/Colonel Osmond Luxmoore Jones   Cheshire Regt.
                                                   2/I.C. 1st A/Lng. Bde.

Appendix 3/2

Awards to Glider Pilot Regiment : Sicily

Operation "Turkey Buzzard" (May–June, 1943)
Air Force Cross
11.11.43   Capt. (T/Major) Astley John Cooper   52601   Cheshire R.
             (K.I.A. Sicily 10.7.43)

Air Force Medal
11.11.43   1608391   Cpl. (A/Sgt.) Sotirios Antonopoulos
11.11.43   1779297   Cpl. (A/Sgt.) Denis Arthur Hall

Operation "Ladbrooke" (July 9/10.7.43 on)
Distinguished Service Order
21.10.43   Major (T/Lt.-Col.) George James Stewart Chatterton   91149

Military Cross
Lt. (T/Capt.) Thomas Dermot Brockbank McMillen   85618
21.10.43   Lieut.   Frank Horace Barclay   99951
(Killed in air crash S. France + 11 G.P.R. 5.12.44)
23.12.43   Lieut. Walter James Carn   179140
21.10.43   Lieut. Bernard Holt Hallsal   134176   *(BD42)*
21.10.43   Lieut. Foster Robson   182390

Distinguished Flying Cross
11.11.43   Lieut. William Nicolson Barrie   138718   *(D.O.W. Arnhem 2.10.44)*
11.11.43   Lieut. Arthur Francis Boucher-Giles   190924
11.11.43   Lieut. James Alexander Dale   149290

Distinguished Conduct Medal
24.8.44   25902073 Sgt. Edward Ivan Garratt   *(W.D. 9.7.43)*

Military Medal
23.12.43   T/81376 S/Sgt. John Alfred Ainsworth
24.8.44   4541252 Sgt. Thomas Raymond Moore   *(W.D. 9.7.43)*

Distinguished Flying Medal
11.11.43   911619   C/Sgt. (A/W.O.II) Dennis Patten Galpin
(Landed at the P.G. Bridge)
11.11.43   2874921 Sgt. (A/W.O.II) William Masson, M.M.

11.11.43 2078059 S/Sgt. Harold Norman Andrews *(BD24)*
11.11.43 5254139 S/Sgt. Harold George Protheroe
11.11.43 5500999 S/Sgt. Frank Herbert White

Awards of the 1st Parachute Brigade at Primosole Bridge, Sicily 13/14.7.43

2nd Bar to the D.S.O.
23.12.43 Major (T/Lt. Col.) Alastair Stevenson Pearson, D.S.O., M.C.
(BD 158)   62792   C.O. 1st Bn.

Distinguished Service Order
23.12.43 Brigadier (actg) Gerald William Lathbury, M.B.E.
Ox. & Bucks. L.I.   34834   C.O. 1st Bde.
23.12.43 Capt. (T/Major) Richard Thomas Henry Lonsdale, M.C.
Infantry   69129   "A" 2nd Bn.
(MC 25.10.40 Leics. R. Waziristan Ops 1939)

Military Cross
23.12.43 66302   Capt. (T/Major) David Ronald Hunter
                                        Camerons – Bde. Major
23.12.43 113514 Lt. (A/Capt.) Victor Dover   "A" 2nd Bn.
23.12.43 165617 Lt. (A/Capt.) Stanley Charles Panter   "A" 2nd Bn.
23.12.43 99817   Lieut. Anthony Mutrie Frank   "A" 2nd Bn
                                        Lancashire Fus.

Military Medal
23.12.43 2047962 Sgt. Frederick Wright   2nd Bn.
23.12.43 5339494 Cpl. (A/Sgt.) John Bardwell   2nd Bn.
23.12.43 7897666 Cpl. (A/Sgt.) Graham Errol Douglas Kerr 1st Bn.
23.12.43 4124109 Pte. (A/Cpl.) Neville Leonard Ashley   2nd Bn.
23.12.43 4032087 L/Cpl. John Lewis   "T" 1st Bn.
23.12.43 5884314 Pte. Dennis Aisne Bettle   2nd Bn.
23.12.43 3659183 Pte. William Arthur Hall   "HQ" 2nd Bn.
23.12.43 6351370 Pte. Dudley Keith Stemp   2nd Bn.
23.12.43 880602   Pte. William Henry Joseph White   "H.Q." 2nd Bn.

Mentioned In Despatches
23.4.44   247974   Lieut. J. Gardiner   1st Bn.
23.4.44   100039   Lieut. R. J. Gammon   "R" 1st Bn.
23.4.44   5190388 Cpl. (A/Sgt.) W. Busson
23.4.44   5435354 Pte. A. Roberts *(KIA 14.7.43 Arthur Roberts)*   3rd Bn.

Naval Bombardment Party att. 1 Bde.
23.12.43   172959   Lt. (T/Capt.) Francis Vere Hodge   R. Arty.

1st A/Lng. Anti-Tank Battery, R.A.
Military Cross
23.12.43   258481   Lieut. Edward Eric Clapham

Military Medal
23.12.43   1491303 Sgt. John George Anderson
23.12.43   2061934 L/Bdr. David Reed

1st Parachute Squadron, R.E.
Military Medal
23.12.43   1911484 Spr. Ronald Hall

1st Abn. Div. Signals
Military Medal
23.12.43   2583477 Cpl. Thomas Frederick Wilson   att. 2nd Bn.

16th Parachute Field Ambulance, R.A.M.C.
Distinguished Service Order
23.12.43   52033 Major (T/Lt. Col.) Percival Ross Wheatley, M.B.

Military Cross
23.12.43   122030   Captain John Rutherford, M.B.   R.M.O. 3rd Bn.
23.12.43   104446   Captain Derek Hughes Ridler   A.D. Corps "H.Q."

Military Medal
23.12.43   7373608 S/Sgt. Eric George Stevens, D.C.M.   No. 3 Section
23.12.43   7265224 Cpl. Stanley Tynan   att. 1st Bn.
                     (Died P.O.W. Germany 18.1.45)

181st A/Lng. Field Ambulance, R.A.M.C.
Military Medal
23.12.43   7370806 Pte. Victor Norman Winter

Royal Army Chaplain's Department
Military Cross
23.3.44   Rev. C. F. 4 Bernard Mary Egan   att. 2nd Bn.

Appendix 3/4

Posthumous George Cross Award—10.7.43

George Cross

9.11.43   6287023   Pte. Charles Alfred Duncan   Army Air Corps.

Pte. Duncan was a member of the Signal Platoon, 4th Parachute Battalion in the 2nd Parachute Brigade, which had arrived in North Africa in April, 1943. On the 10th July, 1943, the 1st Air-Landing Brigade was to capture the bridge at Ponte Grande, and the 2nd Parachute Brigade a bridge near Augusta. Thus the Parachute Brigade waited at M'Sakan airfield for the order to fly to Sicily. However due to the speed of the 8th Army linking up with the S.R.S. at Augusta, the 2nd Parachute Brigade's part was cancelled.

The Brigade returned to camp, and back to their billets, where they stripped off equipment and began storing their arms. All the parachutists had live grenades in their pouches, and one of the first tasks was to render them safe. This was done by unscrewing the base plate and removing the fuse. In Duncan's billet, several of the soldiers were engaged in this duty, when one of Duncan's grenade fell onto the floor. As he went to pick it up, he noticed that the safety-pin was missing, and the fuse was already burning. To save his comrades he threw himself onto the grenade and sacrificed his own life.

He was buried at Enfidaville War Cemetery, Tunisia.

(In May, 1972 his medals were presented to the Airborne Forces Museum at Aldershot.)

Chapter IV

BUONGIORNO!

The Background to the 1st Abn. Div. in Italy

BETWEEN May and June, 1943, the other three Brigades had joined the 1st Parachute Brigade to form the 1st Airborne Division under the command of Major-General G. F. Hopkinson, O.B.E., M.C.

Support for Mussolini ended on the 25th July, 1943, and he was imprisoned finally at the hotel "Camp d'Imperatore" in the Gran Sasso mountain range. The King assumed power again, and a government was formed, regardless of the German threat.

On September 3rd, 1943, the 8th Army's 13 Corps landed along the toe of Italy, principally at REGGIO in Calabria, across the Straits of Messina. Slowly the forward elements of the 5th Infantry Division and 1st Canadian Division forced their way inland.

The Landing at Taranto

On September 4th, 1943 Major-General Hopkinson was ordered to make ready for embarkation from BIZERTA to TARANTO—an important Southern Italian sea port on the 8th September.

It was found that there were not enough ships available to take the entire Division to Italy in one go, so the 2nd and 4th Parachute Brigades were to be sent first.

The role of the 1st Airborne Division in ITALY was to be a predominantly ground one, with only three parachute drops: a couple of P.O.W. aid paradrops involving several men, and one by sixty men from the 2nd Parachute Brigade in the latter stages of the campaign, when it had split from the Division, as an Independent Brigade Group.

The first part of the Division left BIZERTA on the 8th September, 1943, the convoy comprised: four ships from the 12th British Cruiser squadron: HMS "Aurora" (Carried Div. H.Q. and Medical Staff); HMS "Penelope" (part of the 4th Para. Bde.); HMS "Dido" and HMS "Sirius" (most of 2nd Para. Bde.). The mine-layer HMS "Abdeil" carried elements of 2nd & 4th Para. Bdes. Five jeeps and crew of Popski's Private Army were on the American U.S.S. "Boise". The convoy arrived in the afternoon of the 9th, escorted by the battleships "Howe" and "King George V", plus a number of destroyers. HMS "Penelope" and U.S.S. "Boise" docked immediately along the quayside, the other ships discharging men and equipment by barges.

There was no opposition, the Germans having left in the morning, and the G.O.C. accepted the surrender of the port from the Italian military governor.

The 2nd Parachute Brigade patrolled the town, whilst the 4th Parachute Brigade started to push outwards.

There then happened just after midnight on the 10th September, an incident that was to mar the peaceful landings. HMS "Abdeil" moving into a new berth, struck a mine, which set off others she was carrying, and the ship blew up, sinking within a matter of minutes. It had been carrying 400 men of the 6th (Royal Welch) Parachute Battalion; the 2nd A/Lng. Anti-Tank Battery, R.A., and the 127th (Parachute) Field Ambulance, R.A.M.C. Casualties were great, including some sixty men of the 6th Battalion killed, including their C.O.—Lt-Colonel J. A. Goodwin, and five officers. The 127th P.F.A. lost its C.O.—Lt-Colonel M. J. Kohane wounded, and the Navy also lost about fifty killed. The wounded, some 200 were evacuated to the Italian Maritime Hospital, and various emergency posts, many afterwards being transferred by sea and air to North Africa.

The Move Inland

The Divisional H.Q. started to send out reconnaissance patrols: "B" Troop of the **1st A/Lng. Recce. Sqn.** covered the right flank up to MARTINA FRANCA, whilst "A" Troop moved north towards MASSAFRA, under the command of Captain T. J. Firbank. Italians were encountered, and disarmed along the various routes.

156th Parachute Battalion seized MOTTOLA, and it was here that the **1st A/Lng. Recce. Sqn.** won its first decoration, in the shape of Cfn. G. E. York (R.E.M.E. att Recce.). As ammunition dwindled, he found an Italian truck, and got it packed with ammunition, and then drove it through shell and machine-gun fire, to the troops on the hillside. In a fight at SAN

BASILIO, Major R. J. L. Pott and Pte. D. Sowden, both of **156th Para. Bn.** won an M.C. and an M.M., and near there Cpl. J. G. "Spud" Taylor of **1st Recce**. won an M.M., with his skill with a Bren gun, when his troop was pinned down.

Contact was made with the **10th Parachute Battalion**, who had been conducting fighting patrols in the area. On the 11th September, 1943, at CASTELLANATA, Major-General Hopkinson was mortally wounded in the head whilst watching the progress of the 10th Battalion, he died the next day.

His place as O.C. 1st Abn. Div. was taken by Major-General E. E. Down. The command of the 2nd Parachute Brigade now passed to Brigadier C. H. V. Pritchard.

On the 12th September, the balance of the Division arrived in TARANTO, it included the 21st Indep. Para. Coy., who were to conduct several reconnaissance patrols in armed jeeps.

On the 13th September, it was learnt that Mussolini had been rescued in Operation "EICHE" by SS- Hauptsturmfuhrer Otto Skorzeny and a mixed Luftwaffe/SS glider-borne force, from the hotel at Gran Sasso.
On the 16th September, the two Battalions of the **4th Para. Bde.** took GIOIA DEL COLLE airfield. There then followed a reconnaissance to BARI, by the **1st A/Lng. Recce. Sqn.**

On the 19th September, the 4th Parachute Brigade was relieved by the **1st Air-Landing Brigade**, plus two sections of the **181st A/Lng. F. A.** The push was on, the enemy being pursued to FOGGIA. The **Border Regiment** now under the command of Lt-Colonel T. Haddon, formed the infantry support of a mobile force, which captured FOGGIA on the 27th September. On the way to FOGGIA, the **21st Indep. Para.** Coy. had a brief skirmish with a German 88mm battery in some woods. Major B. A. Wilson, M.C. rather than waste time on infantry tactics for crossing open ground, which lay before them, by overlapping platoons giving one another covering fire. He put ten men in each of three jeeps, which then sped over the ground, the men hanging on and shouting at the enemy. The Germans quickly evacuated their position without a fight. It was this front-running leadership that gave Major Wilson a Mention In Despatches. Following the capture of FOGGIA, the 21st Indep. Para. Coy. was instructed to send its No. 1 platoon on a reconnaissance to APRICENA. Here, it fought a sharp action, with its O.C.—Lt. R. H. Grierson being wounded, and brought in by another jeep patrol of P. P. A. He had to leave the Company, though was Mentioned In Despatches. The Company was then removed to BARLETTA, then finally to TARANTO.

The **1st Parachute Brigade** in reserve had been moved to ALTAMURA. On the 2nd October, 1943, Captain J. Timothy, M.C. from the 2nd Para. Bn. dropped near PESCARA to try and make contact with Allied P.O.W., and direct them to our lines. This he achieved with his seven man group, though five were captured, but he and two men rejoined the Battalion. He subsequently received the bar to his Military Cross. There was another P.O.W. aid drop on the 3rd October, by eleven men from the 3rd Para. Bn. at ASCOLI.

The **1st Airborne Division** withdrew from Italy in the November 1943, and disembarked at Philippeville. However, the **2nd Parachute Brigade** remained in Italy as an Independent Brigade Group. It was under the command of 8th Army, and the Central Mediterranean Force. On the 2nd December, 1943, it was taken under the command of the 2nd New Zealand Infantry Division, commanded by General Sir B.C. Freyberg, V.C., K.C.B., K.B.E., C.M.G., D.S.O.

Appendix 4/1

Awards of 1st Airborne Division
in Italy—September – November 1943

Officer of the British Empire
24.8.44   Major (T/Lt-Col.) John Alexander Goschen 36656   G. Gds.
                                           D.A.Q.M.G. 1st Abn. Div. H.G.

Member of the British Empire
28.8.44   4179274 W.O.II (R.Q.M.S.) John Flanagan   6th Bn.

Bar to the M.C.
20.4.44   Lieut. (T/Capt.) John Timothy, M.C. 164812   2nd Bn.

Military Cross
13.1.44   Lieut. (A/Major) Robert Laslett John Pott   95241   156th Bn.
27.1.44   Capt. (A/Major) Richard Strachan Hargreaves 109259   4th Bn.
4.5.44   Lieut. (T/Capt.) Janes Nash Gourlay 121956   4th Bn.
27.4.44   Lieut. Clifford Denis Boiteaux-Buchanan
               (K.I.A. Arnhem 20.9.44)   148624   2nd Bn.
20.4.44   Lieut. Richard Angus Halstead   203705   1st Bn.
20.4.44   Lieut. Ernest Albert James   247180   3rd Bn.
13.1.44   Lieut. Talbert Alexander Mollison   129454   4th Bn.
               (K.I.A. Italy 22.1.44)

Distinguished Conduct Medal
23.9.43   4543011 Sgt. (A/C.Q.M.S.) William Cook
20.4.44   2328498 L/Sgt. Peter Donald Phillips   1st Abn. Div. Sigs.
20.4.44   6216249 Sgmn. Donald Steward   1st Abn. Div. Sigs.
               (K.I.A. Arnhem 24.9.44)

Military Medal
20.4.44   961896   Sgt. Harold William Jack Guest   1st Bn.
13.1.44   3323481 Cpl. (A/Sgt.) Kenneth McGregor Cameron   10th Bn.
13.1.44   6976789 Cpl. (A/Sgt.) Patrick Diver   4th Bn.
20.4.44   2881271 L/Cpl. Paul Quilliam   1st Bn.
20.4.44   5724427 Pte. Harold Henry Cook   Bn.
13.1.44   1727069 Pte. Ernest Gordon Minter   4th Bn.
13.1.44   5671286 Pte. Donald Sowden   156th Bn.

Mentioned In Despatches (24.8.44)

Brigadier (temp) J. W. Hackett, D.S.O., M.B.E., M.C.	52752	R.A.C. C.O. 4th Bde.
Major (T/Lt-Col.) Sir W. R. De B. Des Voeux	52592	G. Gds. C.O. 156 Bn.
Major (T/Lt-Col) K. B. I. Smyth, O.B.E.	36876	Inf. C.O. 10 Bn.
Capt. (T/Major) P. J. R. Davies	68299	
Capt. (T/Major) M. S. Page	71844	156th Bn.
(K.I.A. Arnhem 20.9.44)		
Capt. (T/Major) M. D. Willis	92546	2/I.C. 2nd Bn.
Lieut. H. M. A. Cambier	226876	156th Bn.
Lieut. L. D. Delacour	179815	156th Bn.
Lieut. E. A. James, M.C.	249180	3rd Bn.
Lieut. O. P. St. Aubyn	132149	156th Bn.
Lieut. P. A. Saunders	217639	10th Bn.
Lieut. J. H. Tatham	226840	
6012810 Sgt. S. H. Cooper		
6289223 Sgt. F. W. Meadows		
6470007 L/Sgt. (A/Sgt.) S. O. Cominetti		
3770630 Cpl. (A/Sgt.) E. T. Kerwin		
2989237 Cpl. (A/Sgt.) T. A. Laughland		2nd Bn.
(for escaping after P.O.W.)		
4801673 Cpl. (A/Sgt.) J. Walker		5th Bn.
3064969 L/Sgt. N. Chapman, M.M.		5th Bn.
4923935 L/Cpl. A. E. Carter		
3959774 Pte. H. T. Harding		
5725728 Pte. A. D. Hartley		
6412155 Pte. F. Jeffery		
3129090 Pte. W. Lannary		5th Bn.
2928799 Pte. F. Neilson		
3135986 Pte. R. S. Ford *(now R. S. Fus.)*		5th Bn.

Awards of 21st Indep. Para. Coy.

Mentioned In Despatches (24.8.44)

Capt. (T/Major) B. A. Wilson, M.C.	43050	C.O. 21 Indep.
Lieut. R. H. Grierson *(W.D. 9.43)*	249461	O.C. 1st Pltn.
7902554 Pte. A. J. Sharman		

(Following his escape and eventual return to the Company in Sicily.)

Awards of 1st Air-Landing Recce Squadron

Military Cross
27.1.44   Capt. (T/Major) Charles Frederick Howard Gough
                                                31420   C.O. Recce Sqn.
13.1.44   Lieut. (T/Capt.) Thomas Joseph Firbank   149129 O.C. "A" Troop

Military Medal
13.1.44   6921700 Tpr. (A/Cpl.) James George Taylor   "A" Troop
13.1.44   1603588 Cfn. George Edwin York   R.E.M.E. att. "A" Troop

Mentioned In Despatches (24.8.44)
Lieut. D. Galbraith   240327   "A" Troop
Lieut. T. V. P. McNabb   245232   Int. Officer—H.Q.
Lieut. J. W. Marshall   245234   "D" Troop
5379474 Sgt. G. E. Holderness   *(K.I.A. Arnhem 25.9.44)*   H.Q.
5345128 L/Sgt. S. J. Haydon   H.Q.
2823483 L/Cpl. G. Storrie   "D" Troop
Tpr. C. M. Simpson   *(W.D. 16.9.43)*   "B" Troop
6853684 Tpr. J. D. Wilkes

Awards to the Glider Pilot Regiment

Distinguished Flying Medal
27.1.44   129586   Sgt. William John Bayley

Awards of the R.A.M.C. Units

Officer of the British Empire (O.B.E.)
24.8.44   Major (T/Lt-Col.) William Carson Alford, M.B. 88813
                                                C.O. 133rd P.F.A.

Mentioned In Despatches—24.8.44
Major (T/Lt-Col.) W. C. Alford, M.B.   88813   C.O. 133rd P.F.A.
Capt. (T/Major) E. Townsend, M.C., M.D.   107206   16th P.F.A.

Awards to 1st Air-Landing Light Regt., R.A.

Military Cross

6.4.44	Capt. (T/Major) Richard Keith Jones	62519
9.3.44	Lieut. Peter William Wilkinson	228466

Military Medal

9.3.44	14257583	Gnr. Dennis Arthur Bowles
9.3.44	6016566	Gnr. George Alfred Taylor
9.3.44	14264493	Gnr. Raymond Edward Webb

Mentioned In Despatches

28.4.44	Capt. (T/Major) J. A. S. Hawkins	53162
28.4.44	Lt. (Qr-Mr.) W. C. Roberts	238506
28.4.44	11006124	Gnr. E. C. Etherton

Member of the British Empire

1.3.45 Capt. (actg) Dennis Bossey Rendell, M.C. 180657   A.A.C.
(Award for escaping following capture 1.12.42 with 2nd Bn. in N. Africa. Sent to Italian P.O.W. Camp, escaped in 1943 and joined Rome Escape Organisation.)

Appendix 5

New Year Honours 1.1.44

Officer of the British Empire
Major (T/Lt.-Col.) Hilary Nelson Barlow 34606   Para Regt., A.A.C.
      (K.I.A. Arnhem 19.9.44)   2/I.C., 1st A/Lng. Bde.

Member of the British Empire
6539551   B.S.M. George Gatland   R. Arty. *(since transferred to A.A.C.)*
      (W.D. Arnhem)   11th Bn.

British Empire Medal
4384424   Sgt. Patrick Partridge   12th Bn.
4386484   Sgt. Charles Simpson   12th Bn.

King's Birthday Honours 8.6.44

British Empire Medal
3649956   A/C.S.M. Joseph McParlan   13th Bn.
861184   Sgt. (A/Col. Sgt.) Harold Robert Grange Standish
4536524   Col. Sgt. (A/C.S.M.) Wilfred Sidney Sykes   156th Bn.
6396504   Pte. Edward George Tomlin   10th Bn.
6984407   Pte. (A/Cpl.) John Fulton R.A.M.C.   195th A.F.A. att. 1/R.U.R.

1st British A.B.N. Corps H.Q.
Office of the British Empire
Colonel (temp) Richard James Moberly   34480   R. Signals
            O.C. 1st Abn. Div. Sigs. 1942-44, then Chief Signal Officer

Chapter VI

A COCKEREL LIBERATED

Formation of 6th Airborne Division

ON May 7th, 1943, Major-General R. N. Gale, O.B.E., M.C. assumed command of the newly raised 6th Airborne Division, which was brought up to strength by the September.

It consisted of the **3rd Parachute Brigade**, under command of Brigadier E. W. C. Flavell, D.S.O., M.C. who gave the command to Brigadier S. J. L. Hill, D.S.O., M.C. , on his appointment to the 5th Parachute Brigade. The **3rd Parachute Brigade** had been formed on the conversion of the 223rd Independent Infantry Brigade, its three infantry battalions became parachute units. The 7th Parachute Battalion, on arrival of the 1st Canadian Parachute Battalion in July, became a unit of the **5th Parachute Brigade**. This brigade was formed in June, 1943, under the command of Flavell, command then passed to Brigadier J. H. N. Poett on the 5th July, 1943. The **6th Air-Landing Brigade** comprised two of the units of the 1st Air-Landing Brigade, that had remained at home, plus an additional Infantry Battalion. The commander was Brigadier the Honourable H. K. M. Kindersley. There was of course, the Divisional Support element from the Arms and Services, among which was the **1st Abn. Light Tank Sqn.**, which in January, 1944, became the 6th Abn. Div. Recce. Regt., and trained with the Tetrarch Light Tank.

Between May, 1943, and June, 1944, there was much training, and the troops realised that something big was coming up. This was the invasion of the coast of FRANCE—Operation "OVERLORD". The landings comprised the British 2nd Army and the American 1st Army, with flank airborne landings : the American 82nd & 101st Abn. Divisions on the West, and the British 6th Airborne Division on the east.

The Initial Landings

Shortly after midnight on the 5th June, 1944, members of the **22nd Independent Parachute Company**, formed in October, 1943, under the command of Major Stockwell, dropped out of the sky, to prepare the dropping and landing zones, for the first lift due to arrive over the following hour.

The two primary tasks were the capture of the two bridges over the CAEN CANAL and RIVER ORNE by a glider force, and the destruction of the gun battery at MERVILLE by a para/glider force. This battery covered the beach area, where the British 1st Corps was to land.

There were to be two lifts, due to the quantity of aircraft available, the aircraft coming from No. 38 and 46 Groups, R.A.F. Also under Major-General Gale's command was the 1st Special Service Brigade, under Brigadier The Lord Lovat, who would move off the beach-head, and reinforce the elements of 5th Parachute Brigade at the Orne.

a) The Bridge Raid

The units for the capture of the bridges comprised the following, under the command of Major John Howard, Oxford & Bucks L. I.:

"B" Company, 2nd Bn., Oxford & Bucks L.I. (2 platoons)

"D" Company, 2nd Bn., Oxford & Bucks L.I.

249th Field Coy. (Abn.), R.E.—Detachment (30 men)

They were carried in six Horsa gliders of "C" Squadron, G.P.R., which left at 2256 hrs. on June 5th from Tarrant Rushton, Dorset. At 0016 hrs., the gliders cast off, the leading one, piloted by S/Sgt. Wallwork, with S/Sgt. Ainsworth landed with a crash, through the perimeter wire defence of the canal bridge, injuring the two pilots. The men of Lt. D. Brotheridge' platoon scrambled out with Major Howard. Lt. Brotheridge was killed after being hit in the neck by a machine-gun bullet, as they raced across the bridge. The second glider piloted by S/Sgt. Hobbs, and S/Sgt. Boland landed at the east end, and Lt. D. Wood's platoon captured the 20mm gun emplacement, though Wood and his Sgt. were wounded and Cpl. Godbold assumed command. The third glider piloted by S/Sgt. Barkway and S/Sgt. Boyle crashed on landing, and the third platoon came across the bridge to form a defence perimeter, on the western end. Both Hobbs and Wallwork received D.F.M.'s.

Of the three other gliders detailed to capture the ORNE BRIDGE, one landed five miles away; the second piloted by S/Sgt. Pearson landed 300 yards north of the bridge, and Lt. Fox's platoon found the bridge undefended. The third glider, with Lt. Sweeney's platoon on board, landed 500 yards away, and secured the bridge, while Fox's platoon moved to Benouville as reserve.

They now awaited the arrival of the parachute force.

b) The Merville Battery

This was to be the task of the **9th Parachute Battalion** of the 3rd Para. Brigade, under the command of Lt-Colonel T. B. H. Otway, (who received the D.S.O. for this action).

The plan was for the battalion to drop onto D.Z. "V" near VARAVILLE and rendezvous, there would be three breaching parties led through the minefield in three marked routes by the taping party. Once the wire was cut, the assault party would follow up, backed by the reserve company, and two sniping parties. The glider assault party comprised three officers and 47 other ranks, plus one officer and 7 other ranks from the **591st Para. Sqn., R.E.**, and would be carried in three gliders, which would crash land on top of the battery itself. There was also a glider-borne support group of five gliders, that would land near the D.Z., with three jeeps and two anti-tank guns. A **Naval Bombardment Party** was to drop with the Battalion, and order the guns of HMS "Arethusa" to open fire an hour after the attack began, should the attack have failed. The attack was timed for 0430 hrs.

Although that was the plan, it didn't all work out that well. Several of the aircraft, which all left at 2310 hrs., took evasive action, and instead of the 1900 yards x 800 yard D.Z., many sticks fell over fifty square miles of Normandy, one stick dropping thirty miles from the battery.

The battery recce and rendezvous, parties dropped on time, but were almost killed in the Lancaster air raid between 0030 and 0040 hrs., when they were charged by a herd of maddened cows. By 0250 hrs., the Battalion only numbered 150—about three companies, with no heavy armament and no mine detectors. Although faced with this problem, Lt-Colonel Otway decided to go through with his task. "A" Company led the way, followed by H.Q., "B" Company and then twenty men of "C" Company, plus the B.M.O. Captain W. E. Church and six orderlies from the **224th P.F.A.**

They met Major G. E. Smith and his recce party, who informed them, that they had penetrated the defences with the taping party under Captain P. Greenway. They had successfully marked the minefield, although equipped with neither mine-detectors or tape, by heel marks in the earth.

At 0430 hrs., they were ready, "B" Company formed two breaching teams, and "A" and "C" were joined together into one assault force of four combat teams; one for each gun of the battery, and each of twelve men. Suddenly six enemy-machine-guns opened up outside the perimeter, and four more inside, started firing. The single Vickers M.G. with the force silenced three of the perimeters machine-guns, and the diversion party of six men, under Sgt. Knight silenced the other three.

Then two of the three gliders could be seen circling over the battery, tracer from the 20mm gun emplacement pouring into them. The third glider had parted company with its tow-rope and landed safely in England. S/Sgt. S. G. Bone, with Captain Gordon-Browne on board mistook the village for the battery, but took evasive action and landed four miles from the objective. The party fought at LE MESNIL, in defence of 3rd Para. Bde. H.Q., and then rejoined the Battalion. The second glider piloted by S/Sgt. Kerr prepared to land among the casemates, but he saw a "MINEN" sign, so overshot, and crash-landed in an orchard, 200 yards from the battery. He and his four wounded passengers, plus the rest of the party under Lt. H. C. Pond stumbled out of the smouldering glider. They immediately took on the German reserve platoon from the 1/736th Regiment, who they kept at bay for four hours.

The assault party stormed the guns, and engaged the gunners, who after a brief struggle, and seeing the parachute wings on the smock sleeves promptly gave up the fight. The four guns were destroyed and were found to be 75mm and not the heavier 150mm calibre, as had been thought. The success signal was lit, and Otway found that he had eighty men unwounded, and thirty wounded, who were tended in a nearby barn. One officer had been killed, and four wounded, and the rest of the force killed or missing.

The 3rd Parachute Brigade

The Brigade's objectives were to capture the Merville Battery; and destroy the bridges over the River Deves, thus denying the enemy the Bois de Bavent ridge.

It had been decided that a portion of Brigade H.Q. and a small party from each Battalion, with one company from the 1st Canadians would drop onto D.Z. "V" and clear part of it of posts, that would have obstructed the glider landings. Sixteen Albemarles carried the party, though several were unable to drop their sticks in the correct place, one was forced to turn back, having been hit by anti-aircraft fire—the shell burst blew the Brigade-Major out, and he dangled below the aircraft. He was pulled back in, and rejoined the Brigade in the evening, after the glider lift.

As most of the Independent Pathfinder's equipment was damaged in the drop, only two green lights appeared on D.Z. "V". Many aircraft carrying the **9th and 1st Can. Para. Battalions** took evasive action, and men were dropped into or close by the River DIVES, as the D.Z. was shrouded in smoke due to the bombing raid on the Merville Battery.

The 8th Battalion was to drop on D.Z. "K" but was also scattered. Its orders were to destroy the bridges at BURE and TROARN, and then withdraw to the woods of BAVENT, and form a defensive sector. Lt-Colonel Pearson, who had been wounded, collected about 180 men, and divided them into two groups, and sent them off to the bridges. Some of the sappers made the rendezvous, and one group under Lt. T. Juckes made for BURE with explosives in hand trolleys. The other party under Major Roseveare commandeered an R.A.M.C. jeep, and sped off in the direction of TROARN, with seven other ranks hanging on. They blew the bridges, and both groups moved on foot to the second rendezvous at LE MESNIL.

By the evening, the 8th Battalion in the BOIS DE BAVENT numbered about 250, and Lt-Colonel Pearson then conducted fighting patrols, including cratering the road at ROUCHEVILLE.

The 1st Canadian Battalion's "C" Coy. attacked VARAVILLE, the O.C.—Major H. M. McLeod being killed. His place was taken by Captain J. P. Hanson, who was awarded a Military Cross. Sgt. Minard was awarded an M.M. as a platoon commander and Pte. W. Ducker was awarded one, for outstanding performance as a stretcher bearer, he was later fatally wounded. The Canadian's **"B" Coy.** attacked ROBEHOMME, and blew up target bridges.

Although at first, the sappers of **2nd Troop, 3rd Para. Sqn., R.E.** had difficulty in locating their explosive containers, since many of them had dropped into the flood waters, east of VARAVILLE. However, Lt. Inman and 12 sappers met, and reached VARAVILLE, blew up the bridge, and then the Lieutenant with five sappers went to ROBEHOMME, and blew a hole in that one as well.

Of the 17 strong glider force from "E" and "F" Squadrons, G.P.R.—the 6 attached to 8th Battalion, only three reached D.Z. "K"; two landed on D.Z. "N" and one crashed on landing, killing all on board. The remaining

11, which were the heavy support for Merville; three cast off too early; four landed on D.Z. "N" and four near D.Z. "V".

The **9th Battalion** following its success at MERVILLE, now took LE PLEIN, and although reduced to about 100 men, took a defensive position in the Chateau d'Amfreville, and were relieved by No.6 Commando in the evening.

Brigadier Hill had landed in a flooded field near CABOURG. He and twenty men, after swimming the Dives, met Captain T. Robinson and a small party from the 9th Battalion near VARAVILLE. Here they met Lts. Paters and Catlin, and men from the mortar platoon, and "A" Company, also of the 9th Bn., making the party forty-two. They decided to make for Merville, but were bombed by Allied bombers, and only seven survived, including Captain Robinson and Brigadier Hill—who had been wounded in the left buttock. Captain Robinson was captured, but escaped, rejoining his Battalion on the 9th June.

The 5th Parachute Brigade

Soon after the stick of **22nd Indep. Para. Coy**. under Lieutenant Robert de Latour had marked D.Z. "N", Brigadier Poett and the advance party of the 7th Battalion dropped. They were followed by 110 Albemarles and Stirlings of 38 Group, R.A.F., and 21 Dakotas of 46 Group, R.A.F. Six were shot down, but the others successfully dropped 2,026 men over the D.Z. Also 400 ammunition containers were dropped, and over 60% of these were collected by the Divisional R.A.S.C. Company—716th (Abn.) Light Composite.

At 0050 hrs., the **7th Parachute Battalion** dropped: "C" Company under Major R. Bartlett was to reinforce Major J. Howard's force at the bridges, as soon as they landed. As in nearly all the airborne drops, men were invariably scattered. With the aid of Lt. Roger's Aldis lamp, and Private Chambers' bugle, the men began to rally near LE HOM. By 0230 hrs., Lt-Colonel. Pine-Coffin had about two hundred men at the bridges, but hardly any heavy weapons at all, since the supply containers could not be found. Just before dawn, "A" Company under Major N. Taylor, installed in and around BENOUVILLE was attacked by tanks and infantry, "B" Company under Major R.S. Neale at LE PORT was also in action. "C" Company under Captain R. Keene, (as Major Bartlett was missing), engaged itself, as part of the reserve, and conducted a couple of fighting patrols. Later at 1300 hrs., Lord Lovat, and his personal piper led the men from the 1st Special Service Brigade to reinforce the bridge over the

CAEN CANAL, which thereafter was called "Pegasus Bridge". At 1400 hrs., Captain Webber, 2/I.C. "A" Company arrived, himself wounded, and reported that they were in need of support at BENOUVILLE, and that there were many wounded, that needed to be evacuated. The wounded had been treated by Captain Wagstaff and his **No. 2 Section, 225th P.F.A.** Casualties on the D.Z. had been treated by Captain D. J. Tibbs, and his **No. 3 Section** in an R.A.P. in the church at RANVILLE, and Captain D. R. Urquhart had set up an A.D.S. near the ORNE Bridge, with a similar one at the CAEN Bridge under Captain Jacobs.

The **12th Parachute Battalion** was to rendezvous near the quarry, half a mile North of the Orne Bridge, marked by a red light flashed by the Intelligence Officer. By 0300 hrs., some 30 men of each company had reached the rendezvous, and Lt-Col. Johnston decided to make for his objective—LE BAS DE RANVILLE. An hour later, the Battalion was digging in: "A" Company just east of the Orne Bridge; "B" Company in the hedges south of LE BAS DE RANVILLE; and "C" Company south of the village itself. A forward position was manned by a patrol of "C" Company—12 men under Captain J. A. N. Sim, plus two men from the **Naval Bombardment Party** in contact with HMS "Mauritius", and an anti-tank gun. At 1030 hrs., the enemy attacked supported by two SP Guns. It was then found that the anti-tank gun's breech was damaged, and the F.O.B. officer, who had called on support from the warship, found that it was firing on another target. The SP Guns opened fire, and soon only Sim, his batman, and Sgts. Millburn and Jones remained unwounded. They held out for a couple of hours, but then had to retire, under mortar cover of "C" Company. Captain Sim was awarded the M.C., and the two sergeants, later killed—the D.C.M.

By mid-afternoon, the two Battalions had been relieved by elements of the 3rd Infantry Division.

The **13th Parachute Battalion** landed in good order, the men rallying to hunting horn blasts. Major Cramphorn's "A" Company, with the **591st Para. Sqn., R.E.** clearing the D.Z. of anti-glider poles, whilst the other two companies took RANVILLE.

General Gale landed safely, in the first of the large scale glider landings, in a glider piloted by Major S. C. Griffiths, who was the 2/I.C., **No. 1 Glider Wing, G.P.R.** The sixty-eight Horsa, and four Hamilcar gliders carried the **3rd & 4th A/Lng. A/Tk. Batteries, R.A.; 211th Bty., 53rd A/Lng. Lt. Regt.,** and also a bulldozer team from **286th (Abn.) Fld. Park Coy., R.E.** plus a detachment from **6th Abn. Div. Wkshps., R.E.M.E.**

Brigadier Poett met General Gale, and Brigadier Kindersley of the 6th Air-Landing Brigade, and they walked to the bridge near D.Z. "N" just before the commandos arrived, and witnessed a gun battle between two gun boats and the mixed Para/glider force. One boat was put out of action and the other retreated.

The 6th Air-Landing Brigade

The Brigade was carried in 256 gliders, including the **6th Abn. Div. Recce. Regt.** in 30 Hamilcars. The Hamilcar Squadron was under the command of Major J. A. Dale, D.F.C. (won at Sicily). The balance of the **Oxford & Bucks. L.I.** landed on L.Z. "W", and the **Royal Ulster Rifles** and Bde. H.Q. on L.Z. "N" between 2051 and 2123 hrs. The **12th Devons.**, (less "A" Company that landed as part of the Armoured Recce. Group, with their jeeps), landed by sea on Queen Beach near OUISTREHAM on June 7th. Also by sea came the other 17 Pdr. anti-tank guns of **3rd A/Lng. A/Tk. Bty.** (three landed the day before); the other two batteries of the **53rd A/Lng. Lt. Regt;** and the Seaborne party of the **195th A.F.A. R.A.M.C.**

Unfortunately most of the Tetrarch light tanks fouled their tracks in the abandoned rigging lines of parachutes that littered the DZ, so could not be used effectively. Most of the crews swapping them for Cromwell tanks a couple of days later.

On the 7th June, the **Oxford & Bucks. L.I.** occupied ESCOVILLE. However, they were fiercely counter-attacked and retired to HEROUVILLETTE. They were accompanied by **No. 4 Section, 195th A.F.A.**

The **Royal Ulsters** left RANVILLE at 0900 hrs. for LONGUEVAL: "A" & "B" Companies under Major Rickord and Vickery, with "C" Company under the 2/I.C: Major J. Drummond, and the F.O.B, plus the company mortars on a hill known as the Ring Contour. LONGUEVAL was occupied, the next objective—St. HONORINE; though the Germans occupied the town, and shelled "C" Company who were forced to retire. The two assault companies also retired from St. HONORINE, leaving 7 killed, 4 officers and 65 other ranks wounded, and about 70 missing.

The Germans counter-attacked with tanks and infantry against the **12th Para. Bn.**'s position near LE BAS DE RANVILLE. After a fierce engagement the Germans withdrew. The Battalion was then relieved by the **12th Devons.**

On June 9th, the Germans pulled out of St. HONORINE, and Brigadier Kindersley ordered an attack to be made. The **Devon's** mortars opened up, and hit an ammunition dump. The **Ulsters** moved forward, Major A. Dyball's "D" Company moving across to COLOMBELLE, and laid an ambush on a German patrol. Captain Donnelly's patrol was attacked, as they entered St. HONORINE, and found that tanks and infantry were moving back into the town. They retired to LONGUEVAL, which was mortared and shelled, many of the Ulsters and 12th Para. Bn. were wounded. The R.A.P. was caught in a cross-fire, and the C.O. of the 195th A.F.A. was wounded whilst making a visit to the post. The **Devon's** were attacked in LE BAS DE RANVILLE, but forced the Germans to retire.

The **Oxford & Bucks. L.I.** also forced back a mixed tank force from HEROUVILLETTE, with the help of the 6 Pdr. and 17 Pdr. guns of the **3rd & 4th A/Lng. A/Tk. Batteries**, who knocked out two Panzer IV tanks and two SP Guns.

There next followed the three day battle for BREVILLE. The **9th Para. Battalion** was at the Chateau St. Come and the BOIS DE MONT—a thickly wooded area.

The Battalions of the **5th Para. Bde.** were solidly attacked, and were supported by tanks from the 13/18th Hussars.

The capture of BREVILLE on June 12th, protected the left flank of the 21st Army Group, and the 6th Abn. Division continued to hold the line from LE PLEIN to the BOIS DE BURES, its strength being brought up to scratch by the 4th Special Service Brigade, the Belgian Brigade and the Royal Netherlands Brigade.

For the next two months, they sat in their defence line; slit trenches and bunkers, and conducted numerous fighting patrols. In one on the 10th July, Sgt. Lucas of "B" Coy., 7th Para. Bn. won a bar to his M.M. by engaging the enemy with a Bren-gun as the patrol withdrew. In another, Lt. de Latour and seven men of the 22nd Indep. Para. Coy. penetrated the BOIS DE BEVENT, and captured several prisoners, without a shot. On the way back, they were fired upon, and de Latour, thought to have been the first Allied soldier to land in France was killed: he was the last surviving officer of the Company.

On the 18th August, the **1st Canadian Para. Bn.'s** "A" Company under Captain Clancey captured the bridge at GOUSTRANVILLE. The **224th P.F.A., R.A.M.C.** had been in the Divisional rest area at ECARDE, and then moved to RIVABELLA, and by the 20th August, with reinforcements from the **195th A.F.A., R.A.M.C.** they were in action. The 3rd **Para. Bde.** crossed the DIVES, and the **8th & 9th Para. Bns.** occupied BURES. The bridge was reconstructed by members of the **3rd Para. Sqn., R.E.** The

Canadians occupied the bridges over the DIVES CANAL, the **9th Para. Bn.**, led by Lt-Col. N. Crookenden, who had relieved Lt-Col. Otway, then occupied DOZULE, although put under shellfire almost immediately and were forced to retire.

The **5th Para. Bde.** passed through the Canadians, but were held up, as the level of water had risen. The **7th Para. Battalion** was pinned down by fire through the impenetrable hedgerows, which also stopped the **12th Para. Battalion** for a time. The 7th & 12th Para. Battalions then occupied PUTOT-EN-AUGE. The **13th Para. Battalion** tried to take Hill 13, but failed to do so, Major R. Tarrant being mortally wounded, as "A" & "B" Companies attacked.

The push continued, the **5th Para. Bde.** passing through the 3rd, on the way to PONT L'EVEQUE. On the 21st August, Lt-Col. N. G. Stockwell, who had taken over from Lt-Col W. A. B. Harris, M.C. who was wounded, sent his **12th Para. Bn.'s** "A" & "B" Companies across the fords of the two rivers, and secured the bridgehead. They were forced back by shellfire, and lack of ammunition.

The **13th Para. Bn.** crossed the first river, but were held up, and forced to retire, when the Germans set the houses on fire. Then, as patrols reported that the Germans were retiring once again, the two Brigades set off, and were soon in PONT AUDEMER, the 5th Para. Bde. being first in.

The Division then left France for Bulford on September 3rd, 1944, for a well-earned rest.

Awards of the 6th Airborne Division
in Normandy—June – September 1944

6th A.B.N. Div. H.Q.
Distinguished Service Order

31.8.44   Major-Gen. (Temp) Richard Nelson Gale, O.B.E., M.C.   20116
late R. Innisk. Fus.   O.C. 6th Abn. Div.

31.8.44   Major (T/Lt-Col.) Robert Napier Hubert Campbell Bray 39414
Duke of Well. Regt.   G.S.O.I. 6th Abn. Div.

1.2.45 Major (T/Lt-Col.) Frank Harrington Lowman, M.B.E.   53650
Royal Engineers   C.R.E.   6th Abn. Div.

Officer of the British Empire

1.2.45   Lieut-Col. John Sydney Lapage Norris, M.C.   17089
Royal Artillery   C.R.A. 6th Abn. Div.

Member of the British Empire

1.2.45   Major William Alexander Carlton Collingwood   64582
R.N. Fus.   Major – 3 Bde.

1.2.45   Capt. (T/Major) Gerald Auguste Charles Lacoste   35228
R. Arty   G.S.O.II (Int.)

3rd & 5th Parachute Brigades
3rd Bar to the D.S.O.

1.2.45 Major (T/Lt-Col.) Alastair Stevenson Pearson, D.S.O., M.C. 62792
CO 8th Bn.

1st Bar to the D.S.O.

29.3.45   Brigadier (Temp) Stanley James Ledger Hill, D.S.O., M.C. 52648
C.O. 3rd Bde.

Distinguished Service Order

29.3.45   Brigadier (Temp) Joseph Howard Nigel Poett   38346
Durham L. I.   C.O. 5th Bde.

31.8.44   Major (T/Lt-Col) Richard Geoffrey Pine-Coffin   40705
Devon R.   C.O. 7th Bn.

31.8.44   Major (T/Lt-Col) Alexander Percival Johnson   52653
(K.I.A. 12.6.44) Suffolk R.   C.O. 12th Bn.

19.10.44 Capt. (T/Major)(A/Lt-Col.) Terence Brandram Hastings Otway
63633   Ryl. Ulster Rifs.   C.O. 9th Bn.

Military Cross

21.12.44	Capt. (T/Major) Alfred Reeves Clark	162409
		O.C. "C" 13th Bn.
21.12.44	Capt. (T/Major) Edward James O'Brien Croker	44846
		Leics. Regt. 12th Bn.
31.8.44	Capt. (T/Major) Ralph Symonds Neale	124898
		O.C. "B" 7th Bn.
21.12.44	Capt. (T/Major) Charles John Vere Shoppee	214537 13th Bn.
19.10.44	Capt. (T/Major) George Edward Smith	70499
		O.C. "B" 9th Bn.
21.12.44	Capt. (T/Major) Reginald Mowlam Tarrant	58149
	Dorset R. *(D.O.W. 28.8.44)*	O.C. "A" 13th Bn.
31.8.44	Capt. (T/Major) John Nigel Taylor	318480
		O.C. "A" 7th Bn.
19.10.44	Lieut. (T/Capt.) John Anthony Noel Sim 112966	"C" 12th Bn.
		York. & Lancs.
31.8.44	Lieut. (T/Capt.) Rupert Archer Keene	143508
		O.C. "C" 7th Bn.
21.3.45	Lieut. (T/Capt.) Herbert Horatio Mills	134321 7th Bn. Int. Sn.
31.8.44	Lieut. (T/Capt.) John James Webber, D.C.M.	138495
		2/I.C. "A" 7th Bn.
31.8.44	Lieut. James Hunter Duthie	12th Bn.
19.10.44	Lieut. Richard Noel Fry	286000 8th Bn.
31.8.44	Lieut. William Frederick Hodgson	262425 13th Bn.
31.8.44	Lieut. Daniel McCowan Hunter	235346 "A" 7th Bn.
19.10.44	Lieut. Thomas Ellemore Miller, M.M.	262296 9th Bn.
19.10.44	Lieut. Herbert Charles Pond	255225 "A" 9th Bn.
31.8.44	Lieut. Edward Gordon Pool *(WD)*	288331 "B" 7th Bn.

Distinguished Conduct Medal

19.10.44	3649956	W.O.II (C.S.M.) Joseph McParlan, B.E.M.	13th Bn.
29.3.45	4391561	Sgt. (A/W.O.II) James Albert Warcup, B.E.M.	
			"C" 12th Bn.
19.10.44	7012426	Sgt. Peter James McCambridge	9th Bn.
28.9.44	4343040	Sgt. Frank Milburn *(K.I.A. 6.6.44)*	"C" 12th Bn.
28.9.44	1120624	L/Sgt. William Jones *(K.I.A. 6.6.44)*	"C" 12th Bn.
1.2.45	14635496	Pte. Sidney Cornell	

MID—changed to award of a D.C.M. for same act of Gallantry

22.3.45	14216814 Pte. Michael John McGee	7th Bn.
	(D.O.W. 6.6.44 Orne Bridge)	

British Empire Medal (BEM)—for hazardous work in a very brave manner

7.7.44	4391561	Sgt. James Albert Warcup	"C" 12th Bn.

Bar to the M.M.

21.12.44	5680156	Sgt. Ernest Alexis Lucas, M.M.	"B" 7th Bn.

Military Medal

31.8.44	6281947	W.O.I George Johnson	7th Bn.
19.10.44	4387903	W.O.II (A/W.O.I) George David Miller	"B" 9th Bn.
19.10.44	4122305	W.O.II (C.S.M.) Bernard MacGuiness	22 Indep.
29.3.45	6025157	Sgt. (A/W.O.II) Sidney George Knight	"B" 9th Bn.
19.10.44	6398348	C.Q.M.S. Leonard Arthur Graham	9th Bn.
29.3.45	4395919	Sgt. John William Dobson	12th Bn.
31.8.44	6853662	Sgt. Eric George Frost	9th Bn.
21.12.44	14632835	Sgt. John Goodall	"B" 13th Bn.
1.2.45	328084	Sgt. John Arthur Holmes	12th Bn.
21.12.44	3769990	Sgt. Stanley Hughes	13th Bn.
21.12.44	2884928	Sgt. Eric James Rutherford Lindores	22 Indep.
19.10.44	5680156	Sgt. Ernest Alexis Lucas	"B" 7th Bn.
19.10.44	6008160	Sgt. Patrick McGeever	9th Bn.
29.3.45	4625881	Sgt. Reginald Morgan North	12th Bn.
19.10.44	3309526	Sgt. Patrick Robert O'Connell	
19.10.44	5120931	Sgt. Allan George Reading	8th Bn.
19.10.44	6976552	Sgt. John Sanderson	9th Bn.
29.3.45	6014032	Sgt. Arthur James Joseph Taylor	9th Bn.
19.10.44	5112970	Cpl. (A/Sgt.) Wilfred Errol Miles Littlewood *(K.I.A. 25.8.44)*	8th Bn.
19.10.44	5124320	Cpl. (A/Sgt.) Reginald Harry Mayhew	8th Bn.
21.12.44	1445959	L/Sgt. Bernard Batho	
19.10.44	6013962	L/Sgt. John Trevor Bullock	9th Bn.
31.8.44	5123514	L/Sgt. John Fennell Nankinell	12th Bn.
19.10.44	14526028	Cpl. James McGuiness	9th Bn.
28.9.44	14427403	Cpl. Malcolm Kennedy Walsh *(K.I.A. 9.6.44)*	12th Bn.
31.8.44	6857360	L/Cpl. Dennis William Butt	7th Bn.
19.10.44	6093900	L/Cpl. Ernest Ealham	9th Bn.
31.8.44	4462855	Pte. Ronald James Brennan	"B" 7th Bn.
21.12.44	14660071	Pte. James Glancey	8th Bn.
31.8.44	14399494	Pte. Francis James Hall	"A" 12th Bn.
21.12.44	14530615	Pte. Robert Kennedy	
19.10.44	14605780	Pte. Albert Lewis	7th Bn.
19.10.44	266521	Pte. Joe Millward	"B" 9th Bn.

19.10.44	14407038 Pte. Harry Stevenson	
19.10.44	14401088 Pte. Edward Traynor	7th Bn.

Croix-De Guerre (France)

53049	T/Major John Francis Cramphorn	13th Bn.
129619	T/Major Ian Claude Dyer	9th Bn.
285222	Lieut. Colin William Brown	8th Bn.
189373	Lieut. Denis Gerald Slade	9th Bn.
1136544	Sgt. Dennis Edmund Griss	12th Bn.
14331743	Pte. James Moran	7th Bn.

Awards conferred by President of the U.S.A. (20.6.44)

Legion of Merit—Officer

WS/Colonel (T/Major-Genl.) Richard Nelson Gale, O.B.E., M.C.   20116
R. Innisk. Fus.   C.O. 6th Abn. Div.

Silver Star

WS/Lt-Col. (T/Brigadier) Joseph Howard Nigel Poett   38346
Durham L. I.   C.O. 5th Bde.

Mentioned In Despatches

29.3.45	Lieut-General F. A. M. Browning, C.B., D.S.O. 22588	
	late Gren. Gds. *(BD 203)*	C.O. 1st B.R., Abn. Corps.
22.3.45	Major-General R. N. Gale, D.S.O., O.B.E., M.C. 20116	
	late R. Innisk. F.	C.O. 6th Abn. Div.

Mentioned In Despatches (22.3.45)
Army Air Corps

Major (temp) E. S. Lough	117040	D.A.A.Q.M.G. 5th Bde.
Major A. A. K. Pope	77672	D.A.A.Q.M.G. 3rd Bde.
K.S.L.I. *(K.I.A. 6.6.44)*		
Capt. (temp) D. J. Kypen	258058	8th Bn.
Capt. (temp) I. A. Tait	153407	22nd Indep.
Camn H. *(K.I.A. 9.6.44)*		
Capt. (temp) J. T. Woodgate	156618	Staff. 3rd Bde.
Lieut. W. E. Anderson, M.C.	148939	9th Bn.
Lieut. P. Cattle	180127	
Lieut. D. G. Slade	189373	9th Bn.
7011364 W.O.I(A) W. J. Cunningham	*(KIA 17.6.44)*	9th Bn.
4692027 W.O.II J. W. Kay		12th Bn.

6025157	A/W.O.II S. G. Knight	*(awarded M.M.)*	9th Bn.
4391561	A/W.O.II J. A. Warcup, B.E.M.	*(awarded D.C.M.)*	"C" 12th Bn.
944489	S/Sgt. D. W. M. James		
6206995	S/Sgt. R. C. Creed		9th Bn.
5769851	Sgt. J. W. Hunt		8th Bn.
2047504	A/Sgt. E. Hobson		
4625881	A/Sgt. R. M. North	*(awarded M.M.)*	12th Bn.
5826065	A/Sgt. R. E. Orr		9th Bn.
4801460	Cpl. E. Mills		8th Bn.
5885256	L/Cpl. A. Knibbs		8th Bn.

Parachute Regiment

Capt. (actg.) R. E. V. De Lautour   149121   22nd Indep.
       (Robert Edward Vane De Lautor D.O.W. 20.6.44)

Following had received M.I.D.'s prior to Airborne Service, and were killed in Normandy:

Capt. (T/Major) E. G. Charlton   58172   K.O.Y.L.I. att. 9th Bn.
       (M.I.D. 8.7.43 East Africa. K.I.A. 9.6.44)

4388377   Sgt. D. McKirdy   Green Howards   13th Bn.
       (M.I.D. 27.4.44 in the field. K.I.A. 23.8.44)

5439144   Cpl. F. W. Ball , D.C.L.I.   7th Bn.
       (M.I.D. 27.1.44 N. Africa. K.I.A. 22.8.44)

6th Air-Landing Brigade
Commander of The British Empire

1.2.45   T/Brig. The Hon. Hugh Kenyon Molesworth Kindersley, M.B.E., M.C.
       61108   Scots. Gds. *(W.D.)*   C.O. 6th A/Lng. Bde.

Distinguished Service Order

10.10.44   A/Colonel Robert Goulbourne Parker   17679   Green Howards
       2/I.C. 6th A/Lng. Bde., D.S.O. as T/C.O.   12th Para. Bn.

2nd Bn., Oxford & Bucks. L.I.
Distinguished Service Order

31.8.44   Capt. (T/Major) Mark Darrell-Brown   47522   2/I.C. later C.O.
31.8.44   Capt. (T/Major) Reginald John Howard   155710   O.C. Bridge Raid

Military Cross

31.8.44   Lieut. Charles Anthony Hooper   2711237
31.8.44   Lieut. Richard Arthur Amyas Smith
31.8.44   Lieut. Henry John Sweeney   204283   R.N. Fus. att. 2nd Bn.

Military Medal

31.8.44   2572704   L/Cpl. Lawrence George Stacey   *(W.D. 7.6.44)*

Mentioned In Despatches

10.5.45	36539	Major J. S. R. Edmunds		"B" Coy.
22.3.45	180636	Capt. B. C. E. Priday		"D" Coy.
8.9.44	237676	Lieut. H. D. Brotheridge	*(D.O.W. 6.6.44)*	
10.5.45	6642181	Sgt. C. H. Godbold		"D" Coy.

Croix De Guerre (France)
Awarded with Bronze Palme

155710   Major Reginald John Howard, D.S.O.

Awarded with Bronze Star

5391885   Cpl. Stanley Evans

1st Bn., Royal Ulster Rifles
Military Cross

19.10.44   Capt. (T/Major) Frederick Robert Armstrong Hynds   134847
29.3.45   Lieut. (T/Capt.) Robert Dickson Martin   109577
   (K.I.A. Rhine Crossing 24.3.45)

Military Medal

29.3.45   7012822   W.O.II William James McCutcheon
   (K.I.A. Rhine 24.3.45)
19.10.44   7012420   Sgt. William Hardy
31.8.44   6984231   Rfn. Charles Feeney   *(K.I.A. 24.8.44)*
31.8.44   3853060   Rfn. John Gilliland

Croix De Guerre & Bronze Star

7021622   Rfn. David Cochrane

Mentioned In Despatches (22.3.45)

Lieut-Colonel R. J. H. Carson	44059	C.O. 1st Bn., R.U.R.
Capt. (temp) R. Rigby	176451	
Capt. (temp) H. MacL. Sheane	176459	
Lieut. T. G. W. Houghton	190260	
7016344 Cpl. C. W. Stephenson		
7012477 Cpl. J. T. Uprichard		
7013523 Rfn. F. Purdy		

12th Bn., Devonshire Regiment
Military Cross
29.3.45   Lieut. (T/Capt.) Thomas Dickenson David Bowman   243050
29.3.45   Lieut. Bertram Frederick Horwood   295436
           (K.I.A. Ardennes 6.2.45)
Military Medal
31.8.44   5616813 Sgt. (A/Col. Sgt.) Frank Samuel Bond   "C" Coy.
21.12.44   842515   Sgt. William Edward Coleman
29.3.45   5621727 Cpl. Percy Aplin
31.8.44   5628483 Cpl. Charles Ian Hamilton Jeffrey   "A" Coy
21.12.44   3532888 Pte. Harry Geard

Mentioned In Despatches (22.3.45)
Lieut.-Col. (temp) G. R. Stevens   41437   R. Fus. C.O. 12th Bn.
5628419   Cpl. T. Megee
14567718   Pte. S. Molesworth

Croix De Guerre & Palme (France)
Major (T/Lt.Col.) Paul Gleadell   47571

6th Airborne Division Support Units

6th Abn. Div. Reconnaissance Regiment
Military Cross
21.12.44   Lieutenant Duncan Gordon Shearer   299734   Recce C.

Military Medal
21.12.44   3654658 Sgt. Kenneth Stephen Skidmore   Recce C.
21.12.44   14238690 Tpr. George Bonner Wattam   Recce C.

No.2 Forward Observation Unit, R.A.
Military Cross
29.3.45   Lieut. (T/Capt.) Edward Harrington   155856

53rd Air-Landing Light Regt. R.A.
Military Cross
1.3.45   Captain George William Culley   64507
           (K.I.A. Rhine Crossing 24.3.45)

3rd Parachute Squadron, R.E.
Distinguished Service Order
31.8.44   Capt. (T/Major) John Couch Adams Roseveare 102034 O.C. Sqn.

Military Cross
31.8.44   Lieut. (T/Capt.) Thomas Roland Juckes   100294
        (K.I.A. 28.6.44)
10.10.44 Lieut. Stanley Rannard Shave   229347

Military Medal
10.10.44 1871506 Sgt. Sydney David Shrubsole

Mentioned In Despatches
22.3.45   1875929 Spr. A. W. Peachy

Croix De Guerre (France)
T/Captain Edward Long Fox   242581

591 Parachute Squadron, R.E.
Military Cross
31.8.44   Lieut. (T/Capt.) Roderick Ferguson Semple 237304

6th Abn. Div. Signal Regt.
Croix De Guerre (France)
T/Major George Symes Fenton   95088

Military Medal
31.8.44   4689589 Cpl. Thomas Waters   5 Bde. Sigs.

195th Air-Landing Field Amb. R.A.M.C.
George Medal
2.2.45   7357269 Sgt. Walter Booth
    During the advance on 24th August, 1944, across the River Torques, he (then a Cpl.) and three privates, rescued three badly injured Belgians, from a tank belonging to the Belgian Brigade Group (Brigade Peron), that was in support of the 6th A/Lng. Brigade.

Mentioned In Despatches
22.3.45   Captain A. D. Milne   106839   att. as R.M.O., 2 S.A.S. (6-8/44)
22.3.45   Captain G. P. Shaw, M.B.   257934   No. 3 Section

224th Parachute Field Amb, R.A.M.C.
Distinguished Service Order
31.8.44   Capt. (T/Major) Alastair Donald Young, M.B.   128689
                                                                    2/I.C./C.O.
Member of the British Empire (M.B.E.)
1.2.45   Capt. (T/Major) Richard Lennox MacPherson, M.B.   89932
                                                                    No. 2 Surg. Tm.
Military Cross
19.10.44   Captain Thomas Grant Gray, M.B.   274680   *(W.D.)*
19.10.44   Lieut. Gordon Charles George Philo   179980   R.A.S.C. att.

Mentioned In Despatches
22.3.45   7261957   W.O.I G. M. Green

225th Parachute Field Amb., R.A.M.C.
Distinguished Service Order
31.8.44   Major (T/Lt-Col.) Edward Ian Bruce Harvey, M.B.   33854   C.O.

Military Cross
31.8.44   Captain David John Tibbs   274140   No. 3 Section
31.8.44   Captain Gordon Spencer Sheill   111789   M.O. 716 Coy.
         (K.I.A. Rhine Crossing 24.3.45)

716th (Airborne) Light Composite Company. R.A.S.C.
Member of the British Empire—for gallant conduct
10.11.44   Lieut. (T/Capt.) Arthur Edgar Roberts   126117
         (K.I.A. Rhine Crossing 24.3.45)

Military Cross
31.8.44   Lieut. Frederick John Bland   284108
         (K.I.A. Capt. 22.6.44)

Military Medal
31.8.44   T/3447084   Sgt. William Wilson
The Company also received 12 C-in-C Commendation Certificates.

398 (Airborne) Composite Company, R.A.S.C.
Croix De Guerre & Bze. Star (France)
S/126139 S/Sgt. William Kenneth MacLean

6th Abn. Div. Provost Company, C.M.P.
Croix De Guerre & Bze Star (France)
5947036   Cpl. Charles Stanley Runacres

317 Abn. Field Security Section
Mentioned In Despatches
22.3.45   T/Captain F. G. MacMillan   278881   O.C. Section

Appendix 6/2

Awards of the Glider Pilot Regiment
in Normandy : July – September 1944

Distinguished Service Order

19.10.44   Major (T/Lt-Col.) Iain Arthur Murray   99246
                                                        C.O. No. 1 Glider Wg.

Military Cross

19.10.44   Capt. (T/Major) John Francis Lyne   126104

Bar to the D.F.C.

19.10.44   Capt. (T/Major) James Alexander Dale, D.F.C.   149290
                                                        O.C. Hamilcar Sqn.

Distinguished Flying Cross

19.10.44   Lieut. Aubrey Earle Pickwoad   180092
19.10.44   Lieut. Thomas Whiteley Taylorson   299372

Air Force Cross

11.1.45   Lieut. (T/Capt.) Emrys James Thomas 233883   *(K.I.A. Arnhem)*

Distinguished Conduct Medal

31.8.44   952832   S/Sgt. Raymond Ernest White   *(later K.I.A. Arnhem)*

Military Medal

9.11.44   2765856   S/Sgt. Maurice Alexander Bramah

Distinguished Flying Medal

19.10.44   6468601   S/Sgt. Ernest John Baker
           (cancelled 5.4.45, reinstated 14.11.46.   K.I.A. Arnhem 24.9.44)
19.10.44   6015841   S/Sgt. Richard Banks   *(K.I.A. Arnhem 19.9.44)*
5.4.45   2582663   S/Sgt. Geoffrey Sydney Barkway
                                                "C" Sqn., Bridge Raid
12.10.44   2162082   S/Sgt. Stanley George Bone   "B" Sqn. Merville Battery
19.10.44   3387172   S/Sgt. Edgar England
19.10.44   5509754   S/Sgt. Williams Charles Herbert   *(BD64)*
19.10.44   6897785   S/Sgt. Phillip Allan Hobbs   *(W.D.)*
                                                "C" Sqn. Caen Bridge
19.10.44   14200103 S/Sgt. Roy Allan Howard   "C" Sqn. Orne Bridge

12.10.44	3387884	S/Sgt. David Fisher Kerr	"B" Sqn. Merville Battery
19.10.44	7895376	S/Sgt. Stanley Pearson	"C" Sqn. Orne Bridge
19.10.44	903986	S/Sgt. James Horley Wallwork	"C" Sqn., Caen Bridge

Mentioned In Despatches

22.3.45   Capt. (actg.) I. C. Muir   172724   1st Wing
(Iain Colquhuon Muir K.I.A. Arnhem 25.9.44)

22.3.45   Capt. (temp) D. H. Shuttleworth   174177

22.3.45   6088816 S/Sgt. W. G. Bridgewater

22.3.45   6457896 S/Sgt. G. E. Redway

22.3.45   2045308 S/Sgt. C. D. Richardson *(K.I.A. Arnhem)*

Croix De Guerre (France)

212052 S/Sgt. F. W. Baacke

1449953 S/Sgt. O. F. Boland

2765856 S/Sgt. M. A. Bramah, M.M.

4749795 S/Sgt. L. Guthrie

Chapter VII

BATTLE OF THE BRIDGES

Events Leading Up To Arnhem

FOLLOWING the liberation of PARIS and BRUSSELS, in the August and September of 1944, General Montgomery put forward a proposal to the Supreme Commander: General Dwight D. Eisenhower, of a dynamic push through Holland, and across the Rhine towards the Industrial Heart of Germany—the RUHR. The Supreme Commander at first rejected it, as it would drain most of the equipment of the Allied Armies in France; there was a high element of risk; he preferred a broad front tactic and consolidation; and also there was still a slight attitude of animosity between the two men, which both Chiefs of Staff tried their best to smooth over. After much discussion, it was put forward that the British 21st Army Group would be given the task, using its 2nd Army under Lt-General Dempsey now pushing into northern Belgium, and principally its own 30 Corps.

The Operation was code-named "MARKET-GARDEN"—

"MARKET" was the Airborne side of the operation, as it had been decided to use them to capture key bridges

"GARDEN" was the ground operation

On 2nd August, 1944 the **1st Allied Airborne Army** was formed under the command of Lt-General Lewis H. Brereton, with the British Airborne Commander—now Lt-General F. A .M. "Boy" Browning, C.B., D.S.O. as his deputy, he was also the commander of the 1st British Airborne Corps.

1st Airborne Division—Maj. Gen. R. E. Urquhart
6th Airborne Division—Maj. Gen. R. N Gale
1st S.A.S. Brigade—Brig. R.W. McLeod

1st Polish Indep. Para. Bde.—Maj. Gen. S. Sosabowski

Operation "Market": The Plan

The United States' **18th Airborne Corps** under Major-General M. Ridgeway was to use two of its Divisions for their side of the operation: the **82nd (ALL AMERICAN) Division**—Maj. Gen. James Gavin, **504th P.I.R.** under Lt-Col. R. Tucker was to drop near the west of the GROESBEEK HEIGHTS near to the GRAVE BRIDGE and capture it.

505th P.I.R. under Lt-Col. B. Vandervoort was to drop onto the GROESBEEK HEIGHTS and capture the bridges over the MAAS-WAAL CANAL.

508th P.I.R. under Lt-Col. R. Lindquist was to drop near to NIJMEGAN and make for the bridge and hold it.

The **101st (SCREAMING EAGLES) Div.**—Maj. Gen. Maxwell Taylor **501st P.I.R.** under Lt-Col. H. W. Kinnaird was to drop near to, and capture the bridge at VEGHEL.

502nd P.I.R. under Lt-Col. J. H. Michaelis was to drop near to ST. OEDENRODE and capture the bridge over the DOMMEL RIVER.

506th P.I.R. under Lt-Col. R. F. Sink was to drop near SON BRIDGE and EINDHOVEN.

The **British 1st Airborne Division**—Maj. Gen. R. E. Urquhart, D.S.O. was given the task of holding the most eastern bridge, that of the ARNHEM road Bridge, and if possible the rail bridge as well.

The 1st Airborne Division Prepares

The Division comprised two Parachute Brigades: the 1st and 4th, and the 1st Air-Landing Brigade, plus Divisional Troops, all based in the Rutland and Lincolnshire areas. Unhappy at its prospect of missing the D-Day invasion, the members of the Division had to still go through the trauma of training for several operations, that never materialized, between June and September, 1944.

On September 10th, 1944, Major-General Urquhart, D.S.O. & Bar, who had taken over from Major-General E. E. Down in the December of 1943, was summoned to his commander—Lt-General Browning's H.Q. at Moor Park, where the objectives were discussed. The 1st Airborne Division was to hold the bridge for two days, and Browning thought they could hold it easily for four. Intelligence reports stated that there was only a garrison of a few infantry battalions, and some troops refitting nearby. However, these later turned out to be the 9th (Hohenstaufen) and 10th

(Frundesburg) S.S. Panzer Divisions of the 2nd S.S. Panzer Corps, under General W. Bittrich, which had pulled out of Normandy to refit in Holland, although later intelligence reports to this effect seemed to have been discounted.

Major-General Urquhart and his Staff began planning in earnest, since the date of the opening of the operation was to be on the 17th September, a mere seven days away. Problems arose, in that the main road bridge, could not be taken by "coup de main" glider-landings, since the R.A.F. knew the surrounding area to be heavily fortified with mobile anti-aircraft guns, also the drops would have to be in daylight, since the aircrews were not used to night drops. He also had been only allotted 519 aircraft, as the American Divisions were being dropped as complete units, so the British and Poles: who had been placed under Urquhart's control, had to be content with three lifts over three days.

We're Off!

On Sunday 17th September, 1944, at 10.00 hrs. on a sunny morning, elements of the **21st Independent Parachute Company** took off in twelve converted Stirling bombers to prepare the Dropping and Landing Zones for the 1st Parachute and 1st Air-Landing Brigades.

The **1st Parachute Brigade** under Brigadier G. W. Lathbury landed in reasonably good order on D.Z. "X" which had been marked by No. 1 Platoon, the Brigade's support element was to land on L.Z. "Z" by glider, which had been marked by No. 2 Platoon, 21st Indep.

The **1st Parachute Battalion** moved up towards Arnhem, along the EDE Road, where German tanks were seen, so they dug in, along the tree-lined road, whilst "R" Company took up position in a nearby wood.

The **2nd Parachute Battalion** moved straight for the bridge, Lt-Colonel Frost and "A" Company leading the way. "C" Company would follow up and seize the railway bridge, and "B" Company would capture the pontoon bridge and the high ground of DEN BRINK. "A" Company passed through HEELSUM, and were fired on near OOSTERBEEK, and halted by this fire, coming from DEN BRINK. They then moved around the back of the houses towards the road bridge at ARNHEM, which they reached by 2100 hrs. The commander of "A" Company—Major A. D. Tatham-Warter was asked by Lt-Colonel Frost to send a platoon under the command of Lt. J. H. Grayburn to seize the southern end of the bridge. Unfortunately the attack failed, when they were forced back by fire from an anti-aircraft-gun and an armoured car, the Lieutenant being wounded in the shoulder, but the last to leave the bridge. Lt-Colonel Frost then established his H.Q. overlooking the bridge in a nearby house, the other platoons were installed in adjoining houses. "C" Company under Major V. Dover, M.C. failed to seize the railway bridge, as part of it was blown, as they arrived. Here, they were joined by some members of the **9th Field Company (Abn.), R.E.** under Captain E. Callaghan, M.C., and the men were ordered to follow "A" Company into Arnhem and capture the area commandant's H.Q.

The **3rd Parachute Battalion's** leading platoon under Captain J. A. S. Cleminson had ambushed a Staff Car, that had the commander of Arnhem in it—Maj. Gen. Kussin—who was killed outright. The Battalion then met heavy opposition from several 75mm self-propelled guns, and by the evening were only on the fringe of OOSTERBEEK.

Major-General Urquhart, after landing with his Staff in a glider piloted by Lt-Colonel I. Murray, D.S.O. found that most, if not all, parties on the ground were experiencing difficulty with their radio sets. Maj. Gen. Urquhart then set off with his batman and signaller in a jeep, in search of Hicks and Lathbury, whom he finally managed to contact in the afternoon.

The **16th Parachute Field Ambulance** having successfully dropped with the 1st Parachute Brigade, moved straight through OOSTERBEEK, and were operating in the St. Elizabeth Hospital by evening.

The 1st **Air-Landing Recce. Sqn.** now had their jeeps equipped with a single Vickers "K" Machine-gun. Major Gough had wanted a double set, but this had been turned down, due to the amount of ammunition that could be carried. They were allotted twenty-two gliders out of the 350, which carried an assortment of jeeps, trailers and supplies. In charge of the glider-party was Captain D. Allsop 2/I.C. of the Squadron. Several gliders crashed on landing, and two failed to make the crossing, but soon most of the jeeps were driving to the Drop Zone, though "A" Troop jeeps were missing. There they met up with the rest of the Squadron, some 150 came floating down with men of the 1st Parachute Brigade. They moved off in the direction of WOLFHEZEN. Here the leading section—No.8 was ambushed, and two jeeps and crews lost, including Lt. P. Bucknall—the section leader and Sgt. T. McGregor. The other jeeps pulled back from the German fire. The unit involved was the 16th SS Pzr-Grenadier Depot Battalion under SS-Sturmbannfuhrer S. Krafft. Major Gough and four jeeps after driving back to the D.Z. in search of Brigadier Lathbury and Maj. Gen. Urquhart, finally got to the Arnhem bridge and joined Lt-

Colonel Frost. He had also been reinforced by men from the **1st Para. Sqn., R.E.**, and a troop from the **1st A/Lng. A/Tk. Bty., R.A.** under Major Arnold. Lt-Colonel Frost ordered Major Crawley, M.C. and his "B" Company, with the anti-tank guns to the high ground. He then lost contact with "B" and "C" Companies, but held the northern end of the bridge, after flame-throwers under Captain E. Mackay, R.E. had destroyed a troublesome pillbox.

1st Air-Landing Brigade

Their Landing Zone L.Z. "S" was prepared by No. 3 Platoon and the Company H.Q. of **21st Indep. Para. Coy.**

The **1st Borders**, now commanded by Lt-Col. T. Haddon, (following Lt-Col. Britten taking up a Staff appointment in July, 1943), landed and took up position to cover the landing area. Unfortunately Lt-Col. Haddon's glider crashed, after its tow-rope broke over Oxford, and he had to wait until the following day to try and rejoin his Battalion. In his absence, Major H. S. Cousens assumed temporary command.

It had been decided that the **2nd S. Staffords** should land in two lifts: the first on the 17th September carried Lt-Col. McCardie; his H.Q. and "B" and "D" Companies; and the second on the 18th, carried the remainder— "A" and "C" Companies under the 2/I.C. Major J. C. Commings. Two gliders failed to arrive, but one which carried Major R. H. Cain, and his "B" Company H.Q. made a safe landing in England, and he was able to rejoin the Battalion the following day. The first lift, then dug in towards the northern edge of the L.Z.

The **K.O.S.B.'s** landed on the L.Z., their pipers playing "Blue Bonnets" to rally them together, they covered the north-west approach to the L.Z. By the evening, all three Battalions could hear the sporadic firing coming from Arnhem, though they were not molested by German patrols until the late evening.

The **181st A/Lng. Fld. Ambulance's** main objective was to set up a Dressing Station near WOLFHEZEN, and then to proceed to the Municipal Hospital in ARNHEM, where the town was occupied. The reserve section, under Captain Doyle, with 23 other ranks would be under the control of the A.D.M.S. of the Division: Colonel G. M. Warrack. The main party, however, was set up by the afternoon, in four houses near to the railway line, south of the L.Z.

Monday 18th September
1st Parachute Brigade

The **1st Parachute Battalion** had marched south-east during the night, after receiving a wireless signal from Lt-Colonel Frost asking for support. They came under heavy fire from the railway station near to St. Elizabeth Hospital. "T" Company tried to assault a factory position, after a heavy fight, the position was cleared by the end of the morning, though the company had been reduced to 22 men. By 1700 hrs., the Battalion was only just west of the Hospital, though severely depleted.

The **1st and 2nd A/Lng. A/Tk. Batteries** had too few guns to deal with the tanks, and later on in the day, the 75mm guns of the **1st A/Lng. Lt Regt.**, under Lt-Col. W. F. K. "Sheriff" Thompson, M.B.E. came into action, but proved to be a poor anti-tank weapon.

Major-General Urquhart and Brigadier Lathbury accompanied Lt-Colonel Fitch's **3rd Para. Battalion** on the march towards ARNHEM. Soon on the outskirts of Arnhem, Major P. Waddy's company in the lead was surrounded, as the Battalion was attacked by tanks and machine-gun fire. The unit was split up in various side-streets and houses. Major Waddy was killed later, searching for a way to the bridge. "C" Company under Major Lewis, which had been detached from the Battalion, entered Arnhem along the railway track.

The **16th Parachute Field Ambulance** safely installed in the St. Elizabeth Hospital operated on casualties, whilst there was fighting going on all around the vicinity. At 0800 hrs SS Troops recaptured the hospital, but the two surgical teams under Major C. J. Longland, with Captains D. H. Ridler, M.C. and A. W. Lipmann-Kessel were allowed to continue, but the C.O. and all other ranks not part of the two teams, were not permitted to stay and were marched off.

"C" Troop of the **1st A/Lng. Recce. Sqn**. had been allotted to the 2nd S. Staffords., whilst "D" Troop and a depleted "A" Troop moved eastwards towards Arnhem, and reached the Hartenstein Hotel, which became the new H.Q. of the Division. Further on they were met with machine-gun fire and took to dismounted action in the OOSTERBEEK area.

The **Divisional H.Q.** moved in towards Arnhem, still without its commander. Lt-Col. C. B. Mackenzie (G.S.O.1. Ops.) on talking it over with the C.R.A. Lt-Col. R. G. Loder-Symonds, D.S.O., M.C. decided to try and make contact with Brigadier Hicks, who on General Urquhart's orders would assume command of the Division, should he be captured.

This was done, and at 0945 hrs., Brigadier Hicks instructed that the two companies of the **2nd S. Staffords.** would come under command of the 1st Parachute Brigade, and be sent to try and relieve the bridge. So **"C" Troop, 1st A/Lng. Recce. Sqn.**, plus **No.1 Platoon, 21st Indep. Para. Coy.**, and fifty men of the **Glider Pilot Regt.** defended REIJERSCAMP on D.Z. "L" in readiness for the drop of the Polish Parachute Brigade, the next day.

1st Air-Landing Brigade

The **1st Bn., Borders** were still in the same position, they had been the day before. "B" Company was severely attacked at noon, in the town of RENKUM, and forced to withdraw, losing all their transport, and quite a few of their number.

The two companies of the **2nd S. Staffords.**—"B" and "D" under Captain R. S. Foot, M.C. (in the absence of Major Cain), and Major J. E. Phillip, pushed forward towards the bridge through sniper and machine-gun fire.

They were stopped in the outskirts of Arnhem until the following morning.

The **K.O.S.B.'s** now on their own on the eastern side of the L.Z., were assaulted by SS troops, many of whom got through, including some multiple barrelled 20mm anti-aircraft guns. Lt-Colonel Payton-Reid led a number of bayonet charges, which were partially successful.

There had been no sign of the second lift, which was still in England at 1100 hrs. due to fog, and didnt appear overhead until the early afternoon.

4th Parachute Brigade

Shortly after landing on D.Z. "Y" which had been prepared by **No. 3 Platoon, 21st Indep. Para. Coy.**, Brigadier Hackett was met by Lt-Colonel Mackenzie, who informed him of the change in command, and that Brigadier Hicks had ordered that his 11th Parachute Battalion was to support the **2nd S. Staffords.**, who had landed on L. Z. "X" were sent after the rest of their Battalion. "A" Company under Major Lane forcing its way through to join "B" & "D" companies and the 1st Para. Battalion, which had lost four-fifths of its strength near to DEN BRINK.

The **156th Parachute Battalion** moved eastwards along the railway line, and was in WOLFHEZEN by midday, followed closely by the 10th Parachute Battalion. The **133rd Para. Fld. Ambulance** had been scattered during the drop, and was trying to regroup near WOLFHEZEN.

Major-General Urquhart in his hiding place at 14, Zwartweg heard British voices, and met several men from the South Staffords. and the 11th Parachute Battalion, who informed him, that the Divisional H.Q. was now the Hartenstein Hotel in OOSTERBEEK, so he and Captain Taylor drove off in a jeep, and were reunited with the Staff. Captain Cleminson went off in search of his 3rd Para Battalion.

By the evening there was no sign of 30 Corps, who's tanks of the Guards Armoured Division were waiting at ZON, after passing through the elements of the 101st Airborne Division, and finding the bridge destroyed.

Tuesday 19th September
1st Parachute Brigade

The **1st Parachute Battalion** near Arnhem fought hand to hand, with "T" Company under Major C. Perrin-Brown, M.C. and "R" Company under Major Timothy, M.C. leading bayonet charges. However, by 0600 hrs. they were attacked by tanks firing point-blank. Lt-Colonel Dobie was wounded entering a house, and his Battalion now comprised "R" Company—six men; "S" Company—fifteen; "T" Company—eight and Battalion H.Q.—ten. He and several others were captured.

The **3rd Battalion** fared little better being reduced to one officer (Captain Cleminson) and thirty-six other ranks.

The **2nd Battalion** still held onto their houses, though Tiger tanks started to fire at them, causing more casualties, including Major Tatham-Warter.

1st Air-Landing Brigade

The **1st Borders** were now in a position west of Arnhem, with the **K.O.S.B.'s** and were both beating off determined attacks by the Germans. The **2nd S. Staffords.** were still fighting their way through Arnhem in an attempt to reach the bridge, but soon were split into platoons, when faced with self-propelled guns. The main portion of the Battalion retired to the perimeter defence being established at OOSTERBEEK.

4th Parachute Brigade

The **11th Parachute Battalion** was surrounded near DEN BRINK, and reduced to 150 all ranks. Two companies managed to withdraw in small groups, among them was the 2/I.C.—Major Lonsdale, D.S.O., M.C.

The **10th Parachute Battalion** was ordered to retake the crossing at WOLFHEZEN, but suffered heavily under shellfire, and was forced to withdraw to the perimeter defence line.

The **156th Parachute Battalion** had supported the 10th Battalion and was also forced back to the perimeter, now numbering about 270 all ranks.

Arrival of Polish Para. Bde.

The Germans had amassed flakguns near to L.Z. "L" and opened up as the Polish glider—borne part of the brigade landed in the afternoon. Gliders broke up in the air, or crashed onto the landing zone spilling out jeeps, anti-tank guns, and many dead and wounded. Members of the **21st Indep's 1st Platoon** directed unwounded members of the glider-borne force to the railway embankment at Oosterbeek, but many parties fought on their own, as the Germans counter-attacked. In the confused fighting, parties of the K.O.S.B. and 10th Battalion, were fired on by Poles, they sought to help.

Now H.Q; No.1 Platoon and No.2 Platoon of the 21st Indep. were dug in to the North of OOSTERBEEK, as part of the perimeter defence.

Formation of Lonsdale Force

By now in the face of many confused actions, small groups were moving back to the Oosterbeek perimeter, after losing officers and N.C.O.'s. Lt-Colonel Thompson had left his command post near Oosterbeek to ascertain how his batteries might be used in an offensive role for a thrust into the town. His 3rd Battery still giving fire-support to the defenders at the bridge. He started to collect remnants of the 1st, 3rd, 11th Para. Battalions and S. Staffords., and herd them towards DEN BRINK. Command of this mixed force, that also included some Glider Pilots, was passed to the senior officer, as Lt-Colonel Thompson retired to the Divisional H.Q. to inform Major-General Urquhart of the position. The Colonel later organised a defence force to protect his own guns in Oosterbeek, composed of mainly Glider Pilots, and known as "Thompson Force".

The senior officer at DEN BRINK was the second-in-command of the 11th Para. Battalion—Major R. T. H. "Dickie" Lonsdale, who had won the M.C. on the North-West Frontier of India, and the D.S.O. at Primosole Bridge in 1943. He looked about him and then withdrew his force to the church at Oosterbeek, where he preached to the men from the battered pulpit,

"Well now, the form is this, I have withdrawn you from the open ground by the river. I want you to rest here for two hours, in which time get a meal from what you have left. Get yourself clean and be prepared to move up to a new position around the houses on the south side of the perimeter. On this position, we must stand or fall, and fight to the last round. This edge of the perimeter is being held by a mixed bag consisting of Lonsdale Force, H.Q. at this church. So far, we have had a good battle against good troops. Troops that are not up to our standard. We have fought them in North Africa, Sicily and Italy and at times against odds. They were not good enough for us then, and I am certain they are not our match now. Get yourselves dug in and shoot to kill. Good Luck".

Wednesday 20th September
The 2nd Para. Battalion
The Battalion now reduced still held onto the North-West end of the bridge, although the area held was being reduced. Lt-Colonel Frost was wounded in the leg, and Major Gough of 1st A/Lng. Recce. assumed command, though he still referred major decisions to Frost. Major Tatham-Warter took over what remained of the 2nd Battalion. Captain J. Logan, D.S.O. and Captain D. Wright, M.C. of the **16th Para. Fld. Amb.** dealt with wounded in their R.A.P. at the school, which was set on fire, and Captain Logan informed Major Gough, that he must surrender or the wounded would be burnt to death. Major Gough accepted this, and the Germans under a flag of truce picked up many of the wounded, including Lt-Colonel Frost, who had removed his rank badges.

The Oosterbeek Perimeter
It was a fact that the 2nd Battalion would not be able to be relieved, so Major-General Urquhart decided to consolidate his perimeter defence, in the hope that the 2nd Army's 30 Corps would show up. He was also being mortared, now at his H.Q. at the Hartenstein Hotel.

The **Borders** fought their way back to the perimeter, Major Breese's "D" Company fighting back from HEVEADORP.

The remnants of the **S. Staffords.** fought with Divisional H.Q., and the Lonsdale Force.

The **K.O.S.B.'s** had moved to the northern edge of the perimeter.
Brigadier Hackett and the remainder of his **4th Parachute Brigade**, had

been engaged, as they tried to reach the perimeter from WOLFHEZEN. Even the Brigadier fought beside his Brigade Major with a rifle as they entered the woods, although Major Dawson was killed soon afterwards. The **10th Parachute Battalion** was ordered to lead the advance, and reached the Divisional H.Q., Lt-Colonel Smyth, who had been wounded, reported to the General, that he had only sixty men left. They were put into some houses to the north-east.

Brigadier Hackett and the **156th Para. Battalion** still fought on through the woods, Lt-Colonel des Voeux having been killed. In the end, they fixed bayonets and charged through, reaching the Border's position on the west of the perimeter. There were seventy men left of the Battalion. Brigadier Hackett set up his H.Q. in the grounds of the Hartenstein.With sixty sappers from the **4th Parachute Sqn., R.E.** the remnants of the 156th took up position, to the south of the 10th Battalion.

The members of the **21st Indep. Para. Coy.** under Major Wilson were now dug in, in positions to the north, and No.1 Platoon under Lt. D. Eastwood had rejoined after marching from WOLFHEZEN.

The remainder of the **1st A/Lng. Recce. Sqn.**, under Divisional H.Q. was sent out to try and make contact with the 7th K.O.S.B. "A" Troop under Lt. Wadsworth made a foot patrol in Cronjeweg, but came under fire from an SP Gun. "D" Troop was also attacked in the Dennekamp woods. The Squadron was then ordered to withdraw to the Sqn. H.Q. at Oranjeweg, where Captain Allsop was being mortared. Another SP Gun appeared, and two jeeps were hit and set on fire. The Squadron then scattered, and were later brought into action in an infantry role.

Lt-Colonel Alford and forty all ranks of the **133rd Para. Fld. Amb.** managed to reach OOSTERBEEK, and became part of the Divisional Medical services with the complete **181st A/Lng. F.A.** The **16th P.F.A.** apart from those still working in the St. Elizabeth Hospital were all prisoners. The surgical teams still functioned under Major Longland, and assisted by Captain Lipmann-Kessel. The responsibility for running the wards and giving treatment was Sgt. (later Colonel) A. V. Tenucci, ably assisted by Dutch nurses who had volunteered to stay.

The Main Dressing Station in the Hotel Schoonhord was then captured, but Lt-Colonel Alford and Lt-Colonel Marrable were given permission to continue to work with a full staff. The hotel was recaptured in the evening by elements of the 4th Parachute Brigade. The only D.S. that had not been overrun was that in the Taffelburg Hotel, where two teams under Major Rigby-Jones, M.C. and Captain James from the 181st A.F.A.

were operating.

On the eastern edge of the perimeter, **Lonsdale Force** was in action. Major Cain immobilised a Tiger Tank, and Lance-Sgt. Baskeyfield destroyed single-handed several tanks with his 6 Pdr. anti-tank gun, before being killed by a supporting tank, he received a posthumous V.C.

Meanwhile General "Jumping Jim" Gavin's 504th P.I.R. had just captured the WAAL bridge, and the tanks of the Guards Armoured Division rumbled across, but they were way behind schedule.

Thursday 21st September

In the horse-shoe perimeter, Major-General Urquhart held a conference, and announced that the perimeter would be divided into two commands—east and west. On the west under Brigadier Hicks, there would be the three companies of the **Borders**; the surviving **K.O.S.B.'s**; the **Indep. Para. Coy**; and the mixed group of Poles, glider pilots and sappers. On the east under Brigadier Hackett, the remnants of the **10th & 156th Para. Battalions**; Lt-Col. Thompson's **Light Regt., R.A**; and the **Lonsdale Force**. Also in the morning, contact was made by Captain MacMillen of the **No.1 Forwards Obs. Unit, R.A.**, and Lt-Colonel Loder-Symonds, who had been visiting the unit, talked with the contacted unit—64th Medium Regiment, R.A., 2nd Army, which was to be invaluable over the next few days, firing long range artillery shots over the perimeter.

The Germans started probing attacks from the north-west, Brigadier Hackett was wounded, whilst visiting a dressing station in Mrs Kate Ter Horst's house, a lady who was to become as famous as the commanders, for her bravery, in tending to the troops. Brigadier Hackett, his new Brigade Major: Major D. J. Madden, and Lt-Colonel Thompson, were chatting on the lawn, when a mortar burst killed Major Madden, and wounded the other two men, Lt-Colonel Thompson quite severely.

Due to continued German attacks, Major Lonsdale brought his men back to Oosterbeek Church, where they were mortared, and as he stood next to the 1st Battalion's padre; Rev. Watkins, he was again wounded, but luckily it was slight. It was then he heard that elements from 30 Corps would attempt to cross the river by the HEVEADORP Ferry, and also the rest of the Polish Parachute Brigade had landed at DRIEL, though had suffered casualties in the drop onto a zone, that was still in German hands.

Both the **Borders** and the **K.O.S.B.** were attacked heavily and forced out of houses in the fierce hand to hand engagements. Major-General Urquhart then pulled back the **K.O.S.B.** and pushed the **21st Indep.**, with some of **4th Para. Sqn., R.E.**, and the remainder of "A" & "D" Troops of **1st A/Lng. Recce.**, that had been placed under the command of Major Powell of 156th Para. Battalion, into the north-east of the perimeter. He also sent the Div. R.A.S.C. to the south-east next to Lonsdale Force. Major Gough had been captured attempting to escape from the bridge, after it had finally fallen to the Germans.

The 10th Para. Battalion was attacked in the evening and forced out of the houses, its last officer being killed, and Lt-Col. Smyth wounded a second time. A re-supply drop was again attempted, and over 50% of the force was lost or damaged. Few panniers reached the perimeter, leaving the R.A.S.C. recovery teams under Lt-Colonel Packe with little to do. Water was now a great problem, since the Germans had cut off the supply. By nightfall, Major-General Urquhart sent the following message to 30 Corp :

"No knowledge elements of Div. in Arnhem for 24 hours. Balance of Div. in very tight perimeter. Heavy mortaring and machine-gun fire followed by local attacks. Main nuisance SP Guns. Our casualties heavy. Resources stretched to utmost. Relief within 24 hours vital."

Friday 22nd–Sunday 24th September

Major-General Urquhart received a signal at dawn from 30 Corps, stating that the 43rd Wessex Division would attempt a relief during the day, by using the ferry position. He therefore sent Lt-Colonel Mackenzie and the C.R.E: Lt-Colonel Myers to make contact with the Poles at DRIEL, and also give a message to Lt-General Browning, who had landed at Nijmegan with his Corps H.Q., stating what a difficult situation the remnant of the Division faced.

Lt-Colonel Mackenzie rowed an inflatable dinghy across the river, and the two men made contact with the Poles, who started to ferry across. This was later abandoned, as the three dinghies became unserviceable, although Lt. Storrs, R.E. had rowed back and forth some 23 times, his dinghy only carried two men at a time. Other home-made rafts sank or were swept away, drowning many of the parachutists, and only about fifty made it across. The two Lt-Colonels in two armoured cars, with one in support drove to Nijmegan, and met Lt-General Browning, although Mackenzie had had a lucky escape, when his armoured car overturned taking evasive action. The Guards Armoured Division had been held up at Elst, so the 43rd Division moved through Oosterhout, and leading elements had reached the river by the Saturday evening.

The Germans now using Tigers and SP Guns made more concerted probing attacks, that became more persistent during the two days. **Lonsdale Force** still in the vicinity of the church fought valiantly, though their numbers were dwindling. The **Glider Pilots** east of the Hartenstein were forced out of their blazing houses, Brigadier Hackett called for artillery support from the 64th Medium Regiment. The **21st Indep. Para. Coy.** had been pulled back to be placed in houses near the Schoonhord Hotel C.C.S., and then on the 23rd September, No. 3 Platoon under Lt. Ashmore relieved the depleted 10th Para. Battalion position close by. They were heavily attacked by infantry, a Panzer IV tank and two SP Guns, No.1 Platoon also received part of this onslaught. Colonel Warrack, A.D.M.S. of the Division, who had been everywhere during the battle, visiting R.A.P.s and hospitals, even when under enemy control, made contact with the German A.D.M.S. and asked that fire be lifted, so that the wounded could be evacuated out of the battle area. This was finally agreed on the Sunday.

The **Borders** were attacked, one company being overrun, and "B" Company was driven back. Major Neill organised a composite unit and drove the enemy back, he subsequently received the D.S.O. The **K.O.S.B.'s** and the **Recce. Sqn**. were forced back, Lt-Colonel Payton-Reid, and a glider pilot Sgt. Tilley, who had become temporary R.S.M. jumped through a window of a house, to land in a cellar to evade capture.

On the 24th September, Brigadier Hackett was making his way back to his H.Q., when he was wounded in the thigh and stomach by a mortar burst. He was evacuated to the St. Elizabeth Hospital, where Capt. Lipmann-Kessel performed a life-saving operation. Lt-Colonel Murray, the glider commander took over his command.

The **4th Bn., Dorsets**. under Lt-Colonel G. Tilley from the 130th Bde., made an assault and crossed the river. Prior to this members of the Airborne Medical Staff under Captain Louis, who was later killed; Lt-Colonel Herford of the 163rd Fld. Amb. temporarily placed under command of the Airborne Corps; and Capt. (Q.M.) Tiernan of the 181st A.F.A. crossed the river with medical supplies. The Dorsets. were supported by fire from a member unit of their Brigade — 5th Dorsets, plus the 5th D.C.L.I. from 217th Bde., plus artillery. They eventually crossed in the early morning of the 25th September, as their boats had been held up along the road. They went across in five three-boat waves, as there were only fifteen craft available. They were heavily machine-gunned, and only 239 out of 420 men reached the bank. They were unable to break out, only a few made it to the perimeter, and virtually all were captured, including the 1st Borders' C.O.—Lt-Colonel T. Haddon. His second attempt to rejoin his Battalion on the 18th had also failed, when his glider crashed near Antwerp, and he had joined the Dorsets to try and rejoin his Battalion.

Monday 25th September—The Evacuation

It was obvious now that what remained of the Division, about 2,500 men must be brought out, and Major-General Urquhart signalled, "Operation Berlin must be tonight". He called a conference of his main commanders: Lt-Col. Murray, Brigadier Hicks, with Lt-Cols Mackenzie, Myers and Loder-Symonds, where preparation were discussed for the withdrawal. Parachute tapes would mark out the two routes available, and glider pilots would act as guides to the meadows, where Lt-Colonel Myers' engineers would guide the parties across the open ground to the boats. These would take parties of 14 apiece.

Lt-Col. Loder-Symonds called for artillery support from the guns of 419th Heavy Battery over the Rhine, when the Divisional H.Q. was threatened and soon shells from the 155mm guns were forcing the enemy back, but only for a time.

At 1030 hrs., the Germans attacked the **21st Indep.** position, and the Taffelberg Hotel was hit, killing four and wounded several others, including Captain James of the 181st A.F.A. The **1st A/Lng. Recce.** received orders to withdraw in groups of twos and threes, Captain Allsop being the last to leave.

Evening came and the guns of 30 Corps in the vicinity opened up— a battery from 7th Medium Regiment; a Troop from 84th Medium Regt; 419th Heavy Battery, and 64th Medium Regiment. On the south side of the Rhine, two field companies of Canadian Engineers, and two from the 43rd Wessex Divisional R.E. were waiting with their assault boats. The Canadians had ones powered by outboard motors, but the British had to rely on paddles.

The unwounded men in small parties began the exodus from the perimeter positions, the wounded and doctors staying behind. At Divisional H.Q., papers were burnt, and the Staff left in the direction of the river, where an anti-aircraft battery from the 43rd Division fired red tracer over the two river routes to guide the weary men. Occasionally firing was heard, as Germans met up with stragglers. The **A/Lng. Light Regt.**, now under command of Major Linton, since Lt-Colonel Thompson was wounded, fired its last shells, and destroyed the breech blocks.

The Aftermath

Out of the Division's 10,000 man force, only 2,163 with 160 Poles, and 75 Dorsets. got back across the river, over 1,200 were killed, and 6,600 missing, wounded or taken prisoner. All the units had suffered severely, of the Parachute Battalions: 1st, 2nd, 3rd, 10th and 156th were down to just scores of men; the 11th had ceased to exist, and following the Arnhem battle, the 4th Parachute Brigade was never reformed. Its remaining personnel were transferred to the 1st Parachute Brigade. The commanders: Dobie was wounded, but later managed to escape; Frost wounded and a prisoner; Fitch, Des Voeux and Smyth dead; Lea wounded and a prisoner. Of the infantry, all three Battalions managed to get more than half their number back, Haddon and McCardie were prisoners, and only Payton-Reid escaped. Captain Mackay after being wounded and captured, escaped only to find that from his 1st Para. Sqn., R.E. of 200 men, only five were with him on the opposite side of the river. The 4th Para. Sqn., R.E. was never reformed, those few who remained were absorbed in the 1st Para. Sqn. Sixty-five out of the 186 all ranks of 21st Indep. Para. Coy. were wounded, killed or missing; the C.O. "Boy" Wilson was wounded during the withdrawal, and the 2/I.C. Captain Spivey taking over. However, Wilson rejoined the company on the other side of the river. The survivors were all sent back to Nijmegan, where personal details were taken, and parades were organised from the remnants of units.

Bombadier Bolden, a medical orderly at Kate Ter Horst's house, and Rev. Thorne deterred a Tiger tank from putting a shell through the house. Many of the wounded were transferred to the Apeldoorn Hospital, which was in fact, the old Caserne William III barracks. It was organised with German help, with Colonel Warrack in charge, with an Administrative Wing commanded by Lt-Col. Marrable, and a Medical Wing by Lt-Col. Alford. It was then that Colonel Warrack proposed that as the number of patients were being reduced, a certain number of officers and other ranks could be permitted to escape if the situation warranted it. Several managed to escape, including Warrack, who with about a hundred others tried to reach the river, but were stopped by German patrols. It was during this fight that the 2/I.C. of the K.O.S.B: Major Coke was killed, but Colonel Warrack evaded capture, and later escaped by canoe, courtesy of the Dutch Resistance movement. Brigadier Lathbury, and Brigadier Hackett, who were both wounded had been hidden by the Dutch and both, although separated managed to escape later in the year.

Other escapers included: Major Deane-Drummond, who had hidden in a cupboard for twelve days in a room that was used by Germans; Major Tatham-Warter of 2nd Battalion; Lt. Heaps, a Canadian attached to 1st Battalion, who was awarded an M.C. for his work with the Dutch Resistance Sgt-Major Grainger of 10th Battalion, with two other soldiers mingled with members from a mental asylum and passed several German patrols, before making an escape across the river.

Mention must also be made of the **S.A.S. Mission** under Captain Fabian King, real name Gilbert Sadi-Kirschen, who with three other men from the Belgian Company landed on the 15th September. Their mission was to try and find the launch sites of V2 missiles and gather information for Operation "Market-Garden". After the battle, he and his men operated closely with the Resistance in hiding the evaders, until escape routes could be used. He also kept in touch, by wireless, with his H.Q. at the War Office, and the Airborne H.Q. giving details of the identities of evaders.

The 1st Airborne Division, now reduced by one Parachute Brigade refitted, and regrouped in England, where it remained until the end of the war, when it was sent to Norway.

Appendix 7/1

Awards of the 1st Airborne Division at
Arnhem—17th - 25th September 1944

1st Abn. Div. H.Q.
Companion of the Bath (C.B.)
Major-General Robert Elliott Urquhart, D.S.O.   17550 O.C. 1st Abn. Div.
 (BD186)

Distinguished Service Order
9.11.44   Major (T/Lt-Col) Charles Baillie MacKenzie 44938
                                    Camerons G.S.O.I. 1st Abn. Div

1st & 4th Parachute Brigades
Victoria Cross
1.2.45 +   Captain Lionel Ernest Queripel   108181
             (Royal Sussex R.)   10th Bn.
25.1.45 + Lieut. John Hollington Grayburn   149002
             (Para R. A.A.C.)   2nd Bn.

Bar to the D.S.O.
24.5.45   Brigadier (temp) John Winthrop Hackett, D.S.O., M.B.E., M.C.
             52752   8th Hussars   (BD186)   O.C. 4th Bde.
20.9.45   Lieut.-Colonel John Dutton Frost, D.S.O., M.C. 53721
             Cameronians   *(W.D./P.O.W.)*   C.O. 2nd Bn.
9.11.44   Capt. (T/Major) Richard Thomas Henry Lonsdale, D.S.O., M.C.
             69129 *(W.D.)* Leicester R.   (att. A.A.C.) formed Lonsdale Force

Distinguished Service Order
20.9.45   Major (temp) Christopher Perrin-Brown, M.C.   121945
                O.C. "T" 1st Bn.
22.3.45   Major (temp) Allison Digby Tatham-Warter   75060
             (WD/escaped) Oxford & Bucks L.I.   (att. A.A.C.) O.C. "A" 2nd Bn.
20.9.45   Major (temp) Peter Esmond Warr,
             (M.B.E. 9.9.42 with 1 S.A.S.)   180556 10th Bn.
19.11.44 Lieut. John Llewellyn Williams   180556   B.T.O. 1st Bn.

Member of the British Empire (M.B.E.)
28.2.46   Major (temp) John Graham Ross, D.S.O.   88111   2nd Bn.

2nd Bar to the M.C.

20.9.45 Major (actg.) John Timothy, M.C.   164812   O.C. "R" 1st Bn.

1st Bar to the M.C.

20.9.45 Major (temp) Douglas Edward Crawley, M.C.   108192
Loyal Regt. *(att. A.A.C.)*   O.C. "B" 2nd Bn.
20.9.45 Capt. (temp) Benjamin Beattie Clegg, M.C.   226920   10th Bn.

Military Cross

Date	Name	No.	Bn.
22.3.45	Major (temp) James Anthony Hibbert	74531	1st Bn.
20.9.45	Major (temp) Mervyn William Dennison	100018	3rd Bn.
9.11.44	Capt. (T/Major) Alan Bush	160544	3rd Bn.
9.11.44	Capt. (T/Major) Geoffrey Stewart Powell	69721	
	Green Howards *(att. A.A.C.)*		156th Bn.
20.9.45	Capt. (temp) Bernard Walter Briggs		G.S.O.II 1st Bde.
20.9.45	Capt. (temp) Francis Kinglake Hoyer-Miller	85212	2nd Bn.
1.3.45	Lieut. James Eric Blackwood	107015	2nd Bn.
20.9.45	Lieut. James Arthur Stacey Cleminson	189294	3rd Bn.
9.8.45	Lieut. Richard John Gammon	100039	1st Bn.
3.5.45	Lieut. Leo Jack Heaps *(CDN/415) Can. Inf. att. A.A.C.*		1st Bn.
9.11.44	Lieut. Oliver Piers St. Aubyn	1322149	156th Bn.

Distinguished Conduct Medal

Date	No.	Name	Bn.
20.9.45	2613715	W.O.I Robert Dennis Gay	156th Bn.
20.9.45	6400234	Sgt. Thomas Cyril Bentley	10th Bn.
9.11.44	2610093	Sgt (A/W.O.II) Leonard Ernest Oxley	1st Bn.
11.4.46	3241840	Cpl. Frank Williamson, M.M.	2nd Bn.
20.9.44	6913223	Pte. Albert Edward Etheridge	10th Bn.

British Empire Medal (B.E.M.)

Date	No.	Name	Bn.
29.3.45	5573750	Cpl. Robert Charles Longman	
29.3.45	5681124	L/Cpl. Laurance Goodman	1st Bn.

Military Medal

Date	No.	Name	Bn.
20.9.45	4622101	Sgt. Herbert Wright Carrier	2nd Bn.
20.9.45	4622740	Sgt. Frank Stanley Manser	"HQ" 1st Bn.
20.9.45	4195046	Sgt. John Richards	"T" 1st Bn.
9.11.44	5678213	Sgt. Alfred William Robus	1st Bn.
9.11.44	3604811	L/Sgt. James Scott Chandler	3rd Bn.
9.11.44	5115286	Cpl. Stanley Lunt	"H.Q." 1st Bn.
9.11.44	4915089	L/Cpl. John Noel Rosenburg	
20.9.45	6856426	Pte. Gerald Flamberg	

93

20.9.45	1441125	Pte. Robert Alfred Lygo		2nd Bn.
13.9.45	1537347	Pte. Edward James Rylands	"A"	2nd Bn.

Mentioned In Despatches

20.9.45	Brigadier (temp) J. W. Hackett, D.S.O., M.B.E., M.C. 52752	
	3rd Hussars *(W.D.)*	O.C. 4th Bde.
20.9.45	Lt-Col. (temp) K. B. I. Smyth, O.B.E. 36876	
	S.W.B. *(D.O.W. 26.10.44)*	C.O. 10th Bn.
20.9.45	Lt-Col. (temp) Sir W. R. de B. Des Voeux Bt. 52592	
	Gren. Gds. *(K.I.A. 20.9.44)*	156th Bn.
20.9.45	Major (temp) C. N. B. Dawson, M.C. 69165	
	R. Berks. *(K.I.A.)*	4th Bde.
20.9.45	Major (actg.) R. P. C. Lewis 77176	
	Kings R.	O.C. "C" 3rd Bn.
20.9.45	Major (temp) E. V. Ritson	41715	11th Bn.
10.5.45	Major (temp) M. S. Page	71844	156th Bn.
	(K.I.A. 20.9.44)		
25.10.45	T/Major D. W. Wallis	93375	2/I.C. 2nd Bn.
	Oxf. & Bucks. *(K.I.A. 18.9.44)*		
20.9.45	Captain A. M. Frank, M.C.	99817	"A" 2nd Bn.
20.9.45	Capt. (temp) J. Clarke	189050	
22.3.45	T/Capt. J. A. S. Cleminson	88532	3rd Bn.
20.9.45	Capt. (temp) B. B. Ingram	105018	R. Fus.
28.2.46	Lieut. E. A. James, M.C.	249180	3rd Bn.
18.4.46	Lieut. E. J. Davies, M.C.	207782 *(W.D.)*	1st Bn.
20.9.45	Lieut. J. A. Russell	189329	2nd Bn.
20.9.45	6395864 W.O.II R. E. Grainger		10th Bn.
20.9.45	AN-4202966 Sgt. A. W. Bennetts		
10.5.45	6400234 Sgt. T. C. Bentley		10th Bn.
20.9.45	30550067 Sgt. H. Campbell		
20.9.45	3316885 Sgt. H. R. Houghton		10th Bn.
20.9.45	6469336 Sgt. A. E. Jackman		2nd Bn.
20.9.45	4623004 Sgt. R. C. B. Mason		"C" 3rd Bn.
20.9.45	3128695 Sgt. G. McCarthy		
20.9.45 ⎱			
21.2.46 ⎰	2878834 Sgt. J. G. Rainnie		1st Bn.
10.1.45	6400271 Sgt. A. L. Sparks		10th Bn.
20.9.45	1440687 Sgt. J. Thompson *(K.I.A. 22.9.44)*		2nd Bn.
20.9.45	72808 Sgt. J. Wallace		2nd Bn.
20.9.45	5725086 A/Sgt. N. A. V. Brady		10th Bn.
20.9.45	3857088 L/Sgt. J. Hamilton		2nd Bn.
28.2.46	3055376 Cpl. A. E. N. McM. Thompson		

10.5.45	5573779	Cpl. W. H. Waite	*(K.I.A. 23.9.44)*	10th Bn.
20.9.45	5110007	L/Cpl. H. Cook		
20.9.45	6400067	L/Cpl. W. Garibaldi	*(K.I.A. 21.9.44)*	10th Bn.
20.9.45	3594586	Pte. S. Barnett		
20.9.45	2766217	Pte. B. J. Diedericks		
20.9.45	4801924	Pte. L. T. Grier		
20.9.45	173497	Pte. W. H. McBeth		
20.9.45	14422713	Pte. F. V. Moore	"H.Q."	2nd Bn.
28.2.46	14362066	Pte. R. W. Peatling		2nd Bn.
20.9.45	1537347	Pte. E. J. Rylands *(awarded M.M.)*		"A" 2nd Bn.

21st Independent Parachute Company
Distinguished Service Order
9.11.44   Capt. (T/Major) Bernard Alexander Wilson, M.C. 43050

O.C. 21 Indep.

Military Cross
9.11.44   Lieut. (T/capt.) Herbert David Eastwood   121135

No. 1 Platoon

9.1144   Lieut. Norman Hugh Harry Ashmore 168938   No. 3 Platoon

Distinguished Conduct Medal
9.11.44   6285245   W.O.II (C.S.M.) James Stewart

Military Medal
9.11.44	3968405	Sgt. Norman Binick *(W.D.)*	No. 1 Platoon
9.11.44	1443162	L/Cpl. Ernest Hewitt	
9.11.44	6298748	Pte. William John Joseph Barclay	

Mentioned In Despatches
10.5.45	Capt. (temp) R. E. Spivey	180067	2/I.C. 21 Indep
10.5.45	14604011 Tpr. J. McBride		

The Glider Pilot Regiment
Member of the British Empire
23.9.45   Capt. (T/Major) Kenneth James Stuart Andrews   121236

Military Cross
9.11.44   Capt. (T/Major) Francis Anthony Stoddard Murray   85686
(W.D./escaped)

Distinguished Flying Cross

11.1.45	Capt. (T/Major) John Frank Bernard Blatch	94149
11.1.45	Capt. (T/Major) Stewart Cathie Griffiths	73789
		2/I.C. No. 1 Glider Wg.
11.1.45	Capt. (T/Major) Thomas Ian Jodrell Toler	47712 O.C. "B" Sqn.
11.4.46	Capt. (temp) Christopher Bradford Dodwell	166383
11.4.46	Lieut. George Rose Innes Masters Stokes	243119

Distinguished Conduct Medal

9.11.44   552600   Sgt. Russell Frederick Tilley   *(att. 7 K.O.S.B. as R.S.M.)*

Military Medal

9.11.44   3968405 S/Sgt. Eric John Holloway   *(K.I.A. 18.9.44)*
11.4.46   920678   S/Sgt. David Bruce Wallace *(D.O.W. 24.9.44)*
9.11.44   14623984 Sgt. Lewis Haig *(believed to be Louis Hagen)*

British Empire Medal

29.3.45   3131087   S/Sgt. Samuel Findlay Johnstone

Bar to the D. F. M.

11.1.45   12078059 S/Sgt. Harold Norman Andrews, D.F.M.

Distinguished Flying Medal

11.4.46   6018787   S/Sgt. Albert Vincent Dance
11.4.46   62606 S/Sgt. William Mather
11.1.45   1077155   S/Sgt. Joseph Alyosious Rye
11.4.46   6297726   S/Sgt. George Frederick Stremes
11.1.45   103586   S/Sgt. Cyril Wilfred Twiggs
11.4.46   3859441   A/S. Sgt. Ronald Reid Calder
11.4.46   809931   A/S.Sgt. Charles Rollett Watkinson
11.1.45   2336371   Sgt. (A/S.Sgt.) Robert Gordon Douglas
11.1.45   6149848   Sgt. (A/S.Sgt.) Samuel Gregory Isaacs

Mentioned In Despatches

22.3.45	Major (temp) K. J. S. Andrews	121236		
20.9.45	Captain T. J. Wainwright	101367		
11.4.46	Captain (temp) G. T. Mills	220201	*(K.I.A.)*	
20.6.46	Captain (temp) F. J. T. Neale	73653	*(K.I.A.)*	
10.5.45	Captain (temp) T. A. Plowman	138799	*(K.I.A. 24.9.44)*	
				1st Wing
10.5.45	Lieut. P. J. Brazier	214774	*(K.I.A. 23-24.9.44)*	2nd Wing
11.4.46	Lieut. C. C. Taylor	174387	*(K.I.A. 20.9.44)*	1st Wing

11.4.46	893156	S/Sgt. E. Phillips	*(K.I.A. 18.9.44)*	2nd Wing
11.4.46	3453001	A/S.Sgt. J. E. P. Naden	*(K.I.A. 24-26.9.44)*	2nd Wing
20.9.45	858565	Sgt. P. J. D. Mahoney		
11.4.46	2598378	A/Sgt. M. A. Gwinn	*(D.O.W. 4.10.44)*	1st Wing
11.4.46	6291394	A/Sgt. J. R. Mann	*(K.I.A. 23.9.44)*	1st Wing

1st Air-Landing Brigade
Commander of the British Empire
29.3.45   Brigadier (temp) Philip Hugh Whitley Hicks, D.S.O., M.C.
15075   O.C. 1st Bde.

1st Bn., The Border Regiment
Distinguished Service Order
9.11.44   Capt. (T/Major) William Neill   200852   "B" Coy.

Military Cross
9.11.44   Lieut. Joseph Stevenson Davidson Hardy   258048

Distinguished Conduct Medal
9.11.44   3650449   Sgt. Sidney Clarke

Military Medal
9.11.44   3057009   Cpl. James Swann   "C" Coy.
9.11.44   3783818   Pte. James Joseph O'Neill

7th Bn., King's Own Scottish Borderers
Distinguished Service Order
9.11.44   Major (T/Lt-Col.) Robert Payton-Reid   13802   C.O. 7th Bn.
20.9.45   Major (temp) Charles Gordon Sherriff   65928   2/I.C. 7th Bn.

Military Medal
9.11.44   4750971   Sgt. Daniel Keyes
9.11.44   14426090 Pte. Alfred Robin Holburn

Mentioned In Despatches
20.9.45   Major (temp) J. S. A'D. Coke 52602
          (K.I.A. Leading breakout of P.O.W.'s 27.9.44)
319373   W.O.II J. Swanston
3325754 Pte. R. J. Burns
319693   Pte. D. J. Craven

2nd Bn, South Staffordshire Regiment
Victoria Cross
2.11.44+ Capt. (T/Major) Robert Henry Cain   129484   R.N. Fus. att.
     (BD 199)

23.11.44+ 5057916   L/Sgt. John Daniel Baskeyfield

Distinguished Service Order
9.11.44   Capt. (T/Major) John Steward Aithchison Buchanan   214085

Member of the British Empire
29.3.45   Lieut. (T/Capt.) Stanley John Busby   153276
29.3.45   4912907   W.O.I (R.S.M.) George Henry Threakall

Military Cross
9.11.44   Lieut. Donald Kenneth Edwards   295840
9.11.44   4909235   W.O.II (C.S.M.) William Robinson

Military Medal
9.11.44   5052629   Pte. Ernest Holt

Mentioned In Despatches
22.3.45   Capt. (temp) E. Deuchar, M.C.   240289
20.9.45   Capt. (temp) E. M. Wyss   148579   *(K.I.A.)* 2/I.C."D" Coy.

1st Air-Landing Recce Squadron, R.A.C.
Military Cross
9.11.44   Lieut. Douglas Galbraith   240327   "A" Troop

British Empire Medal (B.E.M.)
9.1.46   4917622   Sgt. Kenneth Osborne Lapper   Spt. Troop
9.1.46   5378524   Sgt. Harry Venes   "A" Troop

Military Medal
9.11.44   2697025   Sgt. James Pyper   "D" Troop

Mentioned In Despatches
20.9.45   3854428   Sgt. G. Kay   H.Q. Troop

The Airborne Support Units
Ryl. Regt. of Artilley
Distinguished Service Order
9.11.44   Capt. (T/Major)   James Edward Fryer Linton 41143
                              O.C. 2nd A/Lng. Lt. Bty.

| 9.11.44 | Lieut. Adrian Donaldson | 228471 | 2nd A/Lng. Lt. Bty. |

Military Cross

| 9.11.44 | Lieut. (T/Capt) Charles Anthony Harrison | 75273 | "E" Trp, 1 A/Lng. Lt. Bty. |
| 20.9.45 | Lieut. Edward Ernest Shaw | 258511 | 1 A/Lng. Atk. Bty. |

Member of the British Empire

| 29.3.45 | 818590 | W.O.I John Sidney Siely | 1 A/Lng. Lt. R. |

Distinguished Conduct Medal

| 9.11.44 | 6210701 | Sgt. John Joseph Daly | "E" Trp | 1 A/Lng. Lt. Bty |
| 9.11.44 | 11003975 | Sgt. Eric Henry Newland | | 1 A/Lng. Lt. R. |

Military Medal

9.11.44	6769165	W.O.II (B.S.M.) Richard Barrett	1 A/Lng. Lt. R.
9.11.44	759664	Sgt. Charles Abel Thomson	2 A/Lng. Atk. Bty.
9.11.44	998673	L/Sgt. Derrick Lewis Newton	1 A/Lng. Lt. R.
9.11.44	989992	Bdr. Wilfred Wheatley	2 A/Lng. Atk. Bty.
9.11.44	884436	L/Bdr. James Dickson	2 A/Lng. Lt. Bty.
9.11.44	14296661	Gnr. Michael Mannion	2 A/Lng. Atk. Bty.

Mentioned In Despatches

20.9.45	220300	T/Capt. P. R. MacG. Barron	2 A/Lng. Atk. Bty.
20.9.45	105888	T/Capt. P. Chard *(D.O.W. 9.10.44)*	1 A/Lng. Lt. R.
20.9.45	207851	T/Capt. A. D. Llewellyn-Jones	1 A/Lng. Atk. Bty.
20.9.45	93355	Capt. W. S. Whimster	1 F.O.U.
20.9.45	273178	Lieut. P. R. R. De Burgh	H.Q. R.A.
20.9.45	251373	Lieut. R. D. Glover *(K.I.A. 19.9.44)*	2 A/Lng. Atk. Bty.
20.9.45	790163	W.O.II W. A. Goodman	2 A/Lng. Atk. Bty.
20.9.45		Sgt. L. Doughty	1 A/Lng. Atk. Bty.
20.9.45	927881	Bdr. C. R. Curnew	
20.9.45	14285005	L/Bdr. E. C. Bolden	1 A/Lng. Lt. Regt.

Corps of Royal Engineers
Member of the British Empire (gallant & dist. service)

20.9.45 Major (temp) Eric Maclachan MacKay 210907 "A" Trp., 1 Para Sqn.

Bar to the M.C.

1.3.45 Lieut. Frank Willoughby John Cowtan, M.C. 91950 9th Abn. Fd. Coy.

Military Cross
9.11.44   Capt. (T/Major) John Chisholm Winchester 50841
                                          O.C. 9th Abn. Fd. Coy.
9.11.44   Captain Henry Faulkner Brown   235514   4th Para. Sqn.
9.11.44   Lieut. Denis Jackson Simpson   249558   1st Para. Sqn.
9.11.44   Lieut. David Valentine Storrs   251041   att. H.Q. 1st Abn. Div.

Distinguished Conduct Medal
9.11.44   1880512 L/Sgt. Hugh Lake   9th Abn. Fd. Coy.

Military Medal
9.11.44   1930355 Spr. Ronald Thomas Emery (at bridge)   1st Para. Sqn.
1.3.45   5827060 Spr. Philip Andrew Hyatt   4th Para. Sqn.

Mentioned In Despatches
20.9.45   Major (temp) A. J. M. Perkins   77568   O.C. 4th Para. Sqn.
1.3.45   Captain Nigel Beaumont Thomas, M.C. 93266
            (K.I.A. 20.9.44)   4th Para. Sqn.
20.9.45   Capt. (temp) E. C. O'Callaghan, M.C.   243580 9th Abn. Fd. Coy.
20.9.45   Lieut. D. R. Hindley   258859   1st Para. Sqn.
20.9.45   Lieut. D. J. Simpson, M.C.   24958   1st Para. Sqn.

Royal Corps of Signals
Military Medal
9.11.44   2341501 Sgt. John Inglis Patterson   att. 21 Indep. Para. Coy.
9.11.44   2325487 Sign. Eric George Tolhurst

Mentioned In Despatches
20.9.45   Major (temp) A. J. Deane-Drummond, M.C. 71076
3317478 Sign. G. H. Brown

Royal Army Service Corps.
Military Cross
9.11.44   Lieut (T/Capt.) John Launcelot Cranmer-Byng

Royal Army Medical Corps
Distinguished Service Order
24.5.45   Colonel (actg.) Graeme Matthew Warrack   57723   A.D.M.S. 1
                                                   Abn. Div.
20.9.45   Lt-Col. (temp) Arthur Trevor Marrable   67301 C.O. 181 A.F.A.
29.3.45   Major (T/Lt-Col.) Martin Edward Meakin Herford, M.B.E., M.C.
                        175256   C.O. 163 F.A. att. 1st Abn. Corps.

Officer of the British Empire (gallant & dist. services)
20.9.45   Colonel (actg.) Graeme Matthew Warrack, D.S.O.   57723

Member of the British Empire (gallant & dist. services)
20.9.45   Captain Alexander William Lipmann-Kessel   227647
Surgical Team 16 P.F.A.
29.3.45   Lieut. (Qr-Mr.) John Tiernan   244779   181 A/Lng. F.A.

Military Cross
20.9.45   Captain Alexander William Lipmann-Kessel, M.B.E.

Distinguished Conduct Medal
20.9.45   7357051   Sgt. John Frederick Weatherby (at the bridge) 16th P.F.A.
20.9.45   7384504   Cpl. (actg.) Harold Roy Couling   16th P.F.A.

Military Medal
9.11.44   7369364   Pte. William Slater

Mentioned In Despatches
20.9.45   Lt-Colonel (temp) W. C. Alford, O.B.E., M.B.   88813
O.C. 133rd P.F.A.
20.9.45   Captain C. C. M. James, F.R.C.S.   279329   181st A.F.A.
20.9.45   Captain J. Lawson   230831   133rd P.F.A.
20.9.45   Captain V. D. R. Martin, M.B. 260584   R.M.O. 1st A/Lng. R., R.A.
20.9.45   Captain G. F. H. Drayson, M.B. *(K.I.A. 19.9.44)* *181248*
R.M.O. 10th Para. Bn.
20.9.45   7249904   S/Sgt. H. Mason
20.9.45   7263618   Cpl. W. Green
20.9.45   7357488   Cpl. G. Holmes
20.9.45   7361872   L/Cpl. G. V. H. Ellis
20.9.45   7364541   L/Cpl. E. W. Mabbott
20.9.45   7377856   Pte. S. E. Jackson
20.9.45   Major (act.) D. H. Ridler, M.C.   104446   Army Dental Corps
att. 16th P.F.A.

Royal Army Chaplain's Dept
Military Cross
20.9.45   Reverend Daniel McGowan C. F. 4th Cl. 287572   16th P.F.A.
9.11.44   Reverend Robert Talbot Watkins C. F. 4th Cl. 188498   1st Bn.

Mentioned In Despatches
20.9.45   Reverend A. A. Buchanan C.F. 4th Cl.   218713   2nd S/Staffords.
22.3.45   Reverend G. A. F. Pare, B.A. C. F. 4th Cl. 175561 1st Wing G.P.R.

For gallant & distinguished services, whilst a Prisoner-of-War
Member of the British Empire
18.4.46   2613527   W.O.I John Clifford Lord   Para. Regt., A.A.C. 3rd Bn

R.S.M. Lord, an ex-Grenadier Guard, created almost a living legend, at Stalag XIB where he was interned. He was responsible for the upkeep of morale among the men and was respected by both sides in the Camp.

The following members received awards prior to Airborne service and were killed in action or died whilst P.O.W:

Distinguished Conduct Medal—Middle East
24.2.42   6009204   (A/Cpl.) Charles Williams Hayes   Essex R.
(D.O.W. 16.3.45 Germany, Cpl. 156th Bn.)

British Empire Medal—Middle East
23.9.43   2612035   Sgt. (Drum Major) Stanley Edward Watling G. Gds.
(K.I.A. 9.44 Arnhem, Lieut. 156th Bn.)

Military Medal—Middle East
24.9.42   7888782   Sgt. Michael Joseph Elliott   R. Tank R.
(K.I.A. 19.9.44 Sgt. 11th Bn.)

19.8.44   6468016   L/Cpl. Ebenezer Cochran   Ryl. Fusiliers
(K.I.A. 23.9.44 Pte 11th Bn.)

Mentioned In Despatches—during air ops whilst att. to R.A.F.
9.7.42   Lieut. (T/Capt.) Ralph Alexander Maltby 73034   R. Arty.
(K.I.A. 17.9.44, Lieut. Int. Off. No 2 Wing, G.P.R.)
Also awarded U.S.S.R. Order of the Patriotic War.

Appendix 7/2

Victoria Cross Citations for the Battle of Arnhem

L.G. 2.11.44 Page 5015

The King has been graciously pleased to approve an award of the V.C. to:

Capt. (temp Major) Robert Henry Cain 129484   Ryl. North'land Fus.
(att. S. Staffs Regt.) (1 Airborne Div.) (Salcombe, Devon)

In Holland on September 19th, 1944, Major Cain was commanding a rifle company of the South Staffs. Regiment during the Battle of Arnhem, when his company was cut off from the rest of the Battalion and during the next six days was closely engaged with enemy tanks, self-propelled guns and infantry. The Germans made repeated attempts to break into the company position by infiltration and had they succeeded in doing so the whole situation of the Airborne Troops would have been jeopardised.

Major Cain, by his outstanding devotion to duty and remarkable powers of leadership, was to a large extent personally responsible for saving a vital sector from falling into the hands of the enemy.

On 20th September, a Tiger tank approached the area held by his company and Major Cain went alone to deal with it armed with a Piat. Taking up position he held his fire until the tank was only 20 yards away, when he opened up. The tank immediately halted and turned its guns on him, shooting away a corner of the house near where the officer was lying. Although wounded by MG Bullets and falling masonry; Major Cain continued firing until he had scored several direct hits, immobilised the tank and supervised the bringing up of a 75mm howitzer, which completely destroyed it. Only then would he consent to have his wounds dressed.

The next morning this officer drove off three more tanks by the fearless use of his Piat, on each occasion leaving cover and taking up position in open ground with complete disregard for his personal safety.

During the following days, Major Cain was everywhere where danger threatened, moving amongst his men and encouraging them by his fearless example to hold out. He refused rest and medical attention in spite of the fact that his hearing had been seriously impaired, because of a perforated eardrum and was suffering from multiple wounds.

On the 25th September, the enemy made a concerted attack on Major Cain's position, using self-propelled guns, flame-throwers and infantry. By this time the last Piat had been put out of action and Major Cain was armed with only a light 2" Mortar. However by a skilful use of this weapon and his daring leadership of the few men still under his command, he completely demoralized the enemy who, after an engagement lasting more than three hours, withdrew in disorder.

Throughout the whole course of the battle of Arnhem, Major Cain showed superby gallantry. His powers of endurance and leadership were the admiration of all his fellow officers and stories of his valour were being constantly exchanged amongst the troops. His coolness and courage under incessant fire could not be surpassed.

L.G. 1.2.45 Page 669
The King has been graciously pleased to approve the award of V.C. to:

Captain Lionel Ernest Queripel 108181   The Ryl. Sussex Regt.
(1st Airborne Division) (Dorchester)

In Holland, on the 19th September, 1944, Captain Queripel was acting as Company Commander of a composite company composed of three Parachute Battalions.

At 1400 hours on that day, his company was advancing along a main road which ran on an embankment towards Arnhem. The advance was conducted under continuous medium machine-gun fire which, at one period, became so heavy that the company became split up on either side of the road and suffered considerable losses. Captain Queripel at once proceeded to reorganise his force, crossing and recrossing the road whilst doing so, under extremely heavy and accurate fire. During this period he carried a wounded Sergeant to the Regimental Aid Post under fire and was himself wounded in the face.

Having reorganised his force, Captain Queripel personally led a party of men against a strong point holding up the advance. This strongpoint consisted of a captured British anti-tank gun and two machine guns. Despite the extremely heavy fire directed at him, Captain Queripel succeeded in killing the crews of the machine-guns and also recapturing the anti-tank gun. As a result of this the advance was able to continue.

Later in the same day Captain Queripel found himself cut off with a small party of men and took up a position in a ditch. By this time he had received further wounds in both arms. Regardless of his wounds and of the very heavy mortar and Spandau fire, he continued to inspire his men to resist with hand grenades, pistols and the few remaining rifles.

As, however, the enemy pressure increased, Captain Queripel decided that it was impossible to hold the position any longer and ordered his men to withdraw. Despite their protests, he insisted on remaining behind to cover their withdrawal with his automatic pistol and a few remaining hand grenades.

This was the last occasion on which he was seen.

During the whole of a period of nine hours of confused and bitter fighting Captain Queripel displayed the highest standard of gallantry under most difficult and trying circumstances. His courage leadership and devotion to duty were magnificent and an inspiration to all. The officer is officially reported to be wounded and missing.

(In fact, Captain Queripel was Killed-In-Action on 19th September, 1944 and is buried at the Oosterbeek War Cemetery).

L.G. 25.2.45 Page 561/2
The King has been graciously pleased to approve the post-humous award of the V.C. to:

Lieut. John Hollington Grayburn   1490002
(The Parachute Regt., A.A.C.) (Chalfont St. Giles)

For supreme courage, leadership and devotion to duty.

Lt. Grayburn was a platoon commander of the Parachute Battalion, (2nd Btn.) which was dropped on the 17th September, 1944 with the task of seizing and holding the bridge over the Rhine at Arnhem.

The north end of the bridge was captured and, early in the night, Lt. Grayburn was ordered to assault and capture the southern end with his platoon. He led his platoon onto the bridge and began the attack with the utmost determination, but the platoon was met by a hail of fire from two 20mm quick firing guns and from the machine-guns of an armoured car. Almost at once Lt. Grayburn was shot through the shoulder. Although there was no cover on the bridge and in spite of his wounds, Lt. Grayburn continued to press forward with the greatest dash and bravery until casualties became so heavy that he was ordered to withdraw. He directed the withdrawal from the bridge personally and was himself the last man to come off the embankment into comparative cover.

Later his platoon was ordered to occupy a house which was vital to the defence of the bridge and he personally organised the occupation of the house.

Throughout the next day and night the enemy made ceaseless attacks on the house, using not only infantry with mortars and machine-guns, but also tanks and self-propelled guns. The house was very exposed and difficult to defend and the fact that it did not fall to the enemy must be attributed to Lt. Grayburn's great courage and inspiring leadership. He constantly exposed himself to the enemy's fire while moving among and encouraging his platoon and seemed completely oblivious to danger.

On 19th September, 1944 the enemy renewed his attacks, which increased in intensity, as the house was vital to the defence of the bridge. All the attacks were repulsed, due to Lt. Grayburn's valour and skill in organising and encourageing his men, until eventually the house was set on fire and had to be evacuated.

Lt. Grayburn then took command of elements of all arms, including the remainder of his own company, and reformed them into a fighting force. He spent the night reorganising a defensive position to cover approaches to the bridge.

On 20th September, 1944, he extended his defence by a series of fighting patrols, which prevented the enemy from gaining access to the houses in the vicinity, the occupation of which would have prejudiced the defence of the bridge. This forced the enemy to bring up tanks, which brought Lt. Grayburn's position under such heavy fire that he was forced to withdraw to an area further north. The enemy now attempted to lay demolition charges under the bridge and the situation was critical. Realising this, Lt. Grayburn organised and led a fighting patrol, which drove the enemy off temporarily and gave time for the fuses to be removed. He was again wounded, this time in the back but refused to be evacuated.

Finally, an enemy tank, against which Lt. Grayburn had no defence, approached so close to his position that it became untenable.

He then stood up in full view of the tank, and personally directed the withdrawal of his men to the main defensive perimeter to which he had been ordered.

He was killed that night.

From the evening of September 17th until the night of September 20th, 1944, a period of over three days, Lt. Grayburn led his men with supreme gallantry and determination. Although in pain and weakened by his wounds, short of food and without sleep, his courage never flagged. There is no doubt, had it not been for this officer's inspiring leadership and personal bravery, the Arnhem Bridge could never have been held for this time.

L.G. 23.11.44 Page 5375
The King has been graciously pleased to approve the post-humous award of V.C. to:

5057916 Lance-Sgt. John Daniel Baskeyfield   South Staffs. Regt.
(1 Airborne Division) (Stoke-on-Trent)

On 20th September, 1944, during the Battle of Arnehem, Lance-Sgt. Baskeyfield was the N.C.O. in charge of a 6 Pdr. A/Tank Gun at Oosterbeek.

The enemy developed a major attack on this sector with infantry, tanks and self-propelled guns with the obvious intention to break into and overrun the Battalion position. During the early stage of the action the crew commanded by this N.C.O. was responsible for the destruction of two Tiger tanks and at least one Sp Gun, thanks to the coolness and daring of this N.C.O. who with complete disregard for his own safety allowed each tank to come well within 100 yards of his gun before opening fire.

In the course of this preliminary engagement L-Sgt. Baskeyfield was badly wounded in the leg and the remainder of his crew were either killed or badly wounded. During the brief respite after the engagement L-Sgt. Baskeyfield refused to be carried to the Regimental Aid Post and spent his time attending to his gun and shouting encouragement to his comrades in neighbouring trenches.

After a short interval the enemy renewed the attack with even greater ferocity than before, under the cover of intense mortar and shell fire. Manning his gun quite alone, L-Sgt. Baskeyfield continued to fire round after round at the enemy until his gun was put out of action. By this time his activity was the main factor in keeping the enemy tanks at bay. The fact that the surviving men in his vicinity were held together and kept in action was undoubtedly due to his magnificent example and outstanding courage. Time after time the enemy attacks were launched and driven off. Finally when his gun was knocked out L-Sgt. Baskeyfield crawled, under intense enemy fire to another 6 Pdr. gun nearby, the crew of which had been killed and proceeded to man it single-handed. With this gun he engaged an enemy SP Gun, which was approaching to attack. Another solider crawled across the open ground to assist him but was killed almost at once. L-Sgt. Baskeyfield succeeded in firing two rounds at the SP Gun, scoring a direct his, which rendered it ineffective. Whilst preparing to fire a third shot, however, he was killed by a shell from a supporting enemy tank.

The superb gallantry of this N.C.O. is beyond praise. During the remaining days at Arnhem, stories of his valour were a constant inspiration to all ranks. He spurned danger, ignored pain and, by his supreme fighting spirit, infected all who witnessed his conduct with the same aggressiveness and dogged devotion to duty, which characterised his actions throughout.

Appendix 7/3

Decorations Conferred by The Allies for Arnhem
By H.M. The Queen of the Netherlands

1st Abn. Div. H.Q.
Bronze Lion
Major-General (actg) Robert Elliott Urquhart, C.B., D.S.O. 17550
      late H.L.I. O.C. 1st Abn. Div.
Lieut-Colonel Edmund Charles Wolf Myers, C.B.E., D.S.O., B.A. 36717
      Ryl. Engrs. Commander: R.E.

Bronze Cross
Colonel (actg) Michael St. John Packe 66968 Commander: R.A.S.C.

1st & 4th Parachute Brigades
Militaire Willemsorde (the Dutch V.C.)
Lt-Col. (temp) David Theodor Dobie, D.S.O. 67437 W.D. C.O. 1st Bn.
Lieut. John Patrick Barrett 253696 1st P.B. H.Q. Def. Pltn.

Bronze Lion

Major (temp) Ronald Leslie Stark, M.C.	167154	1st Bn.
Capt. (temp) Brian Dean Carr	138170	10th Bn.
Capt. (temp) John Edward Helingoe	268135	1st Bn.
Lieut. Alexis Peter Vedeniapine, M.M.	282332	3rd Bn.
5825299 W.O.II Reginald George Chenery		1st Bn.
4687742 W.O.II Donald Craig McRae		4th P.B. H.Q. Def. Pltn.
5338896 Sgt. Dennis George Barrett		
4387793 Sgt. Francis Edward Brown		10th Bn.
4194322 Sgt. Emyr Glyn Edwards		
6344345 Sgt. Owen George Hughes, M.M.		10th Bn.
4192138 Sgt. Thomas Henry Jones		
6985438 Sgt. William James Kerr		
3854424 Sgt. (actg.) Henry Callaghan		3rd Bn.

Bronze Cross

Lieut. Albert Thomas Turrell	233563	1st Bn.
3130841 Cpl. Joseph Shields Jones		

21st Indep. Para. Copy.
Bronze Cross
7904485   Pte. Frederick John Ronald Patrick Lee

1st A/Lng. Recce Sqn.
Bronze Lion
Capt. (temp) David Allsop   105457

Bronze Cross
6105318   Pte. Charles Cecil Bolton

Glider Pilot Regiment
Bronze Lion
Major Robert Shirley Croot   40686   *(D.O.W.)*
2727183   W.O.II Michael Briody, M.B.E.   *(now Lt. R.A.S.C.)*

Bronze Cross
Capt. (temp) Michael Taylor Corrie   177502
Capt. (temp) Thomas James Wainwright   101367
7948876   Sgt. Walter Hammerton Swift

1st Air-Landing Brigade
Bronze Lion
Major (temp) Robert Gilliam Buchanan   92465   K.O.S.B.
Capt. (temp) Michael Robert Holman   228610   Border

Bronze Cross
3187350   Cpl. Alexander Gunning   K.O.S.B.
14211301 Cpl. William Watson   K.O.S.B.
3443816   L/Cpl. Charles Cavaghan   Border

Royal Regiment of Artillery
Bronze Lion
Major (actg) Dennis Stuart Munford   134902   3rd A/Lng. Lt. Bty.
841449   Sgt. John Joseph O'Neill

Bronze Cross
Lt-Col. (temp) William Francis Kynaston Thompson, M.B.E. 44179
                                                    C.O. 1st A/Lng. Lt. Regt.
802710   Sgt. John Thomas Davis
11455238 Gnr. Edgar Walter Neale

Silver Medal in the House Order of Orange

813694   Sgt. Charles Frederick Foster

884753   Bdr. Albert Alexander Cooke

Corps of Royal Engineers

Bronze Lion

1899732 Cpl. Albert Alexander Lancaster   9th Abn. Fd. Coy.

Bronze Cross

2115925 Cpl. William Alfred Coulsting   2 Tp., 4 Sqn.

Royal Army Medical Corps

Bronze Lion

Captain James Watt Logan, D.S.O., M.B.   188966   R.M.O. 2nd Bn.

7259229 W.O.I Leonard Henry Bryson   181 A/Lng. F.A.

7522555 S/Sgt. Albert Edward Allen

7387144 L/Cpl. Geoffrey Charles Stanners

Bronze Cross

Lt-Col. (temp) Thomas Douglas Victor Swinscow   188263

then M.O. 1st A/Lng. Recce Sqn.

Major (temp) Cedric James Longland, M.C., F.R.C.S.   236049 16th P.F.A.

Captain David Wright, M.C., M.B.   218952   16th P.F.A.

No. 1 Forward Obs. Unit R.A.

Bronze Cross

Capt. (temp) Christopher John Salter MacMillen65826   Essex Regt.

1st Abn. Div. Provost Coy.

Bronze Cross

7686615 Cpl. Peter Charles Dale   C.R.M.P.

By the President of the U.S.A.

1st British Abn. Corps

Legion of Merit—Degree of Commander

Lt-General Sir Frederick Arthur Montague Browning, K.B.E., C.B., D.S.O.

22588   *(Late Gren. Gds)*   C.O. 1 Br. Abn.

Distinguished Service Cross

Brigadier (temp) Gerald William Lathbury, D.S.O., M.B.E.   34834

(W.D./escaped)   C.O. 1st Bde.

Brigadier (temp) Robert Guy Loder-Symonds, D.S.O., M.C.   56606

Commander: R.A. Ryl. Regt. Arty.

Lieut-Col. Charles Fred Osborne BREESE   66138   C.O. 1st Border R.

Major George Francis De Gex   1 A/Lng. Lt. R.

4617711   Cpl. Robert Pearce   2nd Bn., Para. Regt.

14282186 L/Cpl. Francis Mann   1st A/Lng. Recce Sqn.

Silver Star

Major (temp) Anthony Mutrie Frank, M.C.   99817   "A" 2nd Bn. P.R.

Captain Basil Anthony Bethune Taylor   1 A/Lng. Lt. R.

6141287   Sgt. Arthur James Ayres   Para. Regt.

3130008 Cpl. James Clements   Para. Regt.

Bronze Star

Major Allen John Petch   127256   Para. Regt.

6395864   WOI Robert Edward Grainger   10th Bn. P.R.

3246740   WOII William Watt   Glider Pilot Regt.

2929430   Sgt. James Walton   Para Regt.

Chapter VIII

FROM ITALIAN SUNSET TO GRECIAN TWILIGHT

WITH the 1st Airborne Division leaving Italy in November, 1943, the 2nd Para. Brigade remained as an Independent Brigade Group, and was placed under the 2nd New Zealand Division in an infantry role.

They were in action on the left flank of the 8th Army during the crossing of the River Sangro in November. The **5th Para Battalion** was in an exposed position, especially "D" Company under Major C. Dudgeon below ORSOGNA. Pte. Morrice won the Battalion's first decoration covering the withdrawal of a patrol from Orsogna, under Lt. Bruce of "B" Company.

The **4th Para. Battalion** relieved the 5th—who were sent to the ARIELE sector near the River Moro. The fighting patrols continued: Lt. Mortimer won the M.C. by capturing a complete enemy section, and Lt. Deacon won one the next day in close combat. In the same action, Cpl. Walker of **127th P.F.A.** won the M.M. for tending wounded under fire. Following the hard winter conditions, the 4th Battalion moved to Naples for a rest in March, 1944, rejoining the rest of the Brigade there.

Following their rest at GUARDIA, the Brigade moved to the CAS-SINO sector, where more patrols were carried out, some of the places were mined and it cost Lt. Pearson his legs. At the end of May, 1944, the Brigade was sent to a rest camp at SALERNO. On the 1st June, there was a parachute drop near TORRICELLI of 3 officers and 57 other ranks of the **6th Battalion**. In this, Operation "HASTY", Captain Fitzroy-Smith and his men were to prevent the Germans carrying out demolitions during their withdrawal. It was a success, though half the force was captured, trying to return to the Allied lines.

No. 3 Pltn., 21st Indep. Para. Coy. remained with 2nd Brigade and formed the 23rd Indep. Para. Platoon, (later renamed the 1st Indep. Para. Pltn.), under command of Captain P. Baker, with Lt. D'Arifat as 2/I.C. Their strength was supplemented by the addition of a section from each of the Battalions, under Lts. Williams (4th Bn.), Boyd (5th Bn.) and Whiteway (6th Bn.) They trained in Sicily with the 1st Glider Sqn., G.P.R. and returned to the Brigade for the proposed landings in the south of France.

The **1st Indep. Glider Sqn.**, under the command of Major Coulthard was formed from elements of the 3rd and 5th Sqns. of the 1st Glider Bn. "B" Flight was based at COMISO in south-west Sicily, and "A" & "C" at PONTEOLIVO and GERBINI airfields. Shortly after the fall of ROME, they were based in MARCIGLINA and trained for the French landings with anti-tank guns and 75mm howitzers. They then with the 2nd Brigade went to TARGUINIA on the coast, north-west of Rome, where they would take off for the south of France.

South of France

It was proposed that the Allies would land in Southern France, capture MARSEILLES and then move inland through the Rhone Valley to link up with the Allied Forces advancing from the Normandy beaches. The **2nd Brigade** became part of the 1st Airborne Task Force, commanded by Major-General R. T. Frederick, U.S. Army. The rest of the force was American and consisted of: 517th P.I.R., 509th P.I.B., 550th P.I.R., 551st P.I.R. and 463rd Para. Fld. Arty.

The 2nd Brigade in Operation "ANVIL" was to drop between LA MOTTE and LE MUY to prevent the enemy from reaching the coast. They took off from five airfields near Rome in Dakotas of the 51st U.S. Troop-Carrier Wing, with 61 Hadrian and Horsa gliders carrying the artillery support, to follow once the landing zone had been cleared of obstacles. The date for the operation was the 15th August, 1944, the **1st Indep. Para. Pltn.** dropping first at 0330 hrs. to mark the British dropping and landing zones; the Americans using their own pathfinders, who were late.

Weather conditions deteriorated with cloud and fog, the pathfinders dropped about a mile from the D.Z., but marched to it, and set up the beacons, and proceeded to clear some of the anti-glider poles on the nearby landing zone.

The force was soon overhead, of the 106 sticks; 73 dropped onto the D.Z.—the **4th and 6th Battalions** dropped in reasonably good order onto and around the DZ, although most of the **5th Battalion** was scattered over an area of 20 miles near CANNES and FAYENCE due to the cloud conditions and a fault in the leading aircraft.

The elements of the **127th Para. Fld. Amb**. were also scattered, but a theatre was established at a house in LE MITAN at 0730 hrs., though as casualties increased, No.3 section requested that a move to St. MICHEL be made. This was agreed, and finally accomplished by 1930 hrs., as more casualties arrived from the L.Z.

No. 1 Section, 127th P.F.A., with the 4th Battalion dropped near St. MICHEL, and they set up an ADS at GOUTES.

"B" Company of the **5th Battalion** landed on the D.Z. Major Dudgeon of "D" Company was badly wounded by grenade fragments in the thigh and calf, and was treated by Captain E. Morrison, and admitted to the civilian hospital at FAYENCE. In mixed parties, "A", "C", and "D" Companies marched to LE MUY, getting involved in small actions along the way.

The **6th Battalion** fought through to LA MOTTE, and there an A.D.S. was set up by **No.2 Section, 127th P.F.A.** under Captain A. L. Kerr.

At 0930 hrs., the **64th Light Battery, R.A**. landed in their Waco Hadrian gliders, although the Horsa carrying the **300th A/Lng. A/Tk. Bty.** had to turn back, as the Dakotas were running out of fuel due to circling over Corsica, due to bad visibility. They landed the next day. A battle started near FREJUS, the artillery towed by their jeeps set off to give support. The glider pilots helped in the digging of defensive positions. Several pilots were injured on landing, including the Squadron Commander—Major Coulthard.

On the 17th August, the paratroopers linked up with the Seaborne force, and on the 27th the Brigade returned to Italy having embarked at Toulon. They were camped near Rome, and then to Bari, where they trained for their next operation—the invasion of Greece.

The Landings In Greece

Following its operation in the south of France, the Brigade moved from Bari to a camp near SAN PANCRAZIO, 20 miles east of Taranto, on September 8th, 1944. In October, the Germans evacuated Athens, and the Allies decided to set up a friendly pro-Western regime, before the Russians got there via the Balkans. It was planned that the Brigade would drop at KALAMAKI airfield near Athens, and proceed to the capital and gain control whilst the PIRAEUS was cleared of mines in preparation for Seaborne force. Lt. Legge of the 2nd Para. Sqn., R.E. had been dropped near Athens in civilian clothes, to set up communications with the Brigade in Italy, prior to the drop.

The operation was code-named "MANNA", though it would be parachutists and not bread that fell from heaven, onto the plain at MEGARA in gale force winds on 12th October, 1944. H.Q., "C" Company and its mortars of the **4th Para. Battalion** under Lt-Colonel Coxen took off from Brindisi for MEGARA airfield, as the plan for KALAMAKI had been changed the day before. They dropped onto the airfield, over 25% of the group were injured, as they were dragged along by their parachutes in the 30 mph winds, there were three fatalities: Lt. D. C. Marsh and two other ranks. Due to the adverse weather conditions, the rest of the Battalion did not arrive until the 14th October, and the **6th Battalion** also had casualties. It had been decided to transfer a surgical team, and two medical officers and 13 other ranks into gliders, but they didn't arrive until the 16th October. The **5th Battalion** had landed on the 15th October, and with the other two Battalions, marched into Athens. They were received by milling crowds, the situation becoming very tense as temperatures rose, but luckily a sudden cloudburst cooled everybody down and cleared the streets.

The Brigade was then joined by the 23rd Armoured Brigade, which consisted of the 40th, 46th and 50th Royal Tank Regiments and the 11th Battalion, King's Royal Rifle Corps. The policing of the city started at that time, the troops were welcomed, but feelings soon were to go against them, particularly from the one warring faction: E.L.A.S.

E.L.A.S. stood for "Ellinikos Laikos Apploeutherotikos Stratos" and was a Left-Wing guerilla force. Opposed to them was E.A.M. the Greek National Liberation Front—"Ethnikon Apeleutherotikon Metopan" and both factions, that wanted liberation, carried out processions, that often coincided. The result was fighting in the streets, the paratroopers were under strict orders not to intervene, but soon E.L.A.S. went underground, and began a war against the policing forces.

On 17th October, 1944, the **4th Parachute Battalion**, with No. 3 Section 127th P.F.A. under Captain L. S. Bruce, and a section of **S.B.S.** under Major I. Patterson, M.C. became known as "Pompforce". It was ordered to proceed to THEBES in pursuit of the German forces, who were still evacuating Southern Greece, and harass their rearguard units. They reached the town of LEVEDIA, which was full of E.L.A.S. troops, and the reception was very uneasy to start with. For the next week, they moved across country and reached GEVENA on the 25th October. Two days later, **"C"Company, 4th Para. Bn**. under the temporary command of Major Lord Jellicoe, D.S.O. of the S.B.S. was ordered to attack and occupy a mountain above KOSANI, unfortunately, they were repelled by the German force still in residence. Their wounded were treated at the R.A.P. at SIATISTA. On the 15th November, the force returned to ATHENS.

The **5th Battalion** sailed from Athens to SALONIKA on the 4th November, 1944, with Bde. H.Q., the remainder of **127th P.F.A.**, and No.9 (Army) Commando. They then moved to MACEDONIA and THRACE, under the command of the 4th Indian Division. Here they tried to maintain peace between the E.L.A.S. and Nationalist forces. On 2nd December, 1944, the Brigade was withdrawn and was supposed to be sailing for Italy, however, it was recalled to ATHENS, and landed at PIRAEUS, being fired upon by E.L.A.S. patrols.

The **6th Battalion** had moved out to occupy THEBES and some of the smaller towns in the area.

Then suddenly the situation in Athens worsened, and war was declared on E.L.A.S. on the 7th December, 1944, after they had tried to seize control of the city by force on the 4th December. An attempt to blow up the British H.Q. by use of the sewers, was thwarted by Major Vernon and his **2nd Para. Sqn., R.E**. The Battalions were recalled to Athens, and with the 23rd Armoured Brigade, became known as "ARKFORCE", and decided that it would hold the Acropolis, and vital points of the city, since the Acropolis overlooked many of the streets. Lt-Col. Parkinson established a hospital in the Acropolis Museum. Fighting continued throughout the month, streets being slowly cleared, until by the first week in January, 1945, the last remaining E.L.A.S. retreated from the city, along the Piraeus Road. Due to the press distorting facts about alleged butchery by the security troops, the Trades Union Congress sent Sir Walter Citrine to ascertain the true facts. This he did, in favour of the Brigade.

The Brigade was then withdrawn to Italy in early February, 1945. It was ready for action after a fortnight's rest, but had over 30 operations cancelled, and on May 8th, 1945, the war ended. The Brigade returned to England on the 16th June, arriving on the 25th. It was then placed under command of the 6th Airborne Division on 29th August, in readiness for the policing of Palestine, which was to lead to another bloody conflict.

Awards of the 2nd Indep. Para. Bde.
in Italy—November, 1943 - May, 1944

Bar to the M.C.
20.9.45   Major (temp) Michael Walter Hopper Shepherd 73969   5th Bn.

Military Cross
20.9.45	Major (temp) Leonard Arthur Fitzroy-Smith	149818	6th Bn.
7.12.44	Lieut. Frederick Turrall Ashby	255763	6th Bn.
6.4.44	Lieut. Leslie John Deacon	253722	4th Bn.
6.4.44	Lieut. Geoffrey Lansdell Mortimer	164861	4th Bn.
26.10.44	Lieut. Gerald Lionel Pearson *(W.D.)*	103091	6th Bn.
	Lieut. Michael Walter Hopper Shepherd	73969	5th Bn.
21.12.44	Lieut. John Henry Tatham	226840	

Military Medal
29.6.44	5887507	Sgt. George Douglas Daniels	4th Bn.
4.5.44	2937777	Sgt. John Hay Hughes	5th Bn.
5.10.44	4345247	Sgt. Harold Wilmott	4th Bn.
21.12.44	6096731	Cpl. (A/Sgt.) Jack Barter	4th Bn.
26.10.44	3911012	Cpl. (A/Sgt.) William Daniel Jones	6th Bn.
4.5.44	3064969	Cpl. Norman Chapman	5th Bn.
4.5.44	2929758	Pte. (A/Cpl.) Alexander Stewart	5th Bn.
3.8.44	4204963	Fus. (A/Cpl.) John Alexander Mauger	6th Bn.
4.5.44	4196571	L/Cpl. Gomer Francis	6th Bn.
	318294	L/Cpl. Peter Murdoch McLeod	5th Bn.
7.12.44	5511499	L/Cpl. Morley William Mitchell	4th Bn.
4.5.44	6213826	Pte. John Charles Driver	4th Bn.
4.5.44	2934174	Pte. George Morrice	"B" 5th Bn.
3.8.44	5254478	Pte. David Norcup	6th Bn.

Mentioned In Despatches (11.1.45)
Major (T/Lt-Col.) H. B. Coxen, D.S.O., M.C. 73534   C.O. 4th Bn.
Captain (T/Major) C. E. R. Dudgeon   *(W.D. S. Fr.)* 137043 O.C. "D" 5th Bn.
Captain (T/Major) H. L. Jones, M.C.   89372   6th Bn.
Captain J. L. Williams   106457   1st Indep. & 4th Bn.
Lieut. (T/Capt.) J. L. Duncan   115299
Lieut. (T/Capt.) L. A. Fitzroy-Smith   149818   6th Bn.

Lieut. (T/Capt.) H. J. Fuller		160594	
Lieut. (T/Capt.) D. H. Marlow		195317	4th Bn.
Lieut. R. N. Geall		255776	4th Bn.
6200786	Sgt. J. W. Chandler		4th Bn.
5505225	Sgt. A. Hybart		4th Bn.
886982	Sgt. E. G. Jenkins		"A" 6th Bn.
6083934	Sgt. J. Pash		4th Bn.
3247083	Sgt. T. Simpson		5th Bn.
2058541	Sgt. H. E. Tucker		"B" 5th Bn.
3964224	Cpl. (A/Sgt.) D. W. Willetts		6th Bn.
6757288	L/Sgt. N. J. Dixon		4th Bn.
2935727	Cpl. F. Richardson		5th Bn.
4203912	Cpl. T. E. Salisbury		6th Bn.
3909860	L/Cpl. J. H. Jenkins		6th Bn.
255446	Pte. W. J. Kimber		4th Bn.
7592948	Sgt. P. C. J. Sheath		R.E.M.E. att 4th Bn.

Military Medal

4.5.44	7262210	Cpl. William Cuthell	127 P.F.A.
13.1.44	2012435	Cpl. Thomas Crawford McCaughie	2 Para. Sqn., R.E.
6.4.44	7347033	Cpl. William Walker	127 P.F.A.
21.9.44	1873646	Spr. (A/Cpl.) George Albert Dogherty	2 Para. Sqn., R.E.

Mentioned In Despatches

11.1.45	838842	Sgt. L. J. Spencer	64 A/Lng. Lt. Bty., R.A.

Awards of the 2nd Indep. Para. Bde.
in the South of France—August, 1944

Military Cross

5.10.44   Capt. (T/Major) Ralph Douglas Cameron McCall   129038

5th Bn.

Bar to the M.M.

21.12.44   4345247   Sgt. Harold Wilmott, M.M.   4th Bn.

Military Medal

14.9.44	3130602	Cpl. Henry Burgess	5th Bn.
14.9.44	4975448	Cpl. Thomas Davies	"A" 6th Bn.
5.10.44	3130993	L/Cpl. James Warnock	"D" 5th Bn.

Mentioned In Despatches

22.2.45	Major (temp) J. A. Blackwood	153408	"B" 5th Bn.
22.2.45	Major (temp) L. A. Fitzroy-Smith, M.C.	149818	6th Bn.
22.2.45	Major (temp) (Q.M.) C. Langelaan	P/173768	
22.2.45	Major (temp) J. W. Pearson	203343	6th Bn.
22.2.45	Lieut. J. R. Greenhalgh 251655		4th Bn.
22.2.45	2937596 Sgt. G. L. Scrimgeour		"B" 5th Bn.
22.2.45	3247083 Sgt. T. Simpson		5th Bn.
22.2.45	3129090 Cpl. (actg.) W. Lannary		5th Bn.
22.2.45	267305 Pte. K. Senerat-Kadigawe		"C" 5th Bn.
22.2.45	5349616 Pte. W. A. Young		4th Bn.
22.2.45	Major (temp) G. A. R. Coulthard	53795	*(W.D.)*
			O.C. 1st Indep. Sqn
22.245	Lieut. Col. (temp) J. P. Parkinson, M.B.		74165 C.O. 127th
			P.F.A., R.A.M.C.
16.11.44	Captain J. P. Irwin	202416	127th P.F.A. R.A.M.C.

Distinguished Flying Medal

962438   S/Sgt. Andrew McCulloch   G.P. Regt.

Appendix 8/3

Awards of the 2nd Indep. Para. Bde. in Greece—October, 1944 – February, 1945

Distinguished Service Order

Brigadier (temp) Charles Hilary Vaughan Pritchard   38573   R.W.F.   O.C. 2nd Bde.

He was also made a Commander of the Royal Order of King George I with Swords, by the King of the Hellenes.

T/Lt. Col. Vernon William Barlow, O.B.E.   K.S.L.I.   O.C. 6th Bn.

Bar to the M.C.

21.6.45   Major (temp) James Nash Gourlay, M.C.   121956   4th Bn.

Military Cross

10.5.45   Major (temp) Anthony Heritage Farrar-Hockley   251309
                                                              "C" 6th Bn.
10.5.45   Capt. (actg) John Morriss Neill   180599   6th Bn.
10.5.45   Capt. (act.) Nathan Vogelman   S. Afr. F.   6th Bn.
10.5.45   Lieut. George Cassidy   301547   5th Bn.
22.2.45   2926374 W.O.I (R.S.M.) Alexander MacLennan   5th Bn.

Military Medal

10.5.45   3309397 Sgt. John Bryson   5th Bn.
10.5.45   4198458 Sgt. Noel Howarth Fitton   6th Bn.
26.7.45   327096   Sgt. Arthur Munden   4th Bn.
10.5.45   4201547 Sgt. William John Thomas   6th Bn.
10.5.45   3531506 Sgt. Norman Yates   1st Indep. Para. Pltn.
10.5.45   4455797 L/Sgt. Robert August Reiber   4th Bn.
10.5.45   4198199 Cpl. Frank Parry   6th Bn.
10.5.45   5350468 L/Cpl. George William Hurry   6th Bn.
10.5.45   6146456 L/Cpl. Hubert McCarthy   6th Bn.
10.5.45   2700466 Pte. William Anderson   5th Bn.
10.5.45   3137482 Pte. John Fleck   5th Bn.
10.5.45   5125689 Pte. William Jonah Pound   6th Bn.
10.5.45   4274959 Pte. Ralph Wood   6th Bn.

Mentioned In Despatches

23.5.46   Major (temp) N. MacP. Boys   176101   6th Bn.

23.5.46	Captain T. Trevor-Williams	219135	6th Bn.
8.11.45	Capt. (temp) J. H. M. Fane, M.B.E.	69531	G.P.R.
21.6.45	Capt. (temp) A. H. Farrar-Hockley, M.C.	251309	"C" 6th Bn.
23.5.46	Capt. (temp) J. S. Holden	76202	5th Bn.
23.5.46	Capt. (temp) G. H. Seal	301567	6th Bn.
23.5.46	Lieut. E. G. Cole	267598	4th Bn.
23.5.46	Lieut. W. I. Grimsditch	158779	4th Bn.
21.6.45	Lieut. H. W. Phillips	162757	
21.6.45	2937237 W.O.II L. Foxcroft		5th Bn.
23.5.46	2933742 A/W.O.II J. Murray		5th Bn.
23.5.46	5500447 C/Sgt. R. C. Corbin		4th Bn.
23.5.46	5443880 Sgt. L. G. Hayman		4th Bn.
21.6.45	6467926 Sgt. S. Hendon		G. P. R.
23.5.46	6465601 Sgt. C J. Johnson		"A" 6th Bn.
21.6.45	871346 Sgt. W. B. Morrison		G. P. R.
23.5.46	4198026 Sgt. T. E. Rowlands		6th Bn.
21.6.45	3247083 Sgt. T. Simpson		5th Bn.
23.5.46	2933177 Sgt. V. R. G. Webster		5th Bn.
23.5.46	14221094 A/Sgt. J. Howard		
23.5.46	7881158 A/Sgt. W. B. Mitchell		5th Bn.
23.5.46	801591 Cpl. F. H. Clapham		4th Bn.
21.6.45	(BNA) 13302278 Pte. M. Palmer		

Special Boat Service
Mentioned In Despatches
4.1.45 Capt. (T/Major) I. N. Patterson, M.C. 69411   att. 4th Bn.
        (K.Air Crash 23.12.43 Italy)

64th A/Lng. Lt. Bty., R.A.
Military Cross
10.5.45   Lieut. Bryan Morwood   232955

Military Medal
10.5.45   14281861 Gnr. James Chalmers

1st Abn. Div. Sigs.
British Empire Medal (for gallant & distinguished service)
21.6.45   3598717   L/Cpl. John Stephenson   att. 4th Bn.

127th Para. Fld. Amb., R.A.M.C.
Mentioned In Despatches
21.6.45   Captain J. P. Irwin, M.B.   202416   R.M.O. 4th Bn.
(John Philip Irwin was killed by an E.L.A.S. sniper whilst about to tend to wounded in Athens suburb 11.12.44)

Military Medal
10.5.45   7389579   Cpl. Fred Bennett   att. 6th Bn.
10.5.45   7346759   Cpl. Kelly Thomas Tighe   att. 6th Bn.

Appendix 8/4

Awards to 2nd Indep. Para. Bde. in Italy
February - May, 1945

Member of the British Empire (gallant & dist. service)
13.12.45	Major (temp) John Lyne Duncan	115299	
13.12.45	Capt. (Qr.-Mr.) Rees John Price	147941	6th Bn.
13.12.45	Major (temp) John Leslie Williams	106457	4th Bn.

Military Medal
13.12.45	3128558	Sgt. John Gregory	5th Bn.
13.12.45	7962994	Sgt. Edwin Charles Prosser	4th Bn.

Mentioned In Despatches
19.7.45	Major J. L. Duncan	115299	
29.11.45	Major (temp) E. R. Harris	93023	
29.11.45	Major (temp) S. K. Hart	105230	5th Bn.
29.11.45	Captain W. R. Hunter *(W.D.)*	200403	"B" 5th Bn.
19.7.45	Capt. (temp) P. Mackie	113628	
29.11.45	Capt. (temp) G. L. Mortimer, M.C.	164861	4th Bn.
29.11.45	Capt. (temp) D. S. West-Russell	180337	
29.11.45	Lieut. J. Miller	251842	"C" 5th Bn.
29.11.45	46855283 W.O.II A. Stewart		4th Bn.
29.11.45	6012094 W.O.II F. J. Wiggs		4th Bn.
29.11.45	4124891 W.O.II J. H. H. Williamson		6th Bn.
29.11.45	1449951 S/Sgt. H. W. Chambers *(now Lieut.)*		
29.11.45	71027 S/Sgt. T. Cooke		
29.11.45	4913170 S/Sgt. A. Brooks		4th Bn.
29.11.45	601270 Sgt. F. C. Hawkins		
29.11.45	3135482 Sgt. J. Priest		5th Bn.
29.11.45	2938171 Sgt. L. Sanders		5th Bn.
29.11.45	4197838 Sgt. D. E. Thomas		6th Bn.
29.11.45	2982664 Sgt. A. Weir		5th Bn.
29.11.45	3189461 A/Sgt. D. L. McEwan		5th Bn.
29.11.45	7022780 Cpl. K. R. Beare		4th Bn.
29.11.45	5573183 Pte. J. I. Barton		4th Bn.
29.11.45	5836986 Pte. W. Cairns		4th Bn.
29.11.45	14328726 Fus. K. Farnworth		6th Bn.
19.7.45	3260607 Pte. H. Fletcher		5th Bn.
29.11.45	858886 Pte. A. Harman		

29.11.45	3537372	Pte. C. Payton	4th Bn.
19.7.45	265750	Pte. H. E. Ruffles	
29.11.45	4031275	Pte. G. Smith	6th Bn.
19.7.45	14527476	Pte. J. T. Smith	6th Bn.
29.11.45	14527476	Fus. J. T. Smith	6th Bn.

Chapter IX

FROM SNOW TO WATER

The Ardennes

THE 6th Airborne Division rested and trained in the Bulford area, until Christmas Eve of 1944, when, due to increased German pressure on the Americans, which had produced a bulge in the ARDENNES Pocket—it was rushed across the Channel to the transit camp at Ostend, in readiness to support the other Allied Forces.

It was now under the command of Major-General E. L. Bols, D.S.O. The **3rd & 5th Parachute Brigades** were in place near to DINANT and NAMUR; the **6th Air-Landing Brigade** was at DINANT, as was the **195th A.F.A.** under command of Lt-Colonel Anderson, which was to be the first airborne unit in action. Now it was the time for the Allies to go on the offensive. The Airborne Division took over from the 53rd (Welch) Division at ROCHEFORT on the 2nd January, 1945.

An example of the heavy fighting, the Division took part in, is evident in the part played by the **13th Para. Battalion**, who took the village of BURE, after a hard fight in the blizzards on the 3/4th January. Major J. R. B. Watson and "A" Company, followed by "B" Company under Major G. Grantham fought through the town, involved in heavy hand-to-hand and house-to-house fighting. They were later reinforced by "C" Company of the **Oxford & Bucks**. The 13th Battalion's Chaplain—the Reverend Foy, received the M.C. for his part in helping the wounded, and Sgt. Scott of the **225th P.F.A.** received the M.M., after going forward with an ambulance to pick up wounded, and being requested by a commander of a Tiger tank, not to do so again. The **12th Devons.**, now under command of Lt-Colonel Gleadell fought around TELLIN and BURE.

The **7th Para. Battalion** conducted fighting patrols, after capturing

WAVREILLE. Another noted incident, was that concerning Captain Tibbs, M.C. the R.M.O. of the 13th Para. Bn., assisting members of a **22nd Indep. Para. Coy**. patrol, which had wandered into a minefield. Captain Tibbs supporting one wounded soldier, who, it was later found out, had he been laid down would have set off a mine!

It was not all fighting, as the 3rd Parachute Brigade showed, with their Winter Sports meeting held at Roy, organised by Major W. C. Knox-Peebles off 212 Battery, **53rd Light Regt., R.A**. On 30th January, command of the 53rd Light passed to Lt-Colonel R. A. Eden, D.S.O.

Another incident connected with mines happened in early February, when two men of the 22nd Indep. were blown up by mines, and Captain Fisher of **195th A.F.A**. went to their assistance, without the aid of mine detectors, and brought both out safely, he was awarded the M.C.

More patrols were carried out and the Division, now holding part of the west bank of the Meuse, under control of the 8th Corps, returned to Salisbury Plain via Ostend in the February, to train for the crossing of the Rhine in March.

The Crossing Of The Rhine

By the Spring of 1945, the Germans had retreated, and the Allies were poised to cross the Rhine, which would lead into the heart of Germany. The plan of Operation "VARSITY" was to drop an airborne task force, consisting of the British 6th Airborne Division, and the American 17th (GOLDEN TALON) Abn. Division, (which formed the U.S. 18th Abn. Corps, under Major-General M. B. Ridgeway, with Major-General R. N. Gale as deputy), over the Rhine between REES and WESEL, to seize terrain, that would be valuable to the landing forces of the British 2nd Army, and American 9th, and widen their bridgehead.

The British objectives were: the seizure of bridges of the River ISSEL; the capture of HAMMINKELN; and the high ground east of BERGEN, notably the SCHNAPPENBERG FEATURE.

The Parachute Brigades were to drop first, with the glider-borne troops following up. The date set was to be the 24th March, 1945, and the operation would be carried out in daylight, so a lot of resources were needed for fighter-bomber and artillery support. Over 1,100 aircraft and gliders would be used by the 6th Airborne Division alone: 242 being parachute aircraft.

The 3rd Parachute Brigade

After taking off at 0700 hrs., the Brigade dropped north of BERGEN, and was fired upon by light anti-aircraft guns and small arms, despite the precaution of bombings and strafing by the Allied air forces.

As a result, there were many casualties: the C.O. of the 224th P.F.A. had been already briefed on this, and to expect about 600 casualties, almost one-third of the Brigade. Many were shot in the trees, as they tried to struggle free.

The **8th Para. Battalion**, plus No.2 Section, **224th P.F.A** and its C.O.'s "Stick" dropped in the first wave, and had a fierce fight on landing, sustaining eighty of the 270 casualties of the Brigade. Having cleared the D.Z. by 1100 hrs, it moved out, only to be isolated during the fighting until the next day. The **224th P.F.A.** arrived virtually complete, and set up a C.C.P. in the wood, its Q.M. Capt. Anderson was shot in the shoulder, as he helped a wounded man, after dropping from the tree, in which he had been suspended, and the unit anaesthetist—Capt. C.A. Chaundy, A.D.C. was killed, as he reached the unit R.V. At midday, the unit had installed one of its' surgical teams at BERGENFURTH Church. The C.O. of the 8th Para. Bn., had been concussed, after he had landed, by a glider which crashed almost on top of him, as he talked with the Battalion I.O.—Lt. J. K. England, M.B.E., who was killed, after being struck by part of the glider.

The **9th Para. Battalion**, plus No. 3 Section, **224th P.F.A.** moved against the one flank of the SCHNAPPENBERG FEATURE, for a short while, the C.O. led the charge up the incline, astride a German horse, but was forced to join his men on ground level, as the resistance warmed up. The **Canadians** had lost their C.O. on the D.Z. in the trees, and were beside the 9th Battalion, as they stormed the hill. It was during this period, that Corporal Topham, a Canadian medical orderly received the Victoria Cross, for his bravery in tending casualties under fire, and whilst himself was wounded.

The 5th Parachute Brigade

The Brigade dropped north of KOPENHOF, and west of HAMMINKELN at 1000 hrs., and it to suffered casualties during the drop, since mobile anti-aircraft guns had not been destroyed, and fired airburst shells at the white parachutes. Lt. Burkinshaw of the **12th Para. Bn.** and his platoon captured four 88mm guns, that had been firing on the DZ, as the men landed, and the gliders as well amongst them.

The **225th P.F.A**. under Lt-Col. N.J. P. Hewlings, landed in good order and set up an A.D.S. in a large farm near to the DIERSFORDTERWALD, and worked undisturbed until the next day, when peace reigned.

By 1500 hrs., the Brigade was digging in, the 12th & 13th Para. Bns. having secured the surrounding farms, with the 7th Para. Bn. in reserve, although the Brigade lost over 300 casualties in the process.

In support of the drop was a total of 544 guns of 12 Corps, and the Airborne Corps Artillery. Their fire was controlled by officers of the **No.2 Forward Observation Unit,** which had been formed primarily for this operation, from ex-members of the Bombardment Parties, who had dropped on D-Day. The unit had had its' baptism of fire in the Battle of the Bulge, and at Bure. Every Parachute Battalion H.Q. had a party of 2 F.O.U. with it.

The 6th Air-Landing Brigade

Many of the gliders were shot down, the Germans having recovered from the initial shock of bombing and shelling. Some gliders landed in the wrong place, due to smoke and haze over the landing zones, though the "coup de main" gliders landed by the bridges and captured them by 1100 hrs. The "coup de main" tactic had been the idea of Brigadier Chatterton, D.S.O., whereby small sub-units could be landed on top of objectives in readiness for the main force to arrive. Fifteen gliders were allocated from "F" Sqn., **G.P. Regt** of No.1 Glider Wing, commanded by Lt-Col. I. Murray, D.S.O. Eight would carry the Oxford & Bucks. L.I. party, and seven — the R.U.R.'s party. On landing the pilots would then become part of the 6th Air-landing Brigade H.Q. Defence Platoon. Out of the 416 gliders that took part in the operation, only 88 landed undamaged, and 37 were burnt out—most of these were Hamilcars carrying large quantities of petrol, and between 20 and 30% of the pilots were killed, wounded or missing.

The **Royal Ulsters** landed south of HAMMINKELN, and moved to take the town, and reinforce their bridge party. Major B. H. Jackson, O.C. "E" Sqn., G.P.R. and his men fought off some German half-tracks, and destroyed two armoured cars, before being reinforced by men from the Ulsters. Major Jackson later received the D.F.C.

The **Oxford & Bucks**. landed north of HAMMINKELN, as did the No. 3 Section, **195th A.F.A**. under Captain J. S. Binning. The C.O. of the Oxfords., in a glider piloted by Sqn. Ldr. V. H. Reynolds—O.C. "F" Sqn., G.P.R. landed next to a railway station, and captured a flak battery nearby.

The **Devons**. to which part of "A" Troop, 210 Bty., **53rd A/Lng. Lt. Regt., R.A**. under Captain W. B. Godfrey was attached, assaulted HAMMINKELN from the south, which had been captured by 1100 hrs. German counter-attacks from RINGENBERG were contained by a platoon of the Devons; some glider pilots; and four American M22 "Locust" Light Airborne Tanks of the 6th Abn. Div. Armd. Recce. Regt., until the main force moved up the next day.

Out of the 78 gliders carrying the 53rd A/Lng. Lt. Regt: 22 were lost completely, and of the battery commanders—Major Knox-Peebles of 212, and Major G.W. Culley, M.C. of 210 were both killed by M.G. fire, as they emerged from their gliders, and Major J. H. Craigie of 211 was wounded. Casualties amounted to 92 of which over 20 were killed. Capt. D. K. Thomas of "B" Troop, 210 Battery received the M.C. for holding a house, with his party, and stragglers, until his ammunition ran out, after landing 3 miles east of the L.Z. in enemy territory.

Major-General Bols landed in a glider piloted by Major H. T. Bartlett, D.F.C. O.C. "A" Sqn., G.P.R., and had set up his H.Q. at KOPENHOF FARM. The Airborne troops then linked up with the ground forces on the following day.

After this action, they remained in Germany in a ground role.

From the 27th March until the 5th May, the Division advanced across Germany, with the 5th Parachute Brigade in the lead, through BRUNEN, held up at ERLE for a short while, and then through OSNABRUCK. The 12th Para. Bn. had a fight at NATRUP, with Pte. Westerman winning the M.M. for house clearing.

The 3rd Parachute Brigade attacked KLOSTERLUTHERHEIM, and then RHADES, passing LEMBECK on the 28th March. They crossed the DORTMUND-EMS CANAL and captured MINDEN. The Division crossed the ELBE on the 30th April and patrols from the 3rd Para. Bde. contacted Russians near MECKELBERG. It was to be the 3rd Parachute Brigade, who were the first to reach WISMAR, and meet the Russians. Though at first, a delicate situation arose, in that the parachutists had just taken the town, and a Russian column informed them, that they would take the town. Words to the effect of "But we've just taken it" fell on deaf ears, and safety catches on both sides were released. Luckily a timely intervention of an interpreter from Div. H.Q. averted the possibility of a confrontation, due to misunderstandings and celebration took the place of combat.

Soon the war in Europe was over, and the Division returned to the U.K. on the 18th May, 1945, and eyes looked to the East.

Appendix 9/1

Awards to the 6th Abn. Div. in the
Ardennes—December, 1944 – February, 1945

HQ, 6th Airborne Division
Military Cross
29.3.45 Capt. (T/Major) Gerard Henry Dearlove Ford   50944
         (K.I.A. Rhine 24.3.45)   S.Lancs. R.

3rd & 5th Parachute Brigades
Distinguished Service Order
29.3.45 Major (T/Lt-Col.) Peter John Luard   49882   Oxf. & Bucks. L. I.
                                                          C.O. 13th Bn.

Member of the British Empire
1.3.45   Lieut. John Kay England   255222   I.O. 8th Bn.
         (K.I.A. Rhine Crossing 24.3.45)
1.2.45   4386637 W.O.II (R.Q.M.S.) George Alfred Fox   12th Bn.
         (K.I.A. Rhine Crossing 24.3.45)

Military Cross
12.4.45 Major (actg) John Bernard Robert Watson   237916   O.C. "A"
                                                             13th Bn.
12.4.45 Lieut. Percy Priestley Clements, D.C.M., M.M.   327224
                                                          "C" 12th Bn.

Military Medal
12.4.45 2059756 L/Cpl. Ronald Hawthorne   13th Bn.
22.3.45 1443798 Pte. William Hogg Brown
22.3.45 3712934 Pte. John Hand   13th Bn.
12.4.45 14422987 Pte. Eric John Toogood   13th Bn.

Mentioned In Despatches
10.5.45 Lt. Col. N. Crookenden   66121   Ches. R. O.C. 9th Bn.
10.5.45 Major (temp) J. Barker   79713
1.3.45   Major (temp) B. R. Browne   138930   "B" 9th Bn.
10.5.45 Major (temp) J. F. Cramphorn 50249   1st O.C. "A" 13th Bn.
10.5.45 Major (temp) M. A. Lindsay   32017
9.8.45   Major (temp) R. Gordon-Browne 138656   O.C. "A" 9th Bn.
10.5.45 Major (temp) C. C. Norbury   165802   9th Bn.

10.5.45	Major (temp) A. J. M. Parry	69160	9th Bn.
10.5.45	Lieut. J. M. Bewley	180561	
10.5.45	Lieut. R. Grayson	302346	
9.8.45	Lieut. S. B. Kearney (*K.I.A. 27.3.45*)	324298	7th Bn.
10.5.45	Lieut. A. P. Neilson	232037	
10.5.45	Lieut. A. E. Ross	333117	9th Bn.
10.5.45	5101778 W.O.II F. Cooke		8th Bn.
9.8.45	4386637 G. A. Fox, M.B.E.		12th Bn.
	(*R.Q.M.S.—K.I.A. Rhine Crossing*)		
10.5.45	2927108 W.O.II A. J. King		
10.5.45	7686322 C/Sgt. D. M. B. Stroude		
10.5.45	4453090 A/C.Sgt. T. Thomas		12th Bn.
9.8.45	914743 Sgt. A. Bromley		
10.5.45	3193249 Sgt. A. Brown		
10.5.45	7885602 Sgt. R. G. Egan		
10.5.45	2003648 Sgt. S. Graham		
10.5.45	6898077 Sgt. J. Leverett		22 Indep.
10.5.45	1477667 A/Sgt. T. P. Rennie		
10.5.45	324535 A/Sgt. K. N. Sturmay		
10.5.45	14401492 L/Sgt. W. N. Brown		
1.3.45	1463009 L/Sgt. L. H. Cox		7th Bn.
10.5.45	7021988 L/Sgt. V. C. Long		"B" 9th Bn.
10.5.45	4393399 Cpl. G. Beedham		12th Bn.
10.5.45	846834 Cpl. J. H. Corbett		
10.5.45	69701 Cpl. J. L. Hughes		
10.5.45	410633 L/Cpl. J. Bromfield		
10.5.45	4976461 L/Cpl. R. B. Essex		8th Bn.
10.5.45	6843051 L/Cpl. S. J. Webb		9th Bn.
10.5.45	14296495 Tpr. A. J. Clowes		
10.5.45	20229863 Tpr. C. R. Crossfield		
1.3.45	14420195 Tpr. G.D. Gordon		22 Indep.
10.5.45	14643360 Tpr. G. Harwood		
10.5.45	4279165 Tpr. F. McCormick		12th Bn.
10.5.45	14331743 Tpr. J. Moran		
10.5.45	1498071 Tpr. A. E. Scrivener		
10.5.45	4446858 Tpr. C. H. Walker		12th Bn.
10.5.45	6897785 S/Sgt. P. A. Hobbs, D.F.M.		Glider Pilot Regt.

6th Air-Landing Brigade
2nd Bn., Oxford & Bucks. L.I.
Military Medal
1.2.45 5340498 Sgt. Martin Charlie Thornton

C-in-C Certificates for Bure: "C" Coy.

Major J. Granville
Captain J. J. W. Molloy
Lieut. C. T. Cross
5381885   Sgt. Evans
6017727   Cpl. Durbridge
5281380   Cpl. Foster
5439677   Cpl. Joy
5385123   L/Cpl. Wilkinson
5388237   Pte. Weston

1st Bn., Royal Ulster Rifles
Military Medal
1.3.45 14401161 Rfn. William Robert Green

Mentioned In Despatches
10.5.45   Captain (temp) K. E. Clokey   117827
10.5.45   Lieut. J. D. K. Ross   278186

12th Bn., Devonshire Regiment
Mentioned In Despatches
10.5.45   Lieut. E. D. Nuttall   295582

The Airborne Support
No. 2 Forward Observation Unit (Abn.), R. Arty.
Military Cross
3.5.45 Capt. (actg) Kenneth Boss   304014   *(for Bure)*
            (D.O.A.S. Germany 9.6.45 buried Essex)

3rd A/Lng. Anti-Tank Bty., R. Arty
Mentioned In Despatches
10.5.45   14200121 Sgt. Robert Austin Knight   *(K.I.A. Rhine 24.3.45)*

6th Abn. Div. Signals
British Empire Medal (for gallant & dist. service)
21.6.45   14331488 L/Cpl. John William George Evans   R. Signals

Royal Army Chaplain's Department
Military Cross
12.4.45   Reverend Whitfield Foy 263526   C.F. 4th Cl. att. 13th Bn.

Royal Army Medical Corps
Military Cross
3.5.45   Captain John Derbyshire Fisher   250628   195th A.F.A.

Military Medal
29.3.45   7262166 Cpl. (A/Sgt.) Robert Scott   225th P.F.A.
               (K.I.A. Germany 7.4.45)
12.4.45   7360233 Cpl. Charles Bryan   att. 8th Bn.

Mentioned In Despatches
22.3.45   7346272 Cpl. H. Houghton   att. 12th Bn.

Awards Conferred by HRH, Prince Regent of Belgium to A.A.C.
Chevalier of the Order of Leopold II with Palm
Captain Wilfred Davison   324280

Croix De Guerre 1940 with Palm
Captain Wilfred Davison   324280
5680136 W.O.II Victor Alfred Bettle   "B" 7th Bn.
5631068 A/W.O.II Frederick Gilbert Burton Eales
14654479 Cpl. Stanley John Horton

Decoration Militaire, 2nd Class
14369218 L/Sgt. Henry Nicholson
3388217 Cpl. Edgar Thomas Coupe

King's Commendation for Brave Conduct (2.2.45)
6013175 Pte. Ernest Hope
7984492 Pte. Thomas Stanley Symons

Appendix 9/2

Awards of the 6th Airborne Division in the Rhine Crossing to the Baltic Coast

18th U.S. Abn. Corps. H.Q.
Companion of the Bath

Major-General (temp) Richard Nelson Gale, D.S.O., O.B.E., M.C. 20116
    late R. Innisk F. Deputy Commdr.   18 Corps.
18th U.S. Abn. Corps. comprised the British 6th and U.S. 17th Abn. Divs.

6th Abn. Div. H.Q.
Companion of the Bath

5.7.45   Major-Genl. (actg) Eric Louis Bols, D.S.O.   28047
               King's Regt. C.O. 6th Abn. Div.

1st Bar to the D.S.O.

7.6.45   Major-Genl. (actg) Eric Louis Bols, D.S.O.   C.O. 6th Abn. Div.
24.1.46   Colonel Malcolm MacEwen, D.S.O., O.B.E., D.F.C., T.D., M.B.
         R.A.M.C. A.D.M.S.   6th Abn. Div.
3.5.45   Lieut.-Col. (temp) Robert Napier Hubert Campbell Bray
         D. of W. Regt. G.S.0.1 6th Abn. Div.

Distinguished Service Order

11.10.45 Brigadier (temp) William McCausland Tindal Faithfull
         31549 R. Arty. C.R.A.   6th Abn. Div.

Officer of the British Empire

11.10.45 Lieut-Col. (actg) Henry John Darlington   50011
         King's Own Regt. D.A.A.G.   6th Abn. Div.

Member of the British Empire

11.10.45 Lieut.-Col. (temp) Roy Johnson Meech   183238
         R.A.O.C.   C.R.A.O.C.   6th Abn. Div.

Mentioned In Despatches

8.11.45   Major (temp) Peter Percy James Jepson   92531   R. Arty.
         G.S.O.2 (Intelligence)   6th Abn. Div.
         (previously M.I.D. Italy 24.9.44)(K.I.A. Germany 2.5.45)
20.9.45   Major (temp) S. Terrell   92722   G.S.O.2 (Ops)

3rd & 5th Parachute Brigades
Victoria Cross
B39039   Cpl. Frederick George Topham   1st Canadian Para. Bn.

2nd Bar to the D.S.O.
24.1.46   Brigadier (temp) Stanley James Ledger Hill, D.S.O., M.C.
52648   C.O. 3rd Bde.

1st Bar to the D.S.O.
21.6.45   Brigadier (actg) Joseph Howard Nigel Poett, D.S.O.   38346
Durham L.I.   C.O. 5th Bde.
21.6.45   Lieut.-Col. (temp) Richard Geoffrey Pine-Coffin, D.S.O., M.C.
40705   Devon R.   C.O. 7th Bn.

Distinguished Service Order
7.6.45   Lieut.-Col. (temp) Napier Crookenden   66121
Cheshire R.   C.O. 9th Bn.
7.6.45   Lieut.-Col. (temp) Kenneth Thomas Darling   44052
Ryl. Fus.   C.O. 12th Bn.
21.6.45   Lieut.-Col. (temp) George Hewetson   74257   C.O. 8th Bn.
12.7.45   Major Francis Moore Bucher   36301   2/I.C. 12th Bn. R. Scots.

Military Cross
24.1.46   Major (temp) Archibald John Bookless   121646   Adj. 8th Bn.
12.7.45   Major (temp) Clifford Clarence Norbury 165802   9th Bn.
12.7.45   Major (temp) Derrick Rowland Reid   129933 O.C. "B" 7th Bn.
24.1.46   Major (temp) Clarence Weatherill Stephens 174249 "C" 12th Bn.
24.1.46   Captain Eric George Woodman   182357   "B" 7th Bn.
24.1.46   Capt. (temp) William Frank Eardsley Bennett 153136 H.Q. 5 Bde.
31.1.46   Capt. (temp) Frederick James Fowles   117654
24.1.46   Capt. (temp) Peter Warburton Wood   151302
12.7.45   Lieut. Douglas Dudgeon Campbell   256582   22 Indep.
24.1.46   Lieut. Ellis Dean   288761   13th Bn.
24.1.46   Lieut. Harold Max Pollak   237466   13th Bn.
11.10.45 5105371   W.O.I Arthur George Parsons

Military Medal
21.6.45   6031820   Sgt. Phillip Costello   "A" 9th Bn.
11.4.44   6204700   Sgt. Edgar Hancock   9th Bn.
11.4.46   2588320   Sgt. Geoffrey George Moss
12.7.45   5513071   Cpl. George John Burns   9th Bn.
1.8.46   4279165   Cpl. Francis McCormick   12th Bn.

12.7.45	5339353	Tpr. Walter Charles Deane	8th Bn.
12.7.45	2985655	Tpr. Isaac Docherty	
12.7.45	14841779	Tpr. Leroy Herbert Maillard Forter	
21.6.45	11005542	Tpr. Stephen Harris	
21.1.46	14416871	Tpr. Dennis James Hollis	
11.10.45	6344176	Tpr. Arthur John Hose	9th Bn.
12.7.45	993584	Tpr. Nathaniel Kennedy	
12.7.45	1136360	Tpr. Henry Meckin	
12.7.45	1798753	Tpr. James Derek Westerman	"A" 12th Bn.

Mentioned In Despatches

4.4.46	Major (temp) D. M. Freegard	109477	12th Bn.
4.4.46	Major (temp) H. H. Mills, M.C.	134321	7th Bn.
4.4.46	Major (temp) J. N. Taylor, M.C.	138480	O.C. "A" 7th Bn.
4.4.46	Major (temp) R. C. Thompson	235682	
4.4.46	Capt. (Qr-Mr.) E. Clarke	178693	12th Bn.
4.4.46	Capt. T. E. A. Robinson	109081	9th Bn.
4.4.46	Capt. F. J. H. Rogers	256072	7th Bn.
4.4.46	Capt. (temp) N. M. Archdale	277406	7th Bn.
4.4.46	Capt. (temp) C. E. Lepper	162535	9th Bn.
8.11.45	Capt. (temp) G. R. Millar	176150	
4.4.46	Capt. (temp) H. J. Milman	143581	"A" 12th Bn.
4.4.46	Capt. (temp) A. Waldron	342019	
8.11.45	Lieut. P. L. Burkinshaw	264936	"A" 12th Bn.
8.11.45	Lieut. P. J. Fordyce	328195	22 Indep.
8.11.45	Lieut. R. Hinman	324284	7th Bn.
4.4.46	Lieut. D. V. Laws	194600	
8.11.45	Lieut. R. M. Town	229773	13th Bn.
4.4.46	4384424	W.O.I P. Partridge, B.E.M.	12th Bn.
4.4.46	5115959	W.O.II J. Flaherty	8th Bn.
8.11.45	3952374	A/W.O.II A. W. A. Lawley	13th Bn.
4.4.46	3599072	A/W.O.II H. Smith	22 Indep.
4.4.46	1657200	C.Q.M.S. H. J. Ward	
14.2.46	7586544	A/C.Sgt. R. Lawson	7th Bn.
4.4.46	889765	A/C.Sgt. F. C. A. Webb	
14.11.46	5390170	Sgt. F. C. Bridges	8th Bn.
8.11.45	5572460	Sgt. R. A. Dinehart	8th Bn.
4.4.46	13046409	Sgt. H. O. Kendall	
8.11.45	5183855	Sgt. J. Kendrick	8th Bn.
4.4.46	420079	Sgt. H. I. Rhys	
8.11.45	4343685	Sgt. J. Vasey	12th Bn.
8.11.45	4743151	Sgt. S. Wilson	7th Bn.

| 4.4.46 | 3656454 | L/Sgt. A. E. Shelton | 13th Bn. |
| 4.4.46 | 14260957 | Cpl. R. Leonard | |

8.11.45	894084	L/Cpl. R. Gladwell	
4.4.46	4967923	A/L/Cpl. C. Beech Batman to Gen. Gale	
			6th Abn. Div. HQ
8.11.45	7681894	Tpr. J. Corns	
4.4.46	907623	Tpr. S. Hamilton	
6.6.46	5671590	Tpr. T. Lorne	7th Bn.
4.4.46	14539309	Tpr. W. Martin	
8.11.45	4698892	Tpr. J. C. Morton	12th Bn.
4.4.46	5774325	Tpr. M. B. Stanion	9th Bn.
8.11.45	14605875	Tpr. T. Thomas	8th Bn.

Glider Pilot Regiment
Bar to the D.S.O.
16.8.45   Lieut-Col. (temp) Iain Arthur Murray, D.S.O.   98246
C.O. 1st Glider Wing

Distinguished Service Order
27.9.45   Lieut. Michael Donald Keen Dauncey   184738

Distinguished Flying Cross
16.8.45		Major (temp) Burton Henry Jackson	95473	O.C. "E" Sqn.
16.8.45		Major (temp) Hugh Tryon Bartlett	180780	O.C. "A" Sqn.
16.8.45		T/Capt. Frederick Cuthbert Aston	90059	
16.8.45		T/Capt. Maurice William Dallow Priest	138830	
16.8.45	4122908	A/W.O.I Kenneth Mew		
16.8.45	7598921	W.O.II Bertram Richardson Holt		
20.7.45	62421	F/Lt. Edgar Kenelm Peter Ince		R.A.F.V.R. att.
20.7.45	180013	F/Lt. John Edward William Lodge		R.A.F.V.R. att.
20.7.45	164461	F/O. George Atkinson		R.A.F.V.R. att.
20.7.45	166030	F/O. John Thomson Love		R.A.F.V.R. att.
20.7.45	165933	F/O. Michael Julian Odlum		R.A.F.V.R. att.

Conspicuous Gallantry Medal (Flying)
16.8.45   4343733   W.O.II Lawrence William Turnbull   "E" Sqn.

Distinguished Flying Medal
16.8.45	6350228	S/Sgt. Albert Bowman
16.8.45	5387319	S/Sgt. John Ewart Edwards
16.8.45	124150	S/Sgt. Ivor Wyn Evans

16.8.45	1914661	S/Sgt. Thomas Gray
16.8.45	5341633	S/Sgt. Lawrence James Minall
16.8.45	10545541	S/Sgt. Gerald Eric Moorcraft
16.8.45	3131992	S/Sgt. Edgar Raspisson
16.8.45	2589301	S/Sgt. Frank Alan Richards
16.8.45	4694484	S/Sgt. Desmond Ryans
16.8.45	2092974	S/Sgt. John Brian Taylor
16.8.45	1890104	S/Sgt. Leonard Wright *(Had taken part also in D-Day ops.)*

Military Medal
| 20.12.45 | 2881235 | W.O.II Ian James Blackwood |

Mentioned In Despatches
8.11.45	Major (actg) I. A. McArthur	174891	
2.8.45	Capt. (temp) P. McG. Bulwer	186171	
4.4.46	Capt. (temp) J. H. Hooper	130100	
1.11.45	Capt. (temp) A. F. W. Low	180708	
8.11.45	Capt. (temp) A. G. C. Turner, M.B.E.	235670	
6.6.46	Lieut. R. H. Garnett	172350	
4.4.46	5672772 S/Sgt. D. O. E. Attwell		
8.11.45	1916518 S/Sgt. A. C. Baldwin		
8.11.45	14569245 S/Sgt. A. S. Brown		"G" Sqn.
4.4.46	3601755 S/Sgt. G. Campbell		
8.11.45	7663245 S/Sgt. W. G. Moore		
8.11.45	7344366 S/Sgt. G. H. E. Nye		
8.11.45	2889519 S/Sgt. A. B. Wethey		
1.11.45	14291815 Sgt. B. J. F. Haller		
4.4.46	2162344 Sgt. C. Palfreeman		

Conferred by the President of the United States of America in 1947
Silver Star
| Major (temp) Burton Henry Jackson, D.F.C. | 95473 |

Bronze Star
| Capt. (temp) Kenneth Fairley Strathern | 99754 |
| *(K.I.A. Rhine 24.3.45)* | |

6th Air-Landing Brigade Awards
Bar to the D.S.O.
| 11.10.45 | Brigadier (actg) Robert Hugh Bellamy, D.S.O. | 47518 |
| | Duke of Cornwall's L.I. | O.C. 6th A/Lng. Bde. |

2nd Bn., Oxford & Bucks. L.I.
Military Cross
24.1.46   Lieut. Kenneth Gunter   251639   "A" Coy.

Distinguished Conduct Medal
21.6.45   5382330   W.O.II Joseph Stevenson   "D" Coy.

Military Medal
5.7.45   3909816   L/Sgt. John Amiens Burns
21.6.45   4613295   L/Sgt. Lawrence Marshall
5.7.45   14200210 Cpl. Reginald George Turton
21.6.45   5117186   L/Cpl. Harold Hughes
5.7.45   5379336   Pte. Alexander Tranter

Mentioned In Despatches
8.11.45   36539   Major J. S. R. Edmunds   2/I.C.
4.4.46   148588   Major E. H. Nankivell   "C" Coy.
4.4.46   53004   Major G. B. Rahr   "B" Coy.
4.4.46   145422   Major J. M. A. Tillett   "D" Coy.

1st Bn. Royal Ulster Rifles
Distinguished Service Order
24.1.46   Lieut.-Colonel Gerald Percival Rickcord   62664   C.O. 1st Bn.

Military Cross
21.6.45   Major (temp) Anthony John Dyball   90507
24.1.46   Major (temp) Robert Wilson Gordon   96687
5.7.45   Major (actg) Robin Rigby   176451
21.6.45   Capt. (temp) Charles Gibson Alexander   14331
24.1.46   Capt. (temp) Colin O'Hara Murray   155052

Military Medal
24.1.46   7043579   Sgt. (actg) Thomas James McMullan
5.7.45   6984425   Rfn. Robert Hamill

Mentioned In Despatches
8.11.45   Major (temp) E. A. D. Liddle   77480
4.4.46   Major (temp) R. McE. Wilson   143429
4.4.46   Major (actg) R. W. McD. Crockett   165899
4.4.46   Major (actg) B. E. Spiller   130173
4.4.46   Capt. (temp) R. Ellis   262294
4.4.46   Capt. (temp) J. C. Nixon   137050

8.11.45   7013707   Sgt. T. E. Matthews
8.11.45   7013548   L/Cpl. J. O. B. McWilliams
4.4.46   7023040   Rfn. J. A. Mellon

12th Bn., Devonshire Regt.
Distinguished Service Order
7.6.45   Lieut. Colonel (temp) Paul Gleadell   47571   C.O. 12th Bn.

Military Cross
5.7.45   Major (temp) John Rogers   71109

Military Medal
5.7.45   6527606   Sgt. Walter Edwin Crane
21.6.45   14689960 Pte. Leslie Oglivie William Meeks

C-In-C Certificates for N.W. Europe
Major K. J. T. Stoneman
Major C. J. Snell
Captain E. J. Harding
Reverend J. W. Hall
5628788   W.O.II K. C. Atwill
5614750   R.Q.M.S. J. Leverton
5624845   Sgt. J. Howe *(deceased)*
5627868   Sgt. K. Tarren
5615960   Sgt. F. Till
5627490   L/Sgt. A. Collman
5624794   Cpl. E. A. Horrell
5627392   Pte. W. Shapter
5628489   Pte. W. Mills
5629543   Pte. G. Webber
5630752   Pte. H. Webber

6th Abn. Div. Support Units

No. 2 F.O.U.
Military Cross
21..6.45   Capt. Sidney Arthur Mooney   R. Can. Arty.

Military Medal
7.6.45 921274   Bdr. George Halewood   R. Arty.

53rd A/Lng. Lt. Regt., R.A.
Military Cross
11.10.45 T/Captain David Keith Thomas   148317

Military Medal
21.6.45   14600489 Gnr. Ivor Eric Hooper

3rd A/Lng. Atk. Bty., R.A.
Military Cross
5.4.45 T/Major Richmond Ambrose Gorle   44862   O.C. Bty.

6th Abn. Div. Signals
Distinguished Service Order
24.1.46   Lieut-Col. (temp) Peter Edward Moore Bradley 63546   O.C.

British Empire Medal (for gallantry)
24.1.46   2369555 L/Cpl. Raymond Usher Brown   Despatch Rider

Military Medal
11.10.45 14567021 Cpl. Peter Elliott   Line Section
12.7.45   2597638 Cpl. Edward Joseph Landau   5th Bde. Sig. Section

Royal Army Chaplains Department
Military Cross
11.10.45 Reverend John Gwinnett, B.A. 248389   *(BD89)* Cl. att. 9th Bn.
                                                                              C.F. 4th

Royal Army Medical Corps
Distinguished Service Order
7.6.45   Lt.-Col. (temp) Norman James Patrick Hewlings   114840
                                                                   C.O. 225th P.F.A.
Military Medal
21.6.45   7346272 Cpl. Harry Houghton   att. 12th Bn.
5.7.45   97006473 Pte. Paul Morrison Lenton   224th P.F.A.

Mentioned In Despatches
8.11.45   97005977 Pte. T. Downey   224th P.F.A.

Victoria Cross

B39039   Cpl. Frederick George Topham, R.C.A.M.C. att. 1st Canadian
                                                                    Para. Bn.

On 24th March, 1945, Corporal Topham, a medical orderly parachuted with his Battalion onto a strongly defended area, east of the Rhine. At about 1100 hrs., whilst treating casualties in the drop, a cry for help came from a wounded man in the open. Two medical orderlies from a field ambulance went out to this man in succession but were both killed, as they knelt beside the casualty.

Without hesitation, and on his own initiative, Cpl. Topham went forward through intense fire to replace the orderlies, who had been killed before his eyes. As he worked on the wounded man, he himself was shot through the nose. In spite of severe bleeding, and intense pain, he never faltered in his task. Having completed immediate first aid, he carried the wounded man steadily and slowly back through continuous fire to the shelter of the wood.

During the next two hours, Cpl. Topham refused all offers of medical help for his own wound. He worked most devotedly throughout this period to bring wounded in, showing complete disregard for the heavy and accurate enemy fire. It was only when all casualties had been cleared, that he consented to his own wound being treated.

His immediate evacuation was ordered, but he interceded so earnestly on his own behalf, that he was eventually allowed to return to duty.

On his way back to his company, he came across a carrier which had received a direct hit. Enemy mortar bombs were still dropping around, the carrier itself was burning fiercely, and its own mortar ammunition was exploding. An experienced officer on the spot warned all not to approach the carrier.

Cpl. Topham, however, immediately went out alone, in spite of the blasting ammunition, and enemy fire, and rescued the three occupants of the carrier. He brought these men back across the open, and although one died, almost immediately afterwards, he arranged for the evacuation of the other two, who undoubtedly owe their lives to him.

This N.C.O. showed gallantry of the highest order. For six hours, most of the time in great pain, he performed a series of acts of outstanding bravery, and in his magnificent and selfless courage inspired all those who witnessed it.

Decorations conferred by the President of the United States of America

Legion of Merit -Commander

Lieut. Genl. Richard Nelson Gale, C.B., D.S.O., O.B.E., M.C. 20116
late inf. Deputy Commander, 18th Abn. Corps.

Silver Star

Major-Genl. (temp) Eric Louis Bols, D.S.O. 28047 King's Regt. C.O.
6th Abn. Div.

Brigadier (temp) Stanley James Ledger Hill, D.S.O., M.C. 52648
Ryl. Fus. C.O. 3rd Bde.

Major (temp) Frank Lugard Fraser 117076 7th Bn.

Capt. (temp) BernardWilfred Metcalfe 180079 12th Bn.

Bronze Star

4124625 Sgt. John Rookes 8th Bn.

New Year & Birthday Honours 1945-46

Knight Commander of the British Empire (K.B.E.) (1.1.46)

Lieut.-Genl. (temp) Frederick Arthur Montague Browning, C.B., D.S.O.,
22588 late Gred. Gds.

Member of the British Empire

14.6.45 Captain (temp) William Burns Duthie 176103 A.A.C.
14.6.45 Captain (temp) Peter Law 124515 A.A.C. 21 Ind. Para. Coy.
1.1.46 Captain (temp) Peter Noel Fletcher 299274 + A.A.C.
1.1.46 Major (temp) Patrick Graham Harding 156828 + A.A.C.
(+ both G.P. Regt.)

M.B.E. In The Field

1.11.45 Lieut. Albert Edwin Baker 240394 Para. R.

B.E.M. In the Field

18.4.46 13051429 Sgt. Joseph Paul Farrow Para. R.

Chapter X

AN ICY WELCOME

Since Arnhem, the 1st Airborne Division had been taking stock and resting in England. It now only consisted of the 1st Parachute Brigade and the 1st Air-Landing Brigade, with the 1st Polish Parachute Brigade under command.

On the 8th May, 1945, the 1st Parachute Brigade, now under the command of Brigadier E. L. Seawright went to restore law and order, as part of the SHAEF Mission to DENMARK, and returned on the 30th July, when Brigadier S. J. L. Hill, D.S.O., M.C. assumed command. With the Brigade was one section of 133rd Parachute Field Ambulance.

The rest of the Division, with the addition of the S.A.S. Brigade, (since the Polish Brigade remained under orders in England), plus H.Q. 50th Infantry Division; the 303rd & 304th Infantry Brigades, and No. 88 Group, R.A.F. went as the British part of Force 134 to NORWAY, and were placed under Allied Land Forces, Norway, when it was formed.

The 1st Airborne Division landed at GARDEMOEN airfield near OSLO and at STAVANGER. Its' task was to restore law and order, disarm the German troops, and investigate allegations of the population against war criminals. The medical units, which had been reformed had their work cut out, dealing with mainly the hundreds of sick Russian prisoners of war in the camps throughout the country.

There was a large parade to welcome back the King of Norway, in which the S.A.S. and the Airborne Division took part. The S.A.S., now only composed of two regiments went first to ODDA to disarm a number of S.S. troops, and then to BERGEN.

By the end of June, 1945, the Airborne Division started to pull out of the country, and by August most of its' elements were back in England.

Its new role was to be that of the Imperial Strategic Reserve and earmarked for the Middle East. However, this was to be filled by the 6th Airborne Division, and the 1st Airborne Division was disbanded in the October, some of its' units being transferred to the 6th Airborne Division. The **5th Parachute Brigade** became a Brigade Group in July, 1945, and was sent to JAVA from India in late 1945.

The rest of the **6th Airborne Division** went to PALESTINE in September, 1945.

The 1st & 2nd S.A.S. Regiments were disbanded at the end of 1945, though the French and Belgian Squadrons continued within their own armies.

Appendix 10

Decoration Conferred by His Majesty, The King of Norway
Commander with Star, of the Royal Order of St. Olav
Major-General Robert Elliott Urquhart, C.B., D.S.O.   17550
                                                                                            late Inf. Co 1st Abn. Div.

King Haakon VII Liberty Cross
Brigadier (temp) Robert Herbert Bower, C.B.E.   24360
                                                                            late Inf. O.C. 1st A/Lng. Bde.
Brigadier (temp) Robert Guy Loder-Symonds, D.S.O., M.C. 56606 R. Arty.
          (since died—K.I.A. Java)   C.R.A., 1st Abn. Div. H.Q.
Colonel (temp) Edward Ian Bruce Harvey, D.S.O., M.B.   33854
                                                                            R.A.M.C. ex C.O. 225th P.F.A.
Lieut.-Col. Charles Fred Osborne Breese   66138   C.O. 1st Border R.
Lieut.-Col. James Michael Calvert, D.S.O., B.A.   58046
                                                                            R. Engrs. C.O. 1st S.A.S. Bde.
Lieut.-Col. Hugh Christopher Bolt Cook   44621   C.O. 2/Sth. Staffs.
Lieut.-Col. Edmund Charles Wolf Myers, C.B.E., D.S.O.   36717
                                                                            R. Engrs. C.R.E., 1st Abn. Div.
Lieut.-Col. Thomas Cecil Hooke Pearson, D.S.O. 63639   C.O. 1st Bn.
Lieut.-Col Allan John Petch   127256   Int. Corps.

King Haakon VII Liberty Medal
Captain Alexander Arthur Nesling   162566   2nd S.A.S. R.
Captain James Watt Torrance, M.B.E., M.C.   74887   S.F. Det.
405121   Staff Q.M.S. Charles Shaw
7628153   Cpl. George Curry Army Catering Corps   2nd S.A.S. R.
14264324 Cpl. Norman Pateman McLeod
14205769 Cpl. Bernard Weymouth   1st S.A.S. R.

Although awards were given in 1945 they were not gazetted until 19.3.48.

Liberation Certificate
All members of the 1st Abn. Div. in Norway, received a coloured certificates from King Olav commemorating the liberation of Norway, individually named with name, rank, number and unit.

Chapter XI

TO THE EAST

WITH the war in Europe over, the 6th Airborne Division was back in England, making ready to go to the Far East. Tac H.Q. of the Division and the 5th Parachute Brigade H.Q. flew out to India on the 20th July, 1945, arriving in BOMBAY on 27th July. The balance of the Brigade, now designated as an Independent Brigade Group sailed in the "Corfu" on 19th July, and arrived on 5th August. It was then moved to a transit camp at KALYAN, which was midway between Bombay and Poona.

Here the units undertook extensive training in jungle warfare. However, with the dropping of the Atomic bomb on HIROSHIMA and NAGASAKI the Japanese capitulated on 15th August, 1945.

Thus the Brigade's plans were changed and they sailed for Northern Malaya from Bombay on the 9th September in the "Chitral", for a Seaborne assault on the MORIB BEACHES on 17th September. No opposition was encountered in this operation "FIASCO". However the landing craft grounded on sand banks some 500 yards off the shore, and the men had to wade ashore in pouring rain. Had there been opposition, it could have fared badly for the troops. However, a rather wet **7th & 12th Parachute Battalions** were recalled next morning, and the Brigade sailed for SINGAPORE, and garrison duty.

The Japanese were in P.O.W. camps, and the paratroopers helped to restore order, and to reform the civilian police force. The docks were being cleaned by Japanese working parties operating from the camp in KEPPEL ROAD. The guards were from **"C" Company, 7th Parachute Battalion** commanded by Lieutenant Dunsford. Further camps were set up at ROBINSON ROAD and near the amusement park on the outskirts of the city, though these in the main were garrisoned by Indian troops.

Then in December, the Brigade was sent to JAVA. The Brigade arrived in BATAVIA on the 20th December, having embarked on 17th December at Singapore. It was placed under control of the **23rd Indian Division**, and helped in the clearing of BATAVIA—Operation "POUNCE"—arresting and disarming Indonesian Nationalists; and trying to restore order to the chaos, and get food supplies moving.

On 11th January, 1946, the Brigade was despatched to SEMERANG. The city was in chaos following initial British withdrawal of 49th Infantry Brigade. The Indonesians—half of the population of 250,000, had amongst them, Nationalist fanatics. They roamed the streets looting and murdering and generally terrorising the rest of the population, comprising Japanese, Chinese and Dutch Nationals. The Nationalists wanted independence from the Dutch, and a Republic had been declared on 17th August, 1945. They were led by Sukarno and Mohammed Hatta.

The Japanese Garrison had surrendered, but the Nationalists had seized their arms and turned on them, and the population. However, the Japanese Garrison commander was ordered to get his arms back, and this was accomplished, with loss to themselves. The Parachute Brigade then found it had a Japanese Battalion under its control.

They then got down to the job of restoring order, and established food distribution, handled by **716 Lt. Coy., R.A.S.C.**, since there had been a fruitful black market operating. The **225th Para. Fld. Ambulance** established itself in the Dutch Military Hospital, and dealt with local sanitation, as well as countless operations. The **3rd Airborne Squadron, R.E.** restored the public services, as there were no power or water supplies, and the **Signals** helped with the local telephone system.

On the arrival of Dutch forces, the Brigade left Java in May, 1946 returning to SINGAPORE, and then to MALAYA. In July, 1946 its' Tac H.Q. left for PALESTINE, and by August the rest of the Brigade had arrived there, for yet another policing exercise.

British involvement in JAVA ended in November, 1946, with their withdrawal from the country. The Dutch still wanted to hold onto Java and its other territories. However after three years of negotiations and the use of military force, they were forced to retire from Java and the surrounding islands. Sukarno became President of INDONESIA, founded on 27th December, 1949.

Appendix 11/1

5th Indep. Para. Bde. Group Orbat

7th   Parachute Battalion

12th   Parachute Battalion

13th   Parachute Battalion

4th   Air-Landing Anti-Tank Battery, R.A.

3rd   Airborne Squadron, R.E.

5th   Indep. Para. Bde. Park Troop, R.E.

5th   Indep. Para. Bde. Signal Troop

Para Platoon, 716th Light Company, R.A.S.C.

225th Parachute Field Ambulance, R.A.M.C.

5th   Indep. Para. Bde. Provost Company, C.M.P.

22nd Independent Parachute Company

All members of the Brigade were entitled to the award of a bar "S.E. ASIA 1945-46" to the Army General Service Medal, G.V.I.R. 1st type "INDIAE IMP" for their service in Java.

The Parachute Battalions being named "A. A. C." and the Support units —their own Corps designations.

Awards to the 5th Parachute Brigade Group in Java—December, 1945 – May, 1946

13.6.46 King's Birthday Honours

Officer of the British Empire
Lieut.-Col. (temp) Peter John Luard, D.S.O.   49882
      Oxf. & Bucks. L.I. C.O. 13th Bn.

Member of the British Empire
Captain (Qr-Mr.) Ernest Clarke 178693   K.O.Y.L.I. late A.A.C. 12th Bn.
Captain Reginald Percy Harold Fortnum   7th Bn.

British Empire Medal
5214201 . A/Sgt. Arthur Henry Cain
6019028 Col. Sgt. Robert Alfred Jenkins

Mentioned In Despatches
22.8.46	Lieut. C. Wishart	26884	R. Scots. Fus. now Para. R.
22.8.46	Lieut. H. A. L. Gray	323901	Gloster. R. now Para. R.
7.11.46	56400	A/W.O.II P. G. Kent	
7.11.46	1441973	Sgt. H. C. Brogden	
7.11.46	154692	Sgt. D. A. Bruce 7th Bn.	
7.11.46	110207	Sgt. E. A. Titherley	

Chapter XII

BLACK POPPIES

FOLLOWING the end of the war in Europe in May, 1945, the **6th Airborne Division**, as part of the British Liberation Army, was stationed at WISMAR on the Baltic Coast. The 1st Airborne Division was present in Norway, and was earmarked for the Middle East as part of the Imperial Strategic Reserve.

The 6th Airborne Division on the other hand was to go to the Far East, since the war with Japan was far from over. Thus, as has been written in the previous chapter, the Div. Tac H.Q. and the 5th Parachute Brigade H.Q. flew to Bombay, whilst the 5th Brigade Group sailed on the "Corfu" also in July, 1945.

However, internal reorganisation of the army began, following the use of the Atomic bomb, and the end of the war against Japan in the August, and resulted in the disbandment of the **1st Airborne Division** on its return from Norway in November, 1945.

This meant that the 6th Airborne Division, under command of Major-General E. L. Bols, C.B., D.S.O., was now to be sent to the Middle East. Its' Tactical Headquarters flew out on the 24th September, 1945 via Egypt, and established itself in the Nuseirat Hospital Camp on the 27th, with the Main Div. H.Q., which had arrived by sea. However, on the 16th September, the Airborne Division's first representatives arrived in PALESTINE—286th Airborne Park Squadron, Royal Engineers.

The **3rd Parachute Brigade** under Brigadier G. W. Lathbury, D.S.O., M.B.E. arrived on 3rd October, at HAIFA. There then followed the **6th A/ Lng. Brigade** under Brigadier R. H. Bellamy, D.S.O., and the **2nd Parachute Brigade** under Brigadier C. H. V. Pritchard, D.S.O., (this Brigade having been taken under command of the 6th Airborne Division on the

3rd September, replacing the 5th Parachute Brigade then in Malaya and Java). The units were then moved by rail to the camp areas not far from GAZA, near Nuseirat and Al Bureij.

Political Background

Since the First World War, Palestine had had a British administration, under a Mandate of the League of Nations, which had formed a Jewish Agency, and later an elected Assembly, with an inner council—Vaad Leumi. Due to internal troubles between the Arabs and the Jews—who wished for a "National Home", the British trained the Jewish Settlement Police. An underground Jewish Army "The Hagana" had been created following anti-Jewish riots in the 1920's, and was not recognised by the British. Following the 2nd World War, a lot of Jewish ex-servicemen and women joined this organisation, and especially "the Palmach" (Plugot Machatz)—spearhead groups. These groups combined into a Regular armed force, and were highly trained, many of its members having served in the British raised Palestine Regiment, (which was disbanded in 1948). These groups were to be used on specific tasks against the British Government. However the Hagana was not essentially a terrorist organisation, since its instructions were to avoid loss of life to British personnel if possible.

However in 1937, with the question of reprisals against Arab acts of terrorism, there was a split in the Hagana. Result of this was the formation of the I.Z.L. (Irgun Zvai Leumi—**National Military Organisation**. The I.Z.L. claimed that Palestine and Trans-Jordan rightfully belonged to the Jews, and their insignia displayed the fact. In fact it was the I.Z.L. that conducted numerous murderous campaigns against the Government.

Following the outbreak of war, both groups co-operated with the Government, however Abraham Stern and some fifty members opposed this co-operation. They split from the I.Z.L. and began a guerilla campaign against the British, resulting in assassinations of Britons, especially those in the Police. In 1942, Stern was shot dead in a gun battle, and a Pole called Nathan Yellin took over. The gang then called themselves "Lochmei Heruth Israel" (Fighters for the Freedom of Israel), but the Press referred to them as "the Stern Gang". In a letter to the newspapers in April, 1947, they reprimanded the Press for using that title, informing them, that they were the F.F.I. or L.H.I.

Into this uneasy atmosphere of attacks and shootings, was sent the 6th Airborne Division, among other British units, not really knowing if they

152

were protecting the interests of security against or for the Jews, since some of them had fought pre-war in units in the Arab rebellion of 1936.

Deployment

Following acclimatization and brief training in Internal Security duties, such as house searching, road blocks etc., the Brigades were deployed in three of the six Civil Districts of Palestine.

This operation code-named "BENZINE" lasted from the 21st October to 8th November, 1945.

3rd Parachute Brigade

This Brigade would Cover LYDDA District, which also contained TEL AVIV and JAFFA. They left Al Bureij Camp on 21st October, and were joined by Div. Tac H.Q. and the Main H.Q. at Bir Salim.

6th Air-Landing Brigade

The Brigade, (apart from the 1/A. & S. H. still in the U.K.) moved into Lydda in late October, and following the arrival of the 1/A. & S. H. at HAIFA on the 6th November, the other units moved into the SAMARIA District on the 8th, being based at Camp 21 NATHANYA. Under command was the 6th Bn., The Gordon Highlanders at TULKARM.

2nd Parachute Brigade

The Brigade arrived in Palestine at HAIFA on 22nd October, and by the 26th was installed in Nuseirat Ridge Camp in GAZA District, where most of the Divisional Arms & Services were stationed, apart from Batteries of the **53rd A/Lng. Lt. Regt., R.A.** under Lt-Col. R. A. Eden, D.S.O, which were in support of the three Brigades. With the 2nd Para. Bde., was the **127th Para. Fld. Amb., R.A.M.C.** under Lt-Col. F. Murray.

The Troubles Begin

Following a large scale attack on railway communications, and on Lydda Railway Station, by the Palmach on the 30th October, 1945, which incidentally only put the main line out of action for two days, there followed rioting in TEL AVIV on the 14th November. The troubles stemmed from the comments of the British Foreign Secretary relating that Palestine on its' own, could not provide a solution to the Jewish problem, and that there would be consultation with the Arabs to ensure no interruption of Jewish immigration at the monthly rate of 1,500 by the

Arab community. Also there would be an Anglo-American Committee to look into the problems faced by the Jewish resettlement. The Jews felt they had been betrayed by the Government, but the Jewish authorities could not approve a course of violence, since that would have repercussion on the Anglo-American Committee's views.

The Vaad Leumi proclaimed a twelve hour protest strike, however the hooligans were soon out on the streets in TEL AVIV and JERUSALEM—the main Jewish cities.

The **8th Parachute Battalion's** closest company at SARONA was then called into TEL AVIV by the police following an attack on the District Offices at 1815 hrs on 14th November. The company was stoned but held its' fire, however as the situation worsened and casualties suffered by both the company and the police, they had to open fire. This nominal fire made the mob withdraw. At 2040 hrs. the remainder of the Battalion arrived, and a curfew was imposed at 2330 hrs.

The following day, large crowds broke the curfews and the 3rd Brigade was called into the area, with under command "A" Squadron, 3rd The King's Own Hussars in an operation codenamed "BELLICOSE" and law and order was restored. On 16th November, the balance of the **3rd Hussars**, plus the **6th Abn. Armoured Recce. Regt.**, and the **1st Bn., Ryl. Ulsters** joined the 3rd Para. Brigade under command, and by the 20th November the curfew had been lifted.

For his handling of a dangerous situation, and command of his Battalion, Lt-Col. G. Hewetson, D.S.O. was subsequently awarded the O.B.E.

In November, the Division conducted its' first settlement searches following attacks on the coastguard stations at GIVAT OLGA and SIDNA ALI, by Palmach forces. The attacks resulted from the boarding of the S.S. "DEMETRIUS" which was landing illegal Jewish immigrants (I.J.I.'s) on the coast between the two coastal stations, (although 20 Jews were detained, a couple of hundred had evaded capture).

The first attempt by police in entering the settlements of GIVAT HAIYAM and HOGLA in the north; and RISHPON and SHEFAYIM in the south in search of the terrorists resulted in stonings and clubbings. Thus the army units in the vicinity were called in to cordon the settlements, since Jews from neighbouring settlements were pouring into the areas to assist their countrymen.

The Airborne units involved in this operation "GUY FAWKES" were the 3rd Parachute Brigade and the 6th Air-Landing Brigade, (now under command of Brigadier R. H. Bower, C.B.E.), and were deployed as follows :

In the north

1st Bn., The Loyal Regt.	}	both 2nd Inf. Bde.,1st Inf. Div.
2nd Bn., The North Staffords.		(since GIVAT OLGA was in 1st Inf., Div. Sector)

1st Bn., Argyll & Suth'd. H.	}	
1st Bn., Royal Ulster Rifles		6th Air-Landing Brigade

195th A/Lng. Fld. Amb., R.A.M.C.
2/7th Bn., The Middlesex Regiment—under command 6th A.L.
1st Reconnaissance Regiment—under command 6th A.L.
6th Bn., The Gordon Highrs .—under command 6th A.L.
1st Bn., The Hertfordshire Regt.—under command 6th A.L.
3rd, The King's Own Hussars—one Squadron

In the south

8th Parachute Battalion

3rd Parachute Battalion	}	3rd Para. Brigade

224th Para. Fld. Amb., R.A.M.C.
2nd Bn., Oxford & Bucks. L.I. —under command from 6th A/Lng.
3rd, The King's Own Hussars—one Squadron

On 26th November, further attempts to search the settlements succeeded although there were casualties amongst the Security Forces, as well as the Jews themselves, following large groups, some in their thousands attempting to break the cordon at several points.

Following more attacks in JERUSALEM, JAFFA and TEL AVIV on 26/27th December, 1945, RAMAT GAN on the outskirts of TEL AVIV was searched by the **3rd Para. Brigade**, plus the **4th Para. Bn.**, and the police, for suspected terrorists, and 59 were taken into custody, this was Operation "PINTAIL". There then followed Operation "HERON" on 8th January, 1946, and Operation "PIGEON" on 30th January, and smaller operations in support of the police, in the searching of Lydda District and its' settlements.

Also in December, 1945, a Divisional Training Centre was formed, consisting of an Airborne Battle School; Vocational Training Wing, and Airborne Training Wing.

On 25th February, 1946, the I.Z.L. attacked R.A.F. airfields at LYDDA, PETAH TIQVA, and QASTINA destroying many aircraft and damage

155

was estimated at £750,000. As a result of this a curfew and road-blocks were imposed in the District by the **3rd Para. Bde**. There was also an attack on the 6th March, 1946, on the ammunition store of the **3rd Hussars** at SARAFAND by the I.Z.L. However in the shoot-out and pursuit, virtually all of the ammunition was recovered and two wounded I.Z.L. members captured. Captain Barrow, who tried to close the main gate, and grappled with one of the terrorists was subsequently awarded the M.B.E. for his gallantry.

On 5th March, 1946, Major-General A. J. H. Cassells, C.B.E., D.S.O. took over command of the **6th Airborne Division**, and in April, there was a drastic change in the Divisional structure, in that the Division became totally parachute trained.

The **6th Airborne Armoured Recce. Regt**. was disbanded, most of its' personnel transferring to the 3rd Hussars.

The 1st Parachute Brigade arrived in HMT "ORONTES" at PORT SAID, under command of Brigadier R. H. Bellamy, D.S.O. on 1st April, and reached Camp 21 NATHANYA the following week, and took over control from the 6th Air-Landing Brigade of SAMARIA on 8th April.

1st Parachute Brigade
O.C. Bde. —Brigadier R. H. Bellamy, D.S.O.

Units
1st Parachute Battalion—Lt-Col. T. C. H. Pearson
2nd Parachute Battalion—Lt-Col. J. D. Frost, D.S.O., M.C.
17th Parachute Battalion—Lt-Col. W. D. H. McCardie

The **6th Air-Landing Brigade** became the 31st Indep. Inf. Bde. once again, relinquishing its airborne connections. The Brigade was disbanded in November, 1946:
2nd Bn., Oxford & Bucks. L.I.— 3rd Infantry Brigade
1st Bn., Argyll & Suth'd. H.— 8th Infantry Brigade
1st Bn., Royal Ulster Rifles—to Austria (occupation duties)
195th A/Lng. Fld. Amb., R.A.M.C.—retrained as a Parachute Field
Ambulance att. 1st Para. Brigade.

The Car Park Murders
On the night of 25th April, 1946, there occurred a despicable act, that marred the already tense relationship between the Airborne soldiers, and

the Jewish population.

About 25–30 men entered a house opposite a Tel Aviv car park at 2030 hrs. The car park was used by the military and in this instance was guarded by a small section from the 5th Parachute Battalion. The men having held up the occupants of the house, set up fire positions overlooking the entrance of the car park, and the two guard tents.

Fifteen minutes later, a bomb was thrown, and then automatic fire was directed at the sentries, those not killed took cover. Under this rapid short range fire, more gangsters crossed the road. Some entered the first tent, and in their torchlight, shot two of the soldiers, who were off duty and lying on the ground, with bursts from sub-machine guns. The other occupant, a sergeant, who was unlocking a rifle rack feigned death, and the gangsters emptied the arms rack. Two soldiers in the adjoining tent were also shot dead, and two soldiers rushing up to the car park were also killed. Those killed in this attack were:

Pte. J. A. Gilliard	Pte. H. S. McKay
Pte. J. Hope	Pte. A. Morrison
Pte. N. E. Knight	Pte. J. H. Park
Pte. H. Lewis	

The attackers then withdrew, after laying mines. However a trail of blood led into the Yemenite section of the KARTON Quarter. This was searched the following day, and although 79 suspects were detained, no proof of complicity could be found. The Divisional Commander saw the Mayor of Tel Aviv, and asked for assistance from the community, with regard to arresting the criminals of the Stern Gang (F.F.I.). However as no-one wished to aid the soldiers and police, a road curfew was imposed from 6 pm to 6 am and all public places closed from 8 pm to 5 am.

Following members of the Division taking the law into their own hands as QASTINA and BEER TUVYA, all Jewish towns and villages were placed out of bounds to the troops.

During June, Jewish groups attacked railway lines, and trains. Also on 18th June, five officers were kidnapped, three of whom served with the Airborne Division. The officers were released, two on 22nd June, and the remaining three on 4th July, 1946.

On the 29th June, the entire 6th Airborne Division, and indeed most of the Security Forces were involved in Operation "AGATHA". This operation was planned in utmost secrecy, and started with cordons being thrown around settlements, and the Divisional Signals Light Line Troop, escorted by members of the Glider Pilot Regiment, taking control of all

157

the telephone exchanges in the Divisional area. One of the most important assignments was allotted to the **2nd Parachute Brigade**, now under Brigadier J. P. O' Brien Twohig, C.B.E., D.S.O., (who had taken over in April) and they were to go to the addresses of Jews suspected of being members of illegal organisations or involved in the criminal acts, and arrest them.

The **1st Parachute Brigade** in the north, was to search six settlements between NATHANYA and HADERA, and the **3rd Parachute Brigade** in the south, those of GIVAT BRENNER and NO'AR OVED.

Although these early morning "raids" were successful, the Jewish population became more hateful of the British troops, insulting them and in some cases using violence. The Jews compared the tactics to those of the Gestapo, and a song against the Airborne Troops was sung by children in Hebrew, called "Kalanyot" referring to "a red poppy with a black heart" in reference to the headdress of the parachutists.

King David Hotel Blast

The next major incident, which involved members of the Airborne Division, was when on 22nd July, 1946, a party of Jews dressed as Arabs, planted several milk churns full of explosive in the basement of the wing of the King David Hotel in Jerusalem, which was used by the Secretariat of the Government of Palestine, and the H.Q. British Troops in Palestine and Transjordan. No warning had been given, and there were many casualties, as the charges exploded and the wing collapsed. Unfortunately there were no engineers units present, and the **9th Airborne Squadron, R.E.**, under Major E. W. J. Cowtan, M.C., stationed at QASTINA forty miles away, was ordered into the city. They worked for several days in the sweltering heat by day, and cold by night, endeavouring to reach anybody left alive. Only six persons were found alive and ninety-one bodies were recovered.

Their endurance even had praise from some in Jewish quarters, and Major Cowtan later received the M.B.E.

Operation "Shark"

Between 30th July and 2nd August, 1946, the entire 6th Airborne Division, plus eight units under command, plus the Palestine Police, searched the whole of TEL AVIV, screening all the inhabitants, (100,000), and managing to arrest 787 people, amongst them being some prominent members of the I.Z.L. and Stern Gang. Five ammunition and arms dumps were found, one being in the basement of the Great Synagogue. It had been meticulously planned with an outer and inner cordon, and all were in position before dawn broke.

The composition and disposition of the troops involved were as follows:

H.Q. 6th Airborne Division

2nd Infantry Brigade Group—northern sector(Bde. from HADERA)
2nd Bn., The Royal Scots.—inner cordon (north)
1st Bn., The Loyal Regiment—southern part of north sector
2nd Bn., The North Staffords.—northern part of north sector
The King's Dragoon Guards —outer cordon (north)
The Glider Pilot Regt.—detachment of 200 all ranks

1st Parachute Brigade Group —central sector (Bde. from
NATHANYA)
1st Parachute Battalion—western part of central sector
2nd Parachute Battalion— southern part of central sector
17th Parachute Battalion—northern part of central sector
12th Royal Lancers—in support in central sector
1st Bn., King's Shropshire L.I.— in support in central sector

2nd Parachute Brigade Group—southern sector(Bde. from LYDDA)
4th Parachute Battalion
5th Parachute Battalion
6th Parachute Battalion
6th Bn., The Gordon Highlanders
1st Bn., The Hertfordshire Regt.

3rd Parachute Brigade Group—western sector (Bde. from GAZA)
3rd Parachute Battalion
8th Parachute Battalion
9th Parachute Battalion—inner cordon (south)
3rd The King's Own Hussars
6th Airborne Div. Ryl. Arty.—outer cordon (south)
Arms & Services 6th Airborne Division

Arrival of 5th Parachute Brigade Group
On 28th July, 1946, the advance party and Tac. H.Q. of the 5th

Parachute Brigade arrived at Camp 22 Nathanya from South East Asia, and on the 2nd August, the remainder of the Brigade arrived in Egypt, and were in camp by the 5th August. On 21st August, the 7th Parachute Battalion amalgamated with the 17th Parachute Battalion of 1st Brigade, retaining the designation of 7th Parachute Battalion.

Of the remaining units, apart from the 12th & 13th Parachute Battalions which had been disbanded,(some personnel joining other Parachute Battalions, or being demobbed), the changes were as follows :

4th Air-Landing Anti-Tank Bty., R.A. —became part of the 2nd
A/Lng. A/Tk. Regt., R.A.

3rd Airborne Squadron, R.E.—becomes part of Divisional R.E.

5th Indep. Para. Bde. Park Tp., R.E.—disbanded

5th Indep. Para. Bde Signals—became part of Divisional Sign

Para. Pltn. 716th Lt. Company, R.A.S.C.—rejoins Company

225th Para. Fld. Amb., R.A.M.C .— disbanded, members joined
other R.A.M.C. units in the Div.

Throughout the rest of August until November, units of the 6th Airborne Division took part in fifteen searches in Tel Aviv and settlements in all Districts. Of interest were Operations "BREAM" and "EEL" on: the 28th August — 2nd September search of DOROT by **8th Para. Bn.** ; and 29th August, search of RUHAMA by **3rd Para. Bn.**, in which mine-detecting dogs of the C.R.M.P. were used to locate arms caches.

In November following several weeks of railway sabotage, and the deaths of two Royal Engineers' officers — Captain J. M. Newton, 1st Abn. Sqn., (17.11.46) and Captain S. Adamson, 9th Abn. Sqn. (18.11.46), when trying to remove mines, Operation "EARWIG" was put into action. The entire Division was strung out along the railway line, that stretched seventy miles through the Divisional area. The troops patrolled the line in shifts, between posts established, in some cases, only a few hundred yards apart, dependent on if the area was particularly dangerous. This operation lasted a couple of weeks, and the terrorists changed to road mining. On 2nd December, a jeep of the **2nd Forward Observation Unit, R.A.** was mined and four were killed near Jerusalem. Captain G. S. Harrison, 1st Abn. Sqn., R.E. received a G.O.C.'s Commendation for Gallantry following him defusing a mine, which he knew had an anti-handling device fitted, and knowing a similar one had killed a colleague earlier on the same day.

In December, Major-General Cassels relinquished command of the

Division, and Major-General E. L. Bols, C.B., D.S.O. reassumed command on 6th January, 1947.

Following the kidnapping and flogging of the Bde. Major of the 2nd Parachute Brigade, and three N.C.O.'s in two separate incidents on 29th December, 1946, due to an I.Z.L. youth being jailed and flogged for an armed bank robbery, there were two searches for I.Z.L. members. Operation "PRAWN"— **1st Parachute Brigade**, with 8th Parachute Battalion, and 3rd Hussars under command searched PETAH TIQVA; and Operation "NOAH"—**2nd Parachute Brigade** with one squadron of 12th Royal Lancers under command, searched S. E. NATHANYA on the 30th December. Several Jews were detained in both operations.

1947 Into Northern Palestine

In January, the Division moved to the newly designated North Sector, which encompassed the HAIFA and GALILEE Districts. On 24th January, 1947, the **2nd Parachute Brigade** left for England on HMT "Alcantara", and as it was designated a Brigade Group, took some of the Arms & Services units with it.

The **1st Parachute Brigade** was therefore stationed in GALILEE District; the **3rd Parachute Brigade** in HAIFA DISTRICT; the 3rd Hussars to AFULA, and the Divisional Artillery dispersed in the sector. Divisional Headquarters was established at the Carmelite Monastery at STELLA MARIS, overlooking Haifa.

On 22nd January, following the kidnapping of Judge Windham from his court in Tel Aviv, and a Mr. Collins from Jerusalem, in response to the death sentence imposed on an I.Z.L member—Dov Gruner, a cordon and search was carried out on the Jewish HADAR hak CARMEL quarter of Haifa. Those involved were **3rd Parachute Brigade**, with 2nd Bn., East Surrey Regt. and "B" Sqn., 3rd Hussars under command. The two men were later released, and the search was quite peaceful.

The main task of the Haifa units were the protection of the oil refinery and storage plants, and the transshipment of Jewish illegal immigrants. Following the decision of the Government of Palestine to evacuate all non-essential British civilians from Palestine, Operation "POLLY" was put into action 2nd - 7th February, and over 1,500 were evacuated.

Throughout February and March, the Division suffered casualties through road mining. On 16th March, four Jewish criminals, including Dov Gruner were executed at ACRE GAOL, and on the 4th May, the Gaol was attacked by I.Z.L. and Stern Gang members. The Gaol outer wall was

161

breached, and about 250 mixed Arab and Jewish prisoners escaped. Other parties of Jews mined the road, and also mortared the **2nd Parachute Battalion** camp three miles north of Acre. However it was three small bathing parties from the 1st Parachute Battalion; the Divisional Battle School, and the Divisional R.A.S.C., half a mile to the east of the town, who went into action first, setting up road-blocks. The piquet, that protected the bathers under Cpl. J. Powell of 1st Para. Bn. pursued a truckload of gangsters dressed as British troops. In the ensuing chase, the truck crashed. Pte. McCormack from the 1st Parachute Battalion, with several others pursued a second vehicle and after commandeering an Arab car, finally captured five gangsters after a gun battle. Pte. Thorne, also from 1st Parachute Battalion with an officer recaptured three escaped Arab prisoners. For their initiative and gallantry the two Privates were awarded the B.E.M.

Between June and July, 1947, following Britain laying the Palestine Question before the United Nations Organisation in April, a special committee (U.N.S.C.O.P.) was present in Palestine listening to the views of all sides. Their report in September, 1947, recommended that the British Mandate should end, and independence granted as soon as possible. Also that separate Arab and Jewish States be set up, with the city of JERUSALEM under international control. Of course the Jews were very happy at the report, and the Arabs, who had boycotted the committee were far from favourable in their views.

However, the terrorist actions still continued, and on the 28th June, 1947 Captain M. C. Kissane, 9th Para. Bn. was killed in a machine-gun attack on the Astoria Restaurant in Haifa. Two other officers were wounded, and the remaining unwounded officers fired back. Major Liddle, Div. H.Q. was awarded the M.B.E. for his gallantry during this attack.

On the 18th July, 1947 the "President Warfield" carrying about 4,500 illegal Jewish immigrants was boarded and fighting broke out on board, leaving three Jews dead, and members of both sides wounded. On the 19th July, transshipment was complete and the British Transports "Ocean Vigour", "Empire Rival", and "Runnymede Park" sailed for France, where the I.J.I.'s had originally embarked. This had political repercussions, since normally I.J.I.'s were sent to Cyprus to await entry in the normal manner to Palestine. Also the ships were not admitted to land in the south of France, and were diverted to the British sector of Germany, landing at HAMBURG on 8th September, 1947. The I.J.I.'s having to be ejected from the ships with the use of force in some cases.

In August, command of the 6th Airborne Division passed to Major-General H. C. Stockwell, C.B., C.B.E., D.S.O. In November, orders were received for the reduction of the Airborne Division, and amalgamations as follows:

1st Parachute Brigade—1st, 2nd/3rd and 8th/9th Para. Bns.

2nd Parachute Brigade—4th/6th, 5th and 7th Para. Bns. (in England) and the disbandment of the 3rd Parachute Brigade.

Following this decision, there followed certain redeployment in the Divisional area. The **1st Parachute Brigade** was given ACRE Sub-District, as well as keeping HAIFA District; 2nd Bn., The Middlesex Regt. was placed under command for duties near Acre Gaol. **3rd The King's Own Hussars** was given NAZARETH Sub-District. The **Trans-Jordan Frontier Force** under command was in SAFAD and BELSAN Sub-Districts of Galilee. The **17th/21st Lancers** was in TIBERIAS under command.

On 30th November, there was a day of rejoicing in the Jewish quarters, since the day before U.N.O. had agreed to the partition, however this led to rioting between Jews and Arabs, and the Jewish terrorists in the main turned to attacking Arabs instead. From the 5th December until the 19th December, the **1st Parachute Brigade**, with the **66th Abn. A/Tk. Regt**; the **3rd Hussars**, and **17/21st Lancers** were kept busy in HAIFA during outbreaks of violence between the Jews and Arabs, as well as attacks by same on British personnel.

During December, there was trouble in SAFAD Sub-District, and a house curfew imposed by one company of the **8th Parachute Battalion**, and one troop, **T.J.F.F.**, which alleviated the situation of sniping between the Arabs and Jews.

1948 Independence

Following the departure of the T.J.F.F., the Eastern Frontier sub-sector was taken over by "C.R.A. FORCE" commanded by the Divisional Commander Royal Artillery (C.R.A.) Brigadier C. H. Colquhoun, O.B.E. on 16th January, 1948.

C.R.A. Force:

17/21st Lancers — under command 6th Abn.   TIBERIAS
1st Bn., Irish Guards—under command 6th Abn. SAFAD
1st Parachute Battalion   BEISAN

To reinforce the 1st Parachute Brigade, since it lost its 1st Battalion, the 2nd Bn. Middlesex Regiment was placed under command, with one battery from the 1st Regiment, R.H.A. and one from 52nd Observation Regiment, R.A. in HAIFA.

The Arabs and Jews continued to attack various settlements in the Divisional area, and on the 29th January, 1948, an Arab band of about forty, attacked a train near BEISAN, but were surprised by members of the 1st Parachute Battalion, who captured 13, and a further 18 were captured at a road-block manned by 3rd Hussars at AFULA.

On 2nd February, two troops of 17/21st Lancers, and two platoons of 1st Bn., Irish Guards relieved the Jewish settlement of EIN ZEITEM near SAFAD, which was under attack by the Arab Liberation Army. On 4th February, after a ration truck of the 17/21st Lancers was ambushed on the TIBERIAS-ROSH PINNA Road, a party of Syrian members of the A.L.A. were captured by troops of the 1st Bn., Irish Guards.

On 18th February, all ranks of the 6th Airborne Division were informed that on its return to England, the Division would be disbanded.

In January, 1948, 40th Commando, Royal Marines had arrived at HAIFA to protect the port, when evacuation plans were put into action, they were placed under command of the Division.

On 6th March, 1948, advance parties of the Division left Palestine in H.M.T. "Franconia" from Haifa. These were followed by the 87th Abn. Fld. Regt., R.A., and the 9th Abn. Sqn., R.E. on the 9th March aboard the "Samaria"; then H.Q. R.A; 33rd Abn. Lt. Regt., R.A. and the 66th Abn. A/ Tk. Regt, R.A. on the 12th March, aboard the "Otranto".

During April, the 6th Abn. Div. H.Q. closed down, control of the forces passed to H.Q. G.O.C. North Sector. There were more skirmishes between Arabs and Jews in and against settlements. On the 4th April the Headquarters of Divisional R.E; R.A.S.C; R.A.O.C and R.E.M.E.. embarked at Haifa on the "Franconia". On the 10th April, Main H.Q. 6th Abn. Div. left on the "Samaria" for the U.K., and on the 13th April, the Div. Signal Regt., and 716th Abn. Lt. Company, R.A.S.C. embarked on the "Otranto" for U.K.

The **1st Parachute Brigade** handed over control of HAIFA to the 1st Guards Brigade, and on the 16th and 23rd April, its Battalions left on "Empress of Australia" and "Empress of Scotland" for U.K. However, its **1st Parachute Battalion** in the east, formed part of the Divisional rearguard, with the 3rd Hussars; 1st Abn. Sqn., R.E. and 317th Abn. Fld. Security Section.

There was severe fighting in Haifa Port from 21st April, in which the Jews sniped Arab refugees, one shot wounded Lt-Col. J. Chandos-Pole the C.O. of 1st Bn., Coldstream Guards. By the next day, the Jews were in virtual control of Haifa.

The High Commissioner and the last British troops left Jerusalem. In command of the 250 vehicles was the 1st Parachute Battalion—Lt-Col. E. J. B. Nelson, D.S.O., M.C. commanding. All went smoothly, and the units including 17/21st Lancers; 42nd Commando, Royal Marines; 1st Abn. Sqn., R.E. reached Haifa safely. The Mandate ended on 15th May, and on the 18th May, the remaining units of the Division embarked on the "Empress of Australia" for U.K. The 3rd Hussars embarked at Port Said for U.K. on "Strathnaver". The 1st Abn. Sqn., R.E. was among the last British units to leave Palestine on 30th June, 1948.

So ended a three year campaign, that cost the Division 58 killed and 236 wounded. The State of Israel also came into being, though there would still be clashes going on between Jew and Arab thirty years on.

Appendix 12/1

Awards to the 6th Airborne Division in Palestine
September, 1945 – May, 1948

Most of the awards were gazetted 7.1.49, unless otherwise shown.

Headquarters, 6th Abn. Div.
Knight Comander of the British Empire (period 27.3.48 – 30.6.48)
23894 Major General Hugh Charles Stockwell, C.B., C.B.E., D.S.O. O.C. Div.

Officer of the British Empire
63608   T/Lt. Col. Henry Hamilton Van Straubenzee, D.S.O.
(27.3.46 – 26.9.46) G.S.O.I (Operations), 1946   Oxf. & Bucks. L.I.
55743   Lt. Colonel Peter George Francis Young
(27.3.47 – 26.9.47) Asst. Adj. & Qr-Mr. Gen., 1947–48   Oxf. & Bucks. L.I.

Member of the British Empire (Gallantry, 4.11.47)
77480   Capt. (T/Major) Edward Arthur Desmond Liddle   R.U.R.
For gallantry on 28th June, 1947, when terrorists attacked the Astoria Restaurant in Haifa, with machine guns.

Member of the British Empire (27.3.46 – 26.9.46)
96170   T/Major Ronald Dare Wilson, M.C.   R. N. Fus.
Author of "Cordon & Search"—history of 6th Abn. Div. in Palestine, (Gale & Polden, Aldershot, 1949)

Mentioned In Despatches
36316   T/Major-General A. J. H. Cassels, C.B.E., D.S.O.
(27.3.46–26.9.46)   O.C. 6th Abn. Div. 1946
23894   Major-General H. C. Stockwell, C.B., C.B.E., D.S.O.
(27.3.46–26.9.46)   O.C. 6th Abn. Div. 8/47–48

Parachute Brigades
Commander of the British Empire (27.4.47–26.9.47)
33507   T/Brigadier Francis David Rome, D.S.O.   Q.O.R.W. Kents
        O.C., 3rd Bde., 1947   O.C., 1st Bde., 1948

Officer of the British Empire

53752   Lt. Colonel James Henry Hackett   Sh. Foresters 8th Bn.
(27.3.47–26.9.47)   74257
74257   T/Lt. Colonel George Hewetson, D.S.O.   A.A.C. 8th Bn.
For riot control, November 1945   (L.G. 13.6.46)
53116   Lt. Colonel Eustace John Blois Nelson, D.S.O., M.C.Gren. Gds.
(29.4.46–26.3.47)   1st Bn.

British Empire Medal (for gallantry, LG. 7.10.47)

14962339 Pte. Alexander McCormack   A.A.C. 1st Bn.
14488224 Pte. Charles Grantley Thorne   A.A.C. 1st Bn.
Awarded for gallantry, following the Acre Gaol break on 4th May, 1947, when 217 prisoners escaped. The two soldiers were manning a roadblock, which was broken by a truck carrying terrorists in British Army uniforms. They commandeered a car and gave chase, capturing ten men.

British Empire Medal (27.9.46–26.3.48)

5780693 W.O.II Cecil Lawrence   R. Norfolk
4342541 A/W.O.II Thomas Furness   Para. R., A.A.C.

Mentioned In Despatches
Period 27.9.45–26.3.46
14572860 Sgt. R. D. Johnston   A.A.C.

Period 27.3.46–26.9.46
4384   T/Brigadier G. W. Lathbury, D.S.O., M.B.E. Oxf. & Bucks. L.I.
                                          O.C., 3 Bde.
33116   T/Brigadier J. B. O'Brien-Twohig, C.B.E., D.S.O. R. Inn. Fus.
                                          O.C., 2 Bde.
66121   Major N. Crookenden, D.S.O.   Cheshire R. O.C., 9th Bn.
100039   Captain R. J. Gammon, M.C.   Gordons 1st Bn.

Period 27.9.46–26.3.47
6008160 W.O.I P. McGeever, M.M.   A.A.C. 9th Bn.
4076464 W.O.II A. J. Pyke   R. Hamps.

Period 27.3.47–26.9.47
77675   T/Major J. Awdry   Wilts 6th Bn.
365709   Lieut. P. A. L. McHenry   H.L.I.
366619   Lieut. E. Straughan   A.A.C.
4194891 W.O.II R. H. Davies   R.W. Fus.
2321489 W.O.II R. H. Meadows   A.A.C.

| 2325889 | W.O.II F. A. Winter | A.A.C. |

Period 27.9.47–26.3.48

153960	Major P. M. Lawson	R. Sussex
148131	T/Major C. S. Fitzpatrick	E. Surrey
95248	T/Major A. J. Robertson	R. Norfolk
220617	T/Major R. C. Tully-Christie	Bed. & Herts.
129067	Captain P. G. Cliffe	R. Lincoln
341686	T/Captain W. C. Constable	A.A.C.
303313	T/Captain C. E. Eberhardie	R. Norfolk
174530	Captain R. E. Morton	D.C.L.I.
346885	Lieut. W. T. A. Brooks	W. Yorks.
370489	Lieut. M. J. Dawson	Seaforths.
368556	Lieut. P. E. Gray	A.A.C.
366619	Lieut. E. Straughan	A.A.C.
2694494	W.O.II R. H. Thomson, D.C.M.	A.A.C.
2325889	W.O.II F. A. Winter	A.A.C.
2656917	A/W.O.II W. C. Davis	A.A.C.
2992710	A/Col.Sgt. G. R. Mitchell	A.A.C.
14407359	Sgt. J. Atkins	R. W. Kent
4538174	Sgt. F. Kenny	A.A.C.
14908177	A/Cpl. J. G. Edwards	A.A.C.
14464860	Pte. G. W. Johnson	A.A.C.
19133352	Pte. T. J. McMeekin	A.A.C.
19162164	Pte. J. L. Quick	A.A.C.

6th Air-Landing Brigade (left Div 4/46)
Member of the British Empire (27.9.45–26.3.46)

| 167155 | T/Major Charles Henry Styles | 2 Oxf. & Bucks. L.I. |
| 7011211 | W.O.II William James Lutton | 1 R.U.R. |

Mentioned In Despatches

| 47518 | T/Brigadier R. H. Bellamy, D.S.O. | D.C.L.I. O.C., 1945 |
| 24360 | T/Brigadier R. H. Bower, C.B.E. | O.C., 1946 |

The Airborne Support Troops
3rd King's Own Hussars (took place of Arm'd Recce Regt.)
Member of the British Empire (27.3.47–26.9.47)

| 377139 | 2nd Lieut. Francis Joseph Tilbury | |

Mentioned In Despatches

| 63667 | Major A. C. McE. Savage | 27.9.45–26.3.46 |

357727	Lieut. I. H. Gray	27.3.46–26.9.46	
14416735	Cpl. C. Hines	27.3.46–26.9.46	
123542	Captain R. O. N. Chilcott	27.9.46–26.3.47	
14451077	Sgt. R. R. Cotterell	27.9.46–26.3.47	
5834656	Sgt. G. A. V. Harrison	27.9.46–26.3.47	
7891450	Cpl. R. Chorley	27.3.47–26.9.47	
14446885	L/Cpl. A. E. Ballard	27.3.47–26.9.47	
357322	T/Captain A. M. L. Hogge	27.9.47–26.3.48	
190647	T/Captain L. J. Melhuish	27.9.47–26.3.48	
787140	W.O.I N. D. Ellis	27.9.47–26.3.48	

Royal Regiment of Artillery
Mentioned In Despatches
31549	Brigadier W. McC. T. Faithfull, D.S.O.	27.3.46–26.9.46	C.R.A.
26956	Brigadier C. H. Colquhuon, O.B.E.	27.3.47–26.9.47	C.R.A.
44846	Lt. Col. M. I. Gregson, M.B.E.	27.3.47–26.9.47	C.O. 87 Regt.
71008	Major F. S. G. Shore	27.3.47–26.9.47	

Corps of Royal Engineers
Member of the British Empire
(L.G. 28.1.47 Hazardous work in brave manner.)
95190 Capt. (T/Major) Frank Willoughby John Cowtan, M.C.
He commanded 9 Abn. Sqn., and its rescue operations, when the King David Hotel, Jerusalem was devasted on 22nd July, 1946. Part of the hotel was being used by the Government of Palestine, and H.Q. British Troops in Palestine and Transjordan. Jewish terrorist planted bombs in the basement, and killed over a hundred people.

Member of the British Empire (27.9.47–26.3.48)
| 243580 | T/Major Eric O'Callaghan, M.C. | O.C. 9 Abn. Sqn. |

Mentioned In Despatches
1876529	S.Q.M.S. G. Young	27.3.46–26.9.46
6298053	Cpl. E. P. Ratcliffe	27.3.46–26.9.46
1878108	L/Cpl. R. T. Hancock	27.9.46–26.3.47
14455424	Spr. K. H. L. Trego	27.9.46–26.3.47
321813	W.O.II D. Docherty	27.3.47–26.9.47
1876625	Cpl. J. J. N. Johnston	27.3.47–26.9.47
73054	Major D. Ross, O.B.E.	27.9.47–26.3.48
369582	Captain J. St. J. Cadbury	27.9.47–26.3.48
14456387	Spr. F. Berry	27.9.47–26.3.48
14163130	Spr. J. Earley	27.9.47–26.3.48
243580	Captain E. O'Callaghan, M.B.E., M.C.	27.3.48–30.6.48

6th Airborne Divisional Signals
Mentioned In Despatches
6395578	W.O.I E. Jordan	27.9.45–26.3.46
2337641	Sgt. D. H. Titchener	27.9.45–26.3.46
71076	T/Major A. J. Deane-Drummond, M.C.	27.3.46–26.9.46
95088	Major G. S. Fenton	27.3.46–26.9.46
2331857	W.O.II F. S. Shepherd	27.3.46–26.9.46
14935929	Cpl. J. F. Pearson	27.3.46–26.9.46
14557361	Cpl. B. H. Pritchard	27.3.46–26.9.46
217295	T/Major G. Proudman	27.9.46–26.3.47
307988	Captain H. Fairhurst	27.9.46–26.3.47
2575114	W.O.II F. H. Clift	27.9.46–26.3.47
817238	S.Q.M.S. S. J. Glover	27.9.46–26.3.47
50856	T/Lt-Col. D. A. Pringle	27.3.47–26.9.47
2323217	W.O.II W. L. Mayhew	27.3.47–26.9.47
14532667	Sgt. W. H. Fuge	27.3.47–26.9.47
50856	T/Lt-Col. D. A. Pringle	27.9.47–26.3.48
94645	T/Major V. H. Martin, M.C.	27.9.47–26.3.48
95094	T/Major R. C. Pringle	27.9.47–26.3.48
278721	T/Captain W. P. W. Robertson	27.9.47–26.3.48
370493	T/Captain P. H. C. Walker	27.9.47–26.3.48
388019	Lieut. W. J. Robertson	27.9.47–26.3.48
406965	W.O.II E. Bridle	27.9.47–26.3.48
2322166	W.O.II F. G. Hewitt	27.9.47–26.3.48
2325869	Sgt. R. D. Laing	27.9.47–26.3.48
2978145	Sgt. J. Warren	27.9.47–26.3.48
14445928	Cpl. M. M. Gildon	27.9.47–26.3.48

Royal Army Service Corps
Mentioned In Despatches
S/57452	W.O.II N. G. Griffin	27.3.47–26.9.47
S/14715431	Sgt. E. Laycock	27.3.47–26.9.47

224th Para. F. Amb., R.A.M.C.
Mentioned In Despatches
12869	Major A. D. Young, D.S.O.	27.9.46–26.3.47

Ordnance Field Park, R.A.O.C.
Mentioned In Despatches
311613	T/Major A. J. Luke	27.9.46–26.3.47
44948	W.O.I J. H. Rea	27.9.45–26.3.46
7583468	W.O.I J. H. Mullin	27.3.46–26.9.46

317 Abn. F.S.S., Int. Corps.
Mentioned In Despatches
203930   T/Captain J. P. T. Linklater, M.B.E.   27.3.47–26.9.47

Royal Electrical & Mechanical Engineers
Mentioned In Despatches

284631	Major A. M. McKay	27.3.46–26.9.46
7590917	S/Sgt. D. J. V. Howes	27.3.46–26.9.46
7589882	S/Sgt. T. P. McKenzie	27.3.46–26.9.46
10564308	Sgt. A. D. Atkins	27.3.46–26.9.46
5725848	S.Q.M.S. F. W. Lawrence	27.9.46–26.3.47
7597133	Sgt. T. Power	27.9.46–26.3.47
10565028	Pte. D. Beattie	27.9.46–26.3.47
284420	T/Major J. M. Kneem	27.3.47–26.9.47
7588451	W.O.I R. F. Griffiths	27.3.47–26.9.47
7587508	W.O.I G. R. Salisbury	27.3.47–26.9.47
14102469	Cpl. L. Mather	27.3.47–26.9.47
7590931	Cpl. J. R. Melville	27.3.47–26.9.47
2547658	Cpl. M. Robinson	27.3.47–26.9.47
2548077	Cpl. R. H. Ward	27.3.47–26.9.47
262281	T/Capt. C. L. Hunt	27.9.47–26.3.48
868401	S/Sgt. T. A. R. Kavanagh	27.9.47–26.3.48
860721	Sgt. D. J. Bellinger	27.9.47–26.3.48
14087174	L/Cpl. R. H. Scotten	27.9.47–26.3.48
19071782	Cfn. R. Sharples	27.9.47–26.3.48

Sgt. D. Westerley, R.E.M.E. Workshops, commended for gallantry after entering a minefield at Qastina and rescuing a seriously injured Arab child.

Chapter 13

Unit Histories & Insignia Worn

Over the next few pages, I have endeavoured to show in brief, the histories of the units that made up the British Airborne Forces, and the insignia that they wore, including unofficial examples.

Many of the examples mentioned are on display at the Airborne Forces Museum, Browning Barracks, Aldershot, and are classified as (A.B.F.) Also I thank Brian Davis for allowing me to quote page references from his book, regarding illustrations of either recipients of awards mentioned in previous pages, or of the insignia being worn—(B.D. & page number). Many of the individual Corps/Regimental Museums have similar badge displays of course, reflecting their own Airborne connections.

Appendix 13/1   1st Airborne Division & Support Units

Appendix 13/2   2nd Indep. Para. Bde. Group

Appendix 13/3   6th Airborne Division & Support Units

Appendix 13/4   44th Indian Abn. Division & Support

SPECIAL ARMY ORDER

THE WAR OFFICE,
27th February, 1942

ROYAL WARRANT

Formation of the Army Air Corps

GEORGE R.I.

<table>
<tr>
<td>20
General
6006</td>
<td>WHEREAS WE deem it expedient to authorize the formation of a corps to be entitled the Army Air Corps;</td>
<td>A.O. 21
1942</td>
</tr>
<tr>
<td>S.R.O. 325
1942</td>
<td>OUR WILL AND PLEASURE is that the Army Air Corps shall be deemed to be a corps for the purposes of the Army Act, the Reserve Forces Act, 1882, and the Territorial and Reserve Forces Act, 1907;</td>
<td></td>
</tr>
</table>

OUR FURTHER WILL AND PLEASURE is that the Schedule attached to the Warrant of His late Majesty King George V dated 27th February, 1926,* shall be amended as shown in Part I of the Schedule attached to this Our Warrant;

LASTLY, OUR WILL AND PLEASURE is that the rates of pay of personnel of Our Army Air Corps shall be as prescribed in Part II of the Schedule attached to this Our Warrant.

> Given at Our Court at St. James's, this 24th day of February, 1942, in the 6th year of Our Reign.

> By His Majesty's Command,
> **P. J. GRIGG.**

*Army Order 49 of 1926.

2

SCHEDULE

PART I

Under "OTHER BRANCHES" and *above* "Royal Army Service Corps"—

Column I, *insert* "Army Air Corps".

Column 2, *insert* "All units and personnel of the Army Air Corps".

PART II

The rates of regimental pay of officers of the Army Air Corps will be those prescribed for Infantry in Our Warrant for the Pay, Promotion and Non-Effective Pay of the Army, dated 29th February, 1940, Article 268.

The rates of regimental pay of warrant officers, non-commisioned officers and men of the Army Air Corps will be those prescribed for non-tradesmen in Article 829 of the aforementioned Warrant, but soldiers of the Corps duly qualified and mustered as tradesmen within the establishment will be paid at the rates prescribed in Article 838 of that Warrant.

Additional pay may be issued to officers, warrant officers, non-commissioned officers and men of the Army Air Corps at such rates and under such conditions as the Army Council may determine.

By Command of the Army Council,

LONDON

PRINTED AN PUBLISHED BY HIS MAJESTY'S STATIONERY OFFICE

To be purchased directly from H.M. STATIONERY OFFICE at the following addresses

York House, Kingsway, London, W.C.2: 120 George Street, Edinburgh 2;

39-41 King Street, Manchester 2; 1 St. Andrew's Crescent, Cardiff;

80 Chichester Street, Belfast;

or through any bookseller

1942

Price I*d*. net

(10190) Wt. — 36375 3/42 W.O.P. Gp. 339   57—9999

SPECIAL ARMY ORDER

THE WAR OFFICE,

31st August, 1942

20/GENERAL/6006   <u>A.O. 128/1942</u>

Formation of Glider Pilot Regiment and Parachute Regiment

The following regiments have been formed as Units of the Army Air Corps, the formation of which was notified in Army Order 21 of 1942:—

Glider Pilot Regiment with effect from 24th February, 1942.
Parachute Regiment with effect from 1st August, 1942.

By Command of the Army Council,

175

The Army Air Corps:
The Parachute Regiment—See under App. 13/1–3 Battalions.

The Glider Pilot Regiment

Commanding Officers

1st Bn.	1942	Lieut.-Col. J. F. Rock (K.A. Crash c. 9/42)
	1942	Lieut.-Col. G. J. S. Chatterton, D.S.O.
2nd Bn.	1942	Lieut.-Col. G. J. S. Chatterton (until 9/42)
	1942	Lieut.-Col. I. Murray, D.S.O.

In late 1943 after Sicily & Italy operations, the G.P.R. was reorganised—the Battalions became Wings; Companies—Squadrons; and Troops—Flights. Chatterton as T/Brig. Commander, Glider Pilots.

1st Wing	1944	Lieut.-Col. I. Murray, D.S.O.
	1945	Lieut.-Col. R. Q. Gaitley
	1947	Lieut.-Col. F. A. S. Murray, M.C.
	1948	Lieut.-Col. C. J. Deedes, O.B.E., M.C.

2nd Wing 1944 Lieut.-Col. J. Place

Also 1st Indep. Sqn.—formed from No. 3 Sqn., remained in Italy, under Major G. A. R. Coulthard, took part in S. France landings, and in missions to Yugosalvia.

The 1st Wing took part in Normandy assault, and both Wings took part in Arnhem operations, where the Regiment was depleted by 50%. It was ordered to reinforce & retrain for Rhine Crossing in March, 1945, and additional Glider Pilots were found from R.A.F. personnel. Following the end of the war, the 2nd Wing was disbanded, whilst the 1st Wing went to Palestine with the 6th Airborne Division.

On its return to the U.K., the G.P. Regiment had been reduced to a "H.Q.", "A" & "B" Squadrons in 1948.

The Army Air Corps
Insignia The Parachute Regiment
The Glider Pilot Regiment

Beret —All ranks wore the now famous Red Beret, which was introduced in 1942, maroon being chosen in preference to others.
Beret Badge—Both Regiments intially wore the Army Air Corps. badge, which consisted of an eagle, wings outspread, facing left on a laurel wreath

topped by a King's Crown with a semi-circular bar, on which was A.A.C. It was in white—metal for Other Ranks, and hallmarked silver for Officers, and a grey plastic economy issue also existed. The badge was introduced in August, 1942.

In May, 1943, the Parachute Regiment had a badge authorised, which consisted of a pair wings outspread horizontally in the centre of which is an opened parachute, surmounted by the Royal Crest. It was in white-metal for other ranks, and hallmarked silver for Officers. An unpopular grey plastic economy issue also existed.

Shoulder Titles

The men were of course, Airborne, and their titles heralded the fact— "Airborne" light blue on maroon, worn above the Pegasus flash in the same colouration.

Then in August, 1942, the Parachute Regiment was officially formed, and with the Glider Pilot Regiment—new titles appeared—**"Parachute Regiment"** and **"Glider Pilot Regiment"** in dark blue on light blue, first printed types, and later military tailors produced embroidered for best walking-out battledress.

Prior to this, an enterprising manufacturer had listened to the the grumblings of the paratroopers, with their Airborne flashes, and made a dark blue on light blue "Paratroop Regiment", (A.B.F.). However these were not taken into use, as the more favoured Parachute Regiment title was used.

Of course, the first three Parachute Battlalions had favoured their own unofficial shoulder titles, that of "PARACHUTE" with the Battalion numeral below, in light blue on maroon (BD90).

When it was decided that the Glider Pilot Regiment should have Cambridge Blue facings, and the Parachute Regiment, maroon, the shoulder titles of the latter assumed the more recognised pattern of "PARACHUTE REGIMENT" light blue on maroon—being the old racing colours of General "Boy" Browning.

It should be said that from evidence in photographs and reminiscences, the variety of shoulder titles listed above, were all worn at the same time. It would appear that it was a case of supply and demand—the official printed dark blue/light blue types being the most used. The woven types being tailor made for walking out dress were favoured, and brought by those who could afford them.

There was also "ARMY AIR CORPS" dark blue in light blue, printed, and woven types, worn by recruits and personnel who had no commitment to either Regiment. The woven type was readopted for battledress on the reforming of the Army Air Corps in 1957. (ptd A.B.F.).

The Glider Pilot Regiment also wore an example with a blue glider beneath the title in facing pairs (A.B.F.). When No. 2 Wing was established, some of its members had their titles embroidered with a number "2" beneath (A.B.F.).

The Qualification Wings

a) Parachutists

At first an all white parachute and wings were worn by qualified personnel of No. 2 (Army) Commando, later this was changed to light blue wings and a white parachute about 3" wide, and worn on the right arm below the shoulder title, and above the "Pegasus" flash. (BD66).

b) 1st Glider Pilots

This wing introduced in 1942, for Staff Sergeant First Class Pilots, and consisted of large light blue wings, either side of the Royal Crest, on a black background. It was worn above the left breast pocket. Officers' patterns were padded in the R.A.F. style, and about 4" in length, but the Sergeant's pattern was much larger, about $5^1/_2$" and flat (BD64).

c) 2nd Glider Pilots

This wing was introduced in 1944, and was smaller ($2^1/_2$") than the 1st Pilots. It consisted of a gold "G" in a gold circle, with slim light blue wings, and was padded, though flat examples do exist, which are believed to be reproductions.

This badge was also worn on left breast (BD66).

Appendix 13/1

Composition of 1st Airborne Division

Commanding Officers

Major-General F. A. M. Browning	3.11.41—5.4.43
Major-General G. F. Hopkinson	6.4.43—12.9.43 *(K.I.A)*
Major-General E. E. Down	12.9.43—20.12.43
Major-General R. E. Urquhart	10.1.44—1.11.45

Order of Battle

1st Parachute Brigade—   1st Parachute Battalion
2nd Parachute Battalion
3rd Parachute Battalion

4th Parachute Brigade—   10th Parachute Battalion
11th Parachute Battalion
156th Parachute Battalion

1st Air-Landing Brigade—   1st Bn., Border Regiment
2nd Bn., South Staffords.
7th Bn., K.O.S.B.

Plus **Divisional Support Units**

2nd Parachute Brigade—   4th Parachute Battalion
5th Parachute Battalion
6th Parachute Battalion

Became an Independent Parachute Brigade Group, with its own integral support elements in November, 1943.

1st Airborne Division

1ST PARACHUTE BRIGADE

Commanding Officers

5th Sep, 1941	Brigadier R. N. Gale
18th Apr, 1942	Brigadier E. W. C. Flavell
28th Apr, 1943	Brigadier G. W. Lathbury *(W.D. 18.9.44)*
19th Sep, 1944	Lt-Colonel J. D. Frost (actg) *(W.D. 20.9.44)*
23rd Oct, 1944	Brigadier G. W. Lathbury
1st Jun, 1945	Lt-Colonel A. H. Pepys (actg)
12th Jul, 1945	Brigadier E. E. G. L. Searight
30th Jul, 1945	Brigadier S. J. L. Hill

Unit Composition

1st Parachute Battalion	15.9.41 – 31.8.45
2nd Parachute Battalion	30.9.41 – 31.8.45
3rd Parachute Battalion	1.10.41 – 8.5.45

On joining 1st Army in North Africa it was organised as a Brigade Group between September, 1942 and May, 1943 with the following units under command:

1st Parachute Squadron, R.E.

"J" Section 2nd Company, 1st Abn. Div. Signals

16th Parachute Field Ambulance

Whilst an Indpendent Brigade, it served under 1st Army; 5th Corps; 78th Inf. Div; 6th Armd. Div; 46th Inf. Div. and A.F.H.Q.

1st Parachute Brigade

1st Parachute Battalion

Commanding Officers
    1940   Lieut-Colonel C. I. A. Jackson   **11th S.A.S. Btn.**
    1941   Lieut-Colonel E. E. Down
    1942   Lieut-Colonel S. J. L. Hill *(W.D. 11/42)*
    1942   Lieut-Colonel A. S. Pearson *(Ill 7/43)*
    1943   Lieut-Colonel P. Cleasby-Thompson *(temp)*
    1943   Lieut-Colonel D T. Dobie
    1945   Lieut-Colonel T. C. H. Pearson

Brief History
This was the first Parachute Battalion formed. Its original members were from No. 2 Commando, which was selected for parachute training. Those members selected were formed into the 11th Special Air Service Battalion, members of which first dropped at Tragino in 1941. It served through North Africa, Sicily, Italy and finally at Arnhem where it was depleted, though reformed back in the U.K.

It went to Denmark and then to Palestine.

Insignia
The Battalion wore the A.A.C. capbadge, until the new badge came into use on the maroon beret.

For shoulder titles it wore "PARACHUTE" with a number "1" beneath in light blue on maroon, which it wore for all its airborne career, and although orders later specified the removal of unit identification, this was not always adhered to—some of the Battalion undid the stitching and tucked the "1" tablet behind the title!

They also wore Green lanyard as Battalion identification.

2nd Parachute Battalion

Commanding Officers
    1941   Lieut-Colonel E. W. C. Flavell
    1942   Major Gofton-Salmond *(temp) (7/42 – 10/42)*
    1942   Lieut-Colonel J. D. Frost *(W.D. & P.O.W. 9/44)*
    1944   Lieut-Colonel J. E. B. Marshall
    1945   Lieut-Colonel J. D. Frost

Brief History

Formed in 1941, as was the other member battalions of the Brigade. It's "C" Company in 1942, gave the Parachute Regiment its first Battle Honour—BRUNEVAL. The Battalion fought in North Africa, Sicily and Italy and finally at Arnhem, where it held the bridge for several days and almost ceased to exist. It was reformed after the battle in the U.K. and went to Denmark and then Palestine under the 6th Abn. Division.

Insignia

The Battalion wore first the A.A.C. badge and then the authorised beret badge. It's titles were "PARACHUTE" and the numeral "2" beneath and the unit lanyard – yellow, though it was given a golden appearance by enterprising soldiers soaking the cord in Mepocrine tablets!

3rd Parachute Battalion

Commanding Officers

    1941   Lieut-Colonel G. W. Lathbury
    1942   Lieut-Colonel R. Webb *(10/42)*
    1942   Lieut-Colonel R. G. Pine-Coffin (BD90)
    1943   Lieut-Colonel E. C. Yeldham
    1943   Lieut-Colonel J. A. C. Fitch *(K.I.A. 9/44)*
    1945   Lieut-Colonel R. T. H. Lonsdale

Brief History

This Battalion took part in the first action of the North African campaign, that of the drop onto Bone Airfield on the 12th November 1942. It then fought in Sicily, Italy and finally at Arnhem where it was reduced to one officer and 36 other ranks. It was reformed with the remnants of the 11th Battalion, plus reinforcements in U.K. and went to Palestine with the 6th Airborne Division.

Insignia

The Battalion wore the usual A.A.C. beret badge in plastic and white metal, changing in May to the official badge.

The shoulder title was "PARACHUTE" and the numeral "3" below in light blue on maroon. (BD90).

The unit lanyard was a red one.

4TH PARACHUTE BRIGADE

Commanding Officers

6th Dec, 1942	Lt-Colonel K. B. I. Smyth	*(actg)*
4th Jan, 1943	Brigadier J. W. Hackett	
5th Mar, 1943	Lt-Colonel K. B. I. Smyth	*(actg)*
10th Apr, 1943	Brigadier J. W. Hackett	
16th Oct, 1943	Lt-Colonel K. B. I. Smyth	*(actg)*
7th Nov, 1943	Brigadier J. W. Hackett	*(W.D. 24.9.44)*
24th Sep, 1944	Lt-Colonel I. A. Murray	*(actg)*

Unit Composition

156th Parachute Battalion	14.2.43 – 30.9.44
10th Parachute Battalion	23.2.43 – 30.9.44
11th Parachute Battalion	30.4.43 – 30.9.44

The Brigade was formed in the Middle East in December, 1942, and was disbanded on the 10th December, 1944, its remaining personnel being absorbed into the 1st Parachute Brigade.

Units under command whilst in Palestine and Libya
4th Parachute Squadron, R.E.
133rd Parachute Field Ambulance

4th PARACHUTE BRIGADE

156th Parachute Battalion

Commanding Officers
1941   Lieut-Colonel H. R. C. Hose
1943   Lieut-Colonel W. R. de B. des Voeux *(K.I.A. 9/44)*

Brief History
This battalion was formed in India on the 18th October, 1941, from volunteers in that theatre of operations. It was originally numbered 151st Parachute Battalion, but on arrival in the Middle East in 1943, this was changed for some reason to 156th.

It fought in Italy and then at Arnhem, where it ceased to be a fighting unit and was disbanded with the rest of the Brigade in the December of 1944, its remaining personnel being absorbed into the 1st Parachute Brigade.

10th Parachute Battalion

Commanding Officers
1943   Lieut-Colonel K. B. I. Smyth *(K.I.A. 9.44)*

Brief History
This Battalion was formed on the volunteers from the 2nd Btn., Royal Sussex Regiment in the Middle East in early, 1943. It fought in Italy and at Arnhem and was not reformed following the battle.

Insignia note—they wore an epaulette tab of light blue & dark blue.

11th Parachute Battalion

Commanding Officers
1943   Lieut-Colonel R. M. C. Thomas
1943   Lieut-Colonel G. H. Lea

Brief History
The Battalion was formed from a cadre from the 156th P. B. and volunteers from the Middle East theatre of operations. It remained in Palestine, when the rest of the Brigade moved to North Africa, and took part in an airborne assault of the island of Cos in September, 1943. It then joined the Brigade in the U.K. It ceased to exist as a unit after Arnhem, most of its personnel being absorbed by the 3rd Para Battalion.

Insignia note—they wore a lanyard of gold & maroon twists.

31st Independent Brigade Group

This group was raised on 17th July, 1940 and remained under War Office Control until the 31st July, when it became part of 4 Corps and joined it in Iraq. The Brigade left 4 CORPS and returned home February, 1941, when it came under the WESTERN COMMAND, that covered the North-West and North-Midland Counties, and the whole of Wales. On the 27th October, 1941, Brigadier G. F. Hopkinson took over the command of the Brigade from Brigadier H. E. F. SMYTHE—who had commanded the Brigade since its inception.

Unit Composition

+	2nd	South Staffordshires	17.7.40 – 9.12.41
+	2nd	Oxford & Bucks. L.I.	17.7.40 – 9.12.41
+	1st	Royal Ulster Rifles	17.7.40 – 9.12.41
+	1st	Border Regiment	1.12.40 – 9.12.41
	31st	Indep. Bde. Gp. Anti-Tank Coy.	14.9.40 – 1.1.41

The following support elements formed the rest of the Group

Royal Artillery

	75th Field Regiment	20.7.40 – 4.12.41
+	223rd Anti-Tank Battery	20.7.40 – 9.12.41

Royal Engineers

237th Field Company	20.7.40 – 5.8.41
9thField Company	8.12.41 – 9.12.41

Infantry Spt.

	"D" Coy., 5th Devons. (M.G.)	25.8.40 – 13.10.40
	31st Indep. Bde. Gp. M.G. Coy.	14.10.40 – 5.8.41
+	31st Indep. Bde. Gp. Recce Coy.	1.1.41 – 9.12.41 *(from Atk. Coy.)*

Services

+	31st	Indep. Bde. Gp. Coy., R.A.S.C.	5.8.40 – 9.12.41
	39th	Mot. Coach Coy., R.A.S.C.	17.8.40 – 9.12.41

Medical Spt.

	152nd Field Ambulance	20.7.40 – 5.8.41
+	181st Field Ambulance	31.7.40 – 9.12.41

Ordnance

+ 31st Indep. Bde. Gp. Workshops, R.A.O.C.   18.3.41 – 9.12.41
+ 31st Indep. Bde. Gp. Ord. Field Pk.   18.3.41 – 9.12.41

Provost

+ 31st Indep. Bde. Gp. Pro. Secn., C.M.P.   20.7.40 – 9.12.41

On 10th December, 1941, the Brigade was reorganised and became the 1st Air-Landing Brigade Group and units marked + continued within its ranks.

1ST AIR-LANDING BRIGADE

The Brigade was formed on the 10th March, 1943, the units forming the Group having become under 1st Airborne Division control.

Commanding Officers
10th Dec, 1941   Brigadier G. F. Hopkinson
6th Apr, 1943   Brigadier P. H. W. Hicks
11th Dec, 1944   Lt-Col. R. Payton-Reid *(actg)*
14th Dec, 1944   Brigadier R. H. Bower

Unit Composition
1st Btn., Border Regt.	10.12.41 – 31.8.45
2nd Btn., S. Staffords	10.12.41 – 31.8.45
2nd Btn., Oxford & B.	10.12.41 – 15.5.43 *(to 6th A.L.)*
1st Btn., Ryl. Ulsters	10.12.41 – 15.5.43 *(to 6th A.L.)*
7th Btn., K.O.S.B.	10.12.43 – 31.8.45

The unit served under the 1st Airborne Division throughout its existence, except for a few days in Italy when it was under the 78th Infantry Division.

1ST AIR LANDING BRIGADE

1st Btn., The Border Regiment

Commanding Officers
1943   Lieut-Colonel G. V. Britten
1944   Lieut-Colonel T. Haddon
1945   Lieut-Colonel C. F. O. Breese

Brief History
Served in the 1st A/Lng. Bde. for its entire Airborne career, and with the South Staffs., was the first unit to go into battle by Glider in the British Forces, when it landed in Sicily in 1943. It then fought at Arnhem, and was the only unit to return as a virtual complete Battalion.

It later went to Norway and then onto the Army of Occupation in Germny, when the Brigade was disbanded in October, 1945.

Insignia
The beret badge consisted of a diamond cut eight pointed star, topped by a King's Crown. Superimposed on this was a Maltese Cross carrying the Battle Honours of the Regiment on its arms. In the centre a circle inscribed "Arroyo dos Molinos 1811" and within the circle a Dragon with "China" above, the lower part voided and with a red felt backing. Below a scroll inscribed "THE BORDER REGT".

The Battalion should have worn "BORDER" shoulder titles, white on red. However an unofficial one was favoured, consisting of "BORDER" in yellow, on green, with yellow stitching onto purple edging. This was worn above the Pegasus and Airborne tab.

On the lower right forearm, the glider badge in yellow or brown thread on Khaki.

The Battalion also wore shoulder loops as follows:
H.Q. Coy.—Yellow	C Coy.—Red
A Coy.—Green	D Coy.—Dark Blue
B Coy.—White	Spt.—Light Blue

2nd Bn., South Staffordshire Regt.

Commanding Officers
1939   Lieut-Colonel W. C. Green, M.C.
1941   Lieut-Colonel·A. D. Clinch *(from K.O.Y.L.I.)*
1942   Lieut-Colonel O. L. Jones *(from Cheshire Regt.)*

1943 Lieut-Colonel W. D.H. McCardie *(P.O.W. 9/4)*
1944 Lieut-Colonel H. C. B. Cook
1945 Lieut-Colonel D. B. Pike   *C.O. on amalgamation of*
                                    1st & 2nd Bns. in 1948

Brief History

The Battalion had been in India until June 1940, when it returned to England docking at Liverpool from Bombay in July, 1940. It moved to St. Albans in September, 1940, and then in February, 1941, to Pontypool, as part of the 31st Independent Brigade Group.

In December, 1941, the Brigade was renamed the 1st Air-Landing Brigade Group and glider training began.

The Battalion went into action in the first glider assault of the British Army at Sicily, and fought in Italy in 1943. It later fought at Arnhem in Holland in 1944, where two of its members won V.C.'s (these are both on show at the Staffordshire Regimental Museum, along with Major Cain's beret and tunic).

The reformed Battalion following this battle went to Norway in April, 1945 and Germany in 1945-7 as part of 5th Division, where it served its airborne connection.

Insignia

The badge worn on the beret was a white metal Staffordshire Knot, topped by the King's Crown, on a brass scroll inscribed "SOUTH STAF-FORDSHIRE". The knot was backed in Brown holland material. Plastic economy issues were also worn.

Throughout its Airborne career it wore its own special shoulder title—"S. STAFFORDS." embroidered yellow on maroon, above the Pegasus flash and Airborne tab.

On the lower right forearm: the yellow glider on khaki oval.

The Battalion also wore coloured lanyards from the left epaulette as follows:

H.Q. Coy.—White	C Coy.—Blue
A Coy.—Green	D Coy.—Black
B Coy.—Red	Spt. Coy.—Yellow

7th Btn., King's Own Scottish Borderers

Commanding Officer

1939–45 Lieut-Colonel R. Payton-Reid

Brief History

The Battalion was raised in 1939 in Dumfries, and became Airborne in

1943, it fought at Arnhem and was reduced to 150 all ranks.

It was reformed after the battle and served with the rest of the Brigade until disbanded in 1945.

Insignia

It wore the Glengarry badge on the beret, consisting of a circle inscribed "KING'S OWN SCOTTISH BORDERER" with the Castle of Edinburgh in the centre, all upon the Cross of St. Andrew. Surrounded by thistles and topped by the King's Crown. Two motto scrolls one above and one below "IN VERITATE RELIGIONIS CONFIDO" (In true religion my trust) and "NISI DOMINUS FRUSTRA" (Unless the Lord be with me, all is in vain) on Leslie Tartan.

They wore a Tartan Flash above the Pegasus and Airborne Tab, with a blue glider on right lower forearm.

21st Independent Parachute Company

Commanding Officers:
- 1942   Major J. Lander, T.D.   *(K.I.A. 7/43)*
- 1943   Major B. A. Wilson, D.S.O., M.C.   *(W.D. 9/44)*
- 1945   Major R E. Spivey

Formed in June, 1942, from volunteers, a number coming from the Glider Pilot Regiment. Its first action was when members dropped on Sicily. Service in Italy and Holland followed—the Company numbered about 80 all ranks at the start, later rising to about 190. It was reformed after Arnhem and went to Norway and then to Palestine under the 6th Abn. Div., and was disbanded in September, 1946.

Insignia

Many of the early members wore "AIRBORNE" in light blue on maroon. This was then changed to "PARACHUTE" printed dark blue-black on maroon. Major Wilson then acquired from a military tailor woven titles— "PARACHUTE" with "XXI" beneath in light blue on maroon. These were worn on walking-out dress, as orders came for the removal of unit identification so the "XXI" had to be cut off, however this was not always adhered to. The titles were worn above the wings and Pegasus.

They wore the usual "A.A.C." beret badge, later changing to the new Parachute Regiment beret badge. They wore a lanyard with alternate white and blue twists.

The Polish Parachute Brigade (1st Indep.)

Formed in Scotland by Polish volunteers of the 4th Rifle Bde. in early 1941, and assumed title in September, 1941, under command of Major-General S. Sosabowski. Consisted of 3 ParachuteBatalions, and a small glider element.

Placed under command of 1st Airborne Division in June, 1944, and dropped into Arnhem-Driel area, suffering moderate casualites, and striving valiantly to get across the river and aid the 1st Division.

Members of the Brigade were also dropped into Poland to aid the Resistance—the Polish Home Army.

On its return home with the Division to rest and regroup, it remained in the U.K. under orders. It did not go to Norway in May, 1945, and was subsequently disbanded, many of its members remaining in the U.K. rather than return to a Communist Poland.

Insignia

They wore light blue-grey berets, with the metal or plastic crowned Polish Eagle badge. I have seen woven examples on light blue purported to have been worn as well, although I have no actal proof of this at present. They also painted the Eagle on the front of the helmet.

They also wore their own parachute badge—a plunging eagle in dark silver material, and made in Edinburgh by Kirkwood & Son. It was fixed to the tunic, above the breast pocket, by a single screw mount, the brass retaining disc having the maker's name on it. On the reverse of the eagle was the parachutists' serial number, and the motto "TOBIE OJCZYZNO" (For My Country). British battledress was worn, with Polish rank insignia and yellow pointed collar flashes, on which was a white parachute. Also "PO-LAND" in white on red shoulder titles.

Once a combat jump had been completed a gold wreath was fixed to the claws of the eagle. Those who jumped back into Poland wore inside the wreath the combined letters "PW" standing for "POLSKA WALCZLA" (Fighting Poland)—this was unofficial. I have an example of lapel size.

1st Airborne Division Support Units

1st Air-Landing Reconnaissance Sqn., R.A.C.

Commanding Officers
1940   Major T. B. H. Otway
1941   Major C. F. H. Gough *(P.O.W. – escaped 9.44)*

Brief History
Formed in January, 1941, from the 31st Independent Bde. Grp. Anti-Tank company, as the 31st I. B. G. Recce Company. In December, when the Brigade became the 1st Air-Landing Brigade Group, it became the 1st Air-Landing Sqn., Recce Corps.

On 1st January, 1944 it became the 1st A/Lng. Recce Sqn., R.A.C.

Following the Arnhem battle in September, 1944, the unit was reconstituted in the U.K. and served to the end of the war with the Division.

Insignia
They wore the Reconnaissance Corps beret badge, which consisted of a spear flanked by forked lightning above a scroll inscribed with the full title, all in brass. Worn on the maroon beret. Officers in wire.

Their shoulder title was green with "RECONNAISSANCE" in yellow. It was worn above the wings if qualified, and Pegasus Arm Badge, sometimes above the Airborne tab. Officers wore a green and yellow lanyard.

Royal Regiment of Artillery

Insignia
The units wore the field gun badge on the beret, though the collar seven-flamed grenade was worn in gold wire, red scroll "UBIQUE" in gold on maroon ground by Officers. The badge was a field gun, above the wheel ascroll "UBIQUE" (Everywhere) and the gun rests on a three part scroll "QUO FAS ET GLORIA DUCUNT" (Wherever right and glory lead).

They wore the shoulder titles "ROYAL ARTILLERY" scarlet on dark blue, above Parachute wings if qualified, and Pegasus and Airborne tab.

1st Air-Landing Light Regiment

Commanding Officers
2/43 – 7/43   Lt. Colonel R. W. McLeod
7/43 – 9/44   Lt. Colonel W. F. K. Thompson, M.B.E.
9/44 –   Lt. Colonel J. E. F. Linton, D.S.O.

The Regiment was formed on 6th February, 1943, at Bulford, and eventually comprised 41 Officers and 588 O.R.'s.

It comprised three Batteries :

1st Air-Landing Light Bty.   –   1st Air-Landing Brigade
2nd Air-Landing Light Bty.   –   4th Parachute Brigade
3rd Air-Landing Light Bty.   –   1st Parachute Brigade

Insignia note—for a tme the shoulder title "THE LIGHT ARTILLERY" in yellow on dark blue was worn, being locally made. (A.B.F. and BD90).

1st Air-Landing Light Battery

Commanding Officers
Major P. Lloyd

This Battery had formed part of 1st Air-Landing Brigade Group on 10th December, 1941, as 458 Lt. Battery. On 27th July, 1942 it became 1st A/Lng. Lt. Bty.

2nd Air-Landing Light Battery

Commanding Officers
2/43 – 7/43 Major J. G. H. Ward-Jackson
7/43 – Major J. A. S. Hawkins

This Battery was formed on 13th February, 1943 as part of the new Regiment.

3rd Air-Landing Light Battery

Commanding Officers
2/43 – Major D. J. Madden

1st Air-Landing Anti-Tank Regiment

Commanding Officer
Lieut-Colonel R. G. Elliott, M.B.E.

Formed on the 25th March, 1945, and comprised the following:

1st Air-Landing Anti-Tank Bty.

2nd Air-Landing Anti-Tank Bty.
5th Air-Landing Anti-Tank Bty.

1st Air-Landing Anti-Tank Battery

Commanding Officer
12/41 – 11/42   Major T. I. J. Toler
11/42 – 9/44   Major W. F. Arnold
9-12/44   Major H. F. Bear
1-5/45   Major E. A. B. Garrett

Formed in December as part of 1st A/Lng. Bde. Grp., keeping its previous title of 223rd Anti-Tank Battery, (formed from 4th Bn., Kings Own Regiment). This was changed on the 18th June to 1st Air-Landing Atk. Battery. In September it came under the Divisional control and was part of 1st Parachute Brigade at Arnhem, and went to Norway with the Division in 1945.

2nd Oban Air-Landing Anti-Tank Battery

Commanding Officer
    Major J. R. Wilson
– 9/44   Major A. F. Haynes
10/44 –   Major G. B. S. Lardner

Formed on conversion of the 204th Independent Atk. Battery on 23rd October, 1942, and was attached to the 4th Parachute Brigade in Arnhem battle and went to Norway with the Division in 1945.

5th Air-Landing Anti-Tank Battery

Formed on the 20th February, 1945 as Divisional Troops.

Insignia Note—for a time the title "ANTI-TANK ARTILLERY" was worn unofficially—white on blue. (A.B.F. and BD80).

No. 1 Forward Observer Unit

Following the success of the Naval Bombardment Groups, which consisted of an Artillery Officer and Naval telegraphist, the army formed its own unit in 1944. Its first C.O. was Major (later Lt-Colonel) Robert Guy Loder-Symonds, MC. He later became Commander R.A. units of 1st Airborne Division at Arnhem, he was awarded the D.S.O., the American D.S.C. and the

Norwegian Liberty Cross. He was later killed in an aircrash in Java in 1946. Capt. A. E. O'Grady commanded the unit deployed at Arnhem, whilst the C.O.—Major D. R. Wight-Boycott acted as liaison with the ground forces of 30 Corps. The unit went to Norway in 1945.

Corps of Royal Engineers
Insignia

They wore the usual badge in brass or plastic on the maroon beret. It consisted of the Order of the Garter motto on a belt, topped by King's Crown, bordered on both sides by a laurel wreath, with title scroll at the base.

Officers wore the grenade with nine flames in gold wire, above a blue silk scroll "UBIQUE" in gold wire on maroon background.

Their shoulder title was "ROYAL ENGINEERS" in blue on red, worn above the wings if qualified and Pegasus. The Airborne tab was worn by the Airborne units.

1st Airborne Squadron

The 1ST AIR TROOP, R.E. was formed on 3rd November, 1941 and was converted to the 1st Parachute, R.E. on the 19th June, 1942. It joined the 1st Parachute Brigade in North Africa and fought at Arnhem. Following the battle it absorbed the remnant of 4th Para. Sqn., R.E. on the 10th December, 1944. On the 26th March, 1945, it became the 1st Airborne Sqn.

Insignia Note—During its early days it wore an unofficial title "ROYAL ENGINEERS" above "PARACHUTE" red on dark blue.

2nd Parachute Squadron

Formed on conversion of the Holding Company, Kent Corps Troops on the 12th October, 1942, and joined the Airborne Division on the 11th November, 1942. It left the Division to join the 2nd Indep. Para. Bde. on the 16th November, 1943.

3rd Airborne Squadron

Formed at Darlington on 16th December, 1942, and joined the Division on the 19th January, 1943. It left on the 11th April, 1943, to join the 6th Airborne Division, and became an Airborne Squadron on 29th May, 1945.

4th Parachute Squadron

Formed in the Middle East in December, 1943, and came under the command of the 4th Parachute Brigade, until it became Div. Trps. on the 9th June, 1943. It served with 4th Para. Brigade at Arnhem and was disbanded on 10th December, 1944, its personnel being absorbed by the 1st Parachute Squadron.

195

9th Airborne Squadron

This unit was a Regular Army unit, that had its roots back in 1793. Reorganised as Field Company in 1899 for Boer War. It served in France in 1914-18 war and was at Shorncliffe at the outbreak of war in 1939. It served in France in 4th Inf. Division 1939-40, returning to the U.K. with 48th Division. It became the 9th Field Company, (Airborne) on 10th December, 1941 as part of the 1st Air-Landing Brigade, and some of its members took part in the actions at Bruneval and Vermork in 1942.

Became Divisional Troops on the 19th June, 1942 and became an Airborne Squadron on 26th March, 1945.

261st Airborne Park Squadron

Formed on 15th December, 1941 from units from the 45th Infantry Division, T.A. as 261st Field Park Company, (Airborne). It became a Squadron on 25th March, 1945, and placed in suspended animation after the war.

Royal Corps of Signals

Insignia

The members of the Airborne Signals were the Royal Signals' beret badge on the maroon beret:

Officers—Mercury in silver wire, on a blue silk scroll, with motto "CERTA CITO" (Swift & Sure) in gold wire, topped by a K/C in gold wire and coloured jewels, etc., all on a maroon background.

Other Ranks—Mercury, the Messenger of the Gods in w/m, (known as Jimmy within the Corps), on a globe, within an oval band carrying the full title, topped by a K/C all in brass. Plastic issues were also reluctantly worn.

Their shoulder titles were "ROYAL CORPS OF SIGNALS" in white on dark blue, in printed and embroidered types, worn above wings if qualified, Pegasus flash, and sometimes the Airborne tab. In 1944 the pattern was changed to "ROYAL SIGNALS" also in printed or embroidered types. Also examples have been seen, which have been enhanced by painting the letters white, especially for best walking out battledress.

1st Airborne Divisional Signals

Commanding Officers
1942   Lieut-Colonel R. J. Moberly
1944   Lieut-Colonel T. G. V. Stephenson

The Div. Sigs. was formed on 22nd April, 1942, its personnel serving in three Sections attached to the Brigades. They used wireless and pidgeons.

One pidgeon, William of Orange was awarded the Dickin Medal—the animals' V.C. for flying back from Arnhem to England, a total of 260 miles, including 135 miles of open sea in 4 hours 25 minutes.

Royal Army Service Corps

The prinicpal units of the Division were

250th Light Para. Company	63rd (ABN) Comp. Coy. (to 6th Div.)
93rd (Airborne) Company	253rd ABN Re-Supply C.C.A/Lng. Bde.

In early 1944, No.s 749 and 799 Air Despatch Companies were formed, following the demand for air re-supply. Soon an entire A.D. Group had been formed, and supplied units of the S.A.S; the French Resistance, and of course the beleagured 1st Abn. Div. at Arnhem—for which they had their official badge sanctioned— a yellow Dakota aircraft on a Royal Blue square worn on both arms below the title.

Insignia

The beret badge was an eight-pointed star, top point being replaced by a K/C, with the Royal Cypher "G.V.I.R" in the centre of the Garter and motto, with the full title on three scrolls around the base.

Officers wore embroidered versions on a maroon cloth background, whilst Other Ranks wore it in brass or plastic variants.

The shoulder title was "R.A.S.C" yellow on dark blue, in printed and embroidered types, and there is evidence that a full title flash was also worn as well. Below this parachute wings if qualified Pegasus flash. Airborne units wore the Tab below Pegasus and no wings.

Royal Army Medical Corps

Insignia

The beret badge was the rod and serpent of Aesculapius, the Greed God of Medicine, topped by a K/C within a laurel wreath, with the full title on the scroll below. Officers wore an embroidered version in gold & silver wire on a maroon background, and Other Ranks wore all brass and plastic issues.

The title was "R.A.M.C." in white on dull cherry, worn above the usual configuration.

16th ParachuteField Ambulance

Commanding Officers
1941   Lieut-Colonel M. MacEwan, D.F.C., T.D.

197

1943   Lieut-Colonel P. R. Wheatley
1944   Lieut-Colonel E. Townsend, M.C.
1945   Lieut-Colonel N. J. P. Hewlings, D.S.O.

This unit was formed entirely of volunteers from the R.A.M.C. on the 6th April, 1941, and was the first parachute trained medical unit. The number 16 was chosen since a 16th Field Ambulance had existed with the 6th Infantry Division in the First World War.

It served with the 1st Parachute Brigade in all theatres, and was reformed after Arnhem, to serve in Norway. It was disbanded in October of 1945.

Insignia Note—the unit wore the full title on its flashes, above the wings and Pegasus—no Airborne tab. Since the other units in the Brigade wore distinguishing lanyards, the 16th P.F.A. adopted one—dull cherry and sky blue.

133rd Parachute Field Ambulance

Commanding Officer
1943   Lieut-Colonel W. C. Alford

This unit was formed in January, 1943, in Palestine, by the conversion of the 133rd Field Ambulance, which had served under the 44th (Home Counties) Inf. Division that had been disbanded after El Alamein. The unit served with the 4th Parachute Brigade, it was reformed after Arnhem and went to Norway with Force 134. It returned home on 29th June, 1945 and on 15th November it was placed in suspended animation being finally disbanded on 1st December, 1945.

Insignia Note : the unit wore the normal configuration— no tab.

181st Air-Landing Field Ambulance

Commanding Officers
1941   Lieut-Colonel N. G. Hill, M.C., T.D.
1942   Lieut-Colonel G. M. Warrack
1944   Lieut-Colonel A. T. Marrable
1945   Lieut-Colonel I. C. Gilliland   *(3/45 - 7/45)*
1945   Lieut-Colonel A. T. Marrable   *(7/45 – 11/45)*

This unit was formed in December, 1941 on conversion of the 31st Indep. Bde. to the 1st Air-Landing Brigade. It served in Bruneval Raid, Sicily, Italy and Arnhem. It was reformed on 3rd March, 1945, from the seaborne "tail" who tried to reach them at Arnhem, and from those who escaped. They also received reinforcements from the 23rd Field Amb., whilst in Norway. One section went on a voyage to Murmansk caring for Russian P.O.W.'s being repatriated. They returned to the U.K. in September and was disbanded on 14th November.

Insignia note—the unit wore the normal configuration for Abn. units.

Royal Army Ordnance Corps

Ordnance personnel were attached to Division and Brigades, in the form of Ordnance Field Park detachments. Some were parachute trained and others went in by glider.

Insignia

Their badge was the Order of the Garter & Motto, in the centre of which was the shield of Ordnance—three guns and three cannonballs. Below this the full title and topped by K/C in brass, and plastic issues.

The shoulder title was "R.A.O.C." in blue on a scarlet ground, though unofficial full titles were sometimes worn in the same colouration. With the usual Pegasus and wings or Airborne tab.

Royal Electrical & Mechanical Engineers

This unit was formed in 1942 from the R.A.O.C., since the war had made tremendous leaps in technology. All units had R.E.M.E. Workshops attached to them and the 1st Abn. Div. was no exception.

Insignia

Their beret badge in brass or plastic consisted of four shields lettered "R", "E", "M", "E" with a pair of calipers in the centre, topped by the usual K/C. Following the war a new design was approved.

They wore should titles "R.E.M.E." in yellow on dark blue, above Pegasus and Airborne tab.

Corps of Military Police

Besides the "Regimental" police of the Battalions, the Corps provided its own Div. Provost Company, split into sections attached to each Brigade.

Insignia

The Corps' badge the Royal Cypher "G.V.I.R." topped by a K/C between two laurel wreaths, below – a scroll bearing the title "MILITARY POLICE". Following the end of the war, it was made "ROYAL" and the scroll was amended. It was found in brass and plastic.

The shoulder flash was "C.M.P." in dark blue on scarlet, below this the parachute wings, if qualified and Pegasus, sometimes the Airborne tab was worn.

Royal Army Pay Corps

Every unit needs to be paid, and the Division had its own Cash Office, like any other unit.

Insignia
The beret badge was the Royal Crest, above the motto "FIDE ET FIDUCIA" (In faith and trust) in brass and w/m scroll.

The shoulder flash was the full title in yellow on blue, though early in the war an unofficial one was worn that of "R.A.P.C." in blue on yellow.

Army Dental Corps

There was no specific A.D.C. unit within the Airborne, however its personnel served in the R.A.M.C. units a anaesthetists.

Insignia
The Corps' title was "A.D. CORPS." in red on dark green and worn above wings if qualified and Pegasus and Airborne tab.

The beret badge was the monogram "A.D.C." in a laurel wreath, topped by a K/C in brass.

Intelligence Corps

In June, 1942, the first five volunteers from the Int. Corps. formed the nucleus of the 89th Parachute Security Section. They were attached to the 1st Parachute Brigade for North Africa, and then the Section was enlarged to about twenty serving the Division, at Div. H.Q., Brigade and Battalion level. Their purpose being Field Security; Censorship, Interrogation and intelligence tasks—obtaining maps and intelligence of enemy positions, strengths, etc.

Commanding Officers
1942   Captain J. D. Dunbar *(K.I.A. Sicily 9.7.43)*
1943   C.S.M. J. F. Loker *(until return to U.K. 12/43)*

1943 Captain J. E. Killick *(P.O.W. Arnhem 9/44)*
1945 Lieut. Williams

Following service in Denmark and Norway, the Section returned to U.K. and was disbanded 12.8.45.

Insignia

Their beret badge in bronze, brass and plastic consisted of a Rose between a laurel wreath, topped by a K/C below a scroll bearing the full title. Captain Killick wore insignia of the Suffolk Regiment, his previous unit.

Although a shoulder title was produced in 1940, when the Corps was formed, and authorised in 1943, it was not worn until late 1944-45, and was "INTELLIGENCE CORPS" in black on green background.

The intelligence personnel usually wore just the Pegasus, and wings if qualified, since they did not want to draw attention to themselves if captured. Not all were qualified parachutists, since the Section did not operate as a unit, some going by glider. Some also wore the "AIRBORNE" curved should title.

Army Physical Training Corps

Formed in 1940, all units had their own instructors, and the nucleus of the Airborne Forces' Training Staff was composed of Royal Air Force and Army P.T.I.'s. As well as physical fitness, they were also responsible for parachute training.

Insignia

They wore the crossed sabres, topped by K/C in w/m on the beret, with a backing of a black rectangle, with two cherry-red vertical stripes at either end. This stemmed from the connection of red and black hooped shirts the pre-war P.T.I.'s used to wear.

Their shoulder title was the full title, in cherry red on black background.

They also wore the trade badge of crossed sabres on the sleeves of the battledress, above chevrons if N.C.O.'s, or below the Warrant Officers badges. Brass and woven examples were worn (BD56).

Army Catering Corps

Formed in 1941, every unit whatever its size had cooks attached to it, and they were trained just as hard as the next man, so they could perform operational tasks, just as good as any soldier in that unit.

Insignia

The beret badge in brass or plastic was a Grecian brazier, in a circle carrying the Corps' title, with K/C above.

The shoulder titles were of two types, the early one had "ARMY CATERING CORPS" in grey on yellow, the second "A.A.C." in yellow on grey, worn above the usual configuration for Airborne troops.

Royal Army Chaplain's Department

Every unit had a Chaplain of either denomination. They were all Officers, Chaplain 4th Class, being of Captain's rank.

Insignia

The beret badge was in blackened brass or bronze, the centre is the quatrefoil in both cases, the Christian in a Maltese Cross, the Jewish in the Star of David, both topped by a K/C. The Christian one has a motto in the centre "IN THIS SIGN CONQUER". In full dress these badges are in silver, gilt and enamels.

They wore a shoulder title "R.A.Ch.D." in white on purple, though examples of an unofficial type exist with "ROYAL ARMY CHAPLAINS" in white on blue (A.B.F. & BD89). The titles were worn above the usual configurations, and the official type is found in woven and printed form (BD106).

Appendix 13/2

2nd Independent Parachute Brigade Group

Commanding Officers

30th Jul, 1942	Brigadier E. E. Down
11th Sep, 1943	Brigadier C. H. V. Pritchard
1st Mar, 1944	Colonel T. C. H. Pearson *(actg)*
6th Mar, 1944	Brigadier C. H. V. Pritchard
22nd Aug, 1944	Colonel T. C. H. Pearson *(actg)*
29th Aug, 1944	Brigadier C. H. V. Pritchard
13th Nov, 1944	Colonel T. C. H. Pearson *(actg)*
9th Dec, 1944	Brigadier C. H. V. Pritchard
9th Feb, 1945	Colonel H. B. Coxen *(actg)*
28th Feb, 1945	Brigadier C. H. V. Pritchard
1st Jun, 1945	Colonel H. B. Coxen *(actg)*
28th Jun, 1945	Brigadier C. H. V. Pritchard

Unit Composition

4th Parachute Battalion	1.8.42 – 31.8.45
5th Parachute Battalion	1.8.42 – 31.8.45
6th Parachute Battalion	1.8.42 – 31.8.45

Formed in July, 1942, as part of the 1st Airborne Division, but on 17th November, in Italy it became an Independent Brigade Group, with its own support elements.

Whilst independent it served under 8th Army; 2nd N.Z. Division; 8th Indian Inf. Div; 13 Corps; 6th Armoured Div; No. 3 District; US 7th Army; A.F.H.Q. and 3 Corps (as Force 140 in Greece).

2nd Parachute Brigade

4th (Wessex) Parachute Battalion

Commanding Officers
1942   Lieut-Col. M. R. J. Hope-Thompson, M.C. *(1/42-7/42)*
1942   Lieut-Col. J. A. Dene *(P.O.W. 9/43)*
1943   Lieut-Col. H. B. Coxen, D.S.O., M.C.
1945   Lieut-Col. J. L. De V. Martin
1946   Lieut-Col. G. P. Rickcord, D.S.O.
1946   Lieut-Col. P. H. C. Hayward
1947   Lieut-Col H. B. Coxen, D.S.O., M.C.
1948   Lieut-Col J. H. Cubbon, O.B.E. *(as 4/6th Bn.)*

Formed at Derby on the 1st January, 1942 from volunteers from all parts of the U.K., though became known as the Wessex Battalion.

It was originally part of the 1st Para. Bde., though it transferred to the newly formed 2nd Para. Bde. in July, 1942. It served in all the campaigns with the 2nd Para. Bde., and then as part of the 6th Abn. Div. in Palestine until 1947, when it returned to U.K.

In December, 1947 at Cambrai Barracks, Perham Down it amalgamated with the 6th Para. Bn. The 4/6th went to Germany in February 1948, and in June, 1948, the Battalion became the new 1st Para. Bn.

Insignia note—it had the unusual distinction of wearing black webbing equipment and a black lanyard until 8/46.

5th (Scottish) Parachute Battalion

Commanding Officers
1942   Lieut-Col. A. Dunlop
1943   Lieut-Col. C. B. Mackenzie *(to 1st Abn. Div. as G.S.O.1)*
1943   Lieut-Col. D. R. Hunter, M.C.
1945   Lieut-Col. J. N. H. Christie
1947   Lieut-Col. J. Churchill
1947   Lieut-Col. A. G. F. Munro
1948   Lieut-Col. P. S. Sandilands, D.S.O.

Formed on the 7th Bn., Cameron Highlanders in May, 1942. Served in 2nd Para. Bde. all its career. It returned to the U.K. in 1947, and in July, 1948, in Germany the Battalion became the new 2nd Para. Bn.

Insignia note—The Battalion wore the Balmoral bonnet, with "A.A.C." badge on a patch of Hunting Stuart Tartan. The patch was worn on point, with the yellow diagonal stripe, top left to bottom right, and the red diagonal top right to bottom left. They wore this until September 1944, when they adopted the normal Para. Regt. beret and badge, still on the backing. Up to 1944, they also wore the "AIRBORNE" shoulder title, before adopted the usual full Regimental title.

On redesignation the patch was removed, but a blue lanyard was adopted from the field of the standard of St. Andrew. A blue Drop-Zone flash was later adopted to.

6th (Royal Welch) Parachute Battalion

Commanding Officers
    1942   Lieut-Col. C. H. V. Pritchard
    1942   Lieut-Col. J. A. Goodwin *(drowned 9/43)*
    1943   Lieut-Col. V. W. Barlow
    1945   Lieut-Col. A. Tilly
    1946   Lieut-Col. J. H. Cubbon, O.B.E.

Formed on the 10th Bn., Royal Welch Fusiliers in mid-1942. Served in all the campaigns of the 2nd Para. Bde. On its return to the U.K. in 1947 it amalagamated with the 4th Para Bn., and when in Germany in 1948 became the new 1st Para. Bn.

Insignia note—Its personnel were granted permission to wear the Royal Welch Fusiliers black ribbon flash attached to the back of the collar (BD76).

2nd Independent Brigade Support Units

Royal Regiment of Artillery

300th Air-Landing Anti-Tank Battery

Formed in December, 1943 on conversion of the 300th Anti-Tank Battery. It served in a glider borne role with the Brigade.

It then went to Palestine with the Brigade and became one of the Batteries in the 2nd Air-Landing Anti-Tank Regiment, 6th Abn. Div.

64th Air-Landing Light Battery

Formed in June, 1944 in readiness for the landings in France, from the 64th Field Battery. In December, 1944, it became "A" Air-Landing Light Battery, finally adopting its present title in February, 1945.

Insignia—as per usual Artillery units.

Corps of Royal Engineers

2nd Parachute Squadron

Joined the Brigade from 1st Div. Trps. on 17th November, 1943, and served with the Brigade throughout the war. It was disbanded on the 15th November, 1945, its personnel being absorbed into the 1st Airborne Squadron whilst in Palestine.

Royal Corps of Signals

2nd Indep. Para. Bde. Grp. Sigs. was formed on 17th November, 1943 from one of the sections from the 1st Abn. Div. Sigs.

Insignia—as for the usual Signals units—wings, no Airborne tab.

Royal Army Service Corps

751st Para. Bde. Company, R.A.S.C.

This unit was formed on the 18th November, 1943, as the 2nd Indep. Para. Bde. Grp., R.A.S.C. On the 1st July, 1944, it became "T" Company, 2nd Indep. Para. Group, and on the 27th July, the present title.

Insignia—as for usual Para. R.A.S.C. units.

Royal Army Medical Corps

127th Parachute Field Ambulance

Commanding Officers

1942   Lieut-Colonel M. J. Kohane *(W.D. 9/44)*
1944   Lieut-Colonel Parkinson
1945   Lieut-Colonel F. Murray

Formed in July, 1942, from the 127th (East Lancashire) F.A. T.A. which had mobilised on 2nd September, 1939 as part of the 42nd Inf. Div. Following Dunkirk, the unit became a Light Field Amb., with the newly formed 42nd Armoured Div.

It joined the Brigade in November, 1943 from the 1st Abn. Div. and served with it through Italy, South France, Greece and finally in Palestine.

Insignia—as for Para R.A.M.C. units.

Royal Electrical & Mechanical Engineers

2nd Indep. Para. Bde. Grp. Workshops was formed on 20th November and remained with the Brigade throughout its existence, being absorbed into the 6th Abn. Div. Wkshps in Palestine. There was also 4th A/Lng. L.A.D.

Insignia—as for usual R.E.M.E. units.

Corps of Military Police

2nd Indep. Para. Bde. Grp. Provost Section was formed on the 17th November, 1943, from part of the 1st Abn. Div. Provost Company.

2nd Lt. Victor William Wood of the Section was K.I.A. 21.12.43 in Italy on the Sangro River.

1st Independent Parachute Platoon, A.A.C.

Formed in November, 1943, from the 3rd Platoon, 21st Indep. Para. under Captain P. Baker. Its first title being the 23rd Independent Para. Platoon, though this was soon changed to the present title. On its return to U.K. in June, 1945, the Platoon was disbanded though some of its personnel returned to the 21st Indep., now serving with the 6th Abn. Div. in Palestine.

Intelligence Corps Platoon

One Platoon under Sgt. J. Granville, of the 89th Parachute Security Section, remained under command of the 2nd Indep. Bde. following the 1st Airborne Division's withdrawal from Italy, in November, 1943.

No. 3 Forward Observer Unit, R.A.

Formed during June, 1944 for Operation 'Dragoon'—the landing in Southern France, under the command of Major B. D. D. Emslie. Following service in Italy and Greece, the unit was disbanded in October, 1945.

Composition of 2nd Para. Bde. Grp. in 1947
on its return to U.K. from Palestine

4th   Parachute Battalion
5th   Parachute Battalion
6th   Parachute Battalion

"B" Squadron, The King's Own Hussars

211th	Battery, 53rd (Worcestershire Yeo.) A/Lng. Lt. Regt., R.A.
300th	Battery, 2nd A/Lng. A/Tk. Regt. R.A.
No. 1	Section, Forward Observer Unit, R.A.
3rd	Airborne Squadron, R.E.
"K"	Troop, 6th Abn. Div. Signal Regt.
249th	Airborne Park Squadron, R.E.—detachment
63rd	Composite Company (Airborne), R.A.S.C.
127th	Para. Field Ambulance, R.A.M.C.
6th	Abn. Div. Ordnance Field Park, R.A.O.C.—detachment
6th	Abn. Div. Workshops, R.E.M.E. – detachment & 1 A/Lng. L.A.D. R.E.M.E.
6th	Abn. Div. Provost Company, C.M.P.—one section.

later joined by 7th Parachute Battalion on amalgamation of 4/6th.

Appendix 13/3

Composition of 6th Airborne Division

Commanding Officers

Major-General R. N. Gale	7.5.43 – 8.12.44
Major-General E. L. Bols	12.12.44 – 13.2.46
Major-General A. J. H. Cassells	27.2.46 – 14.12.46
Major-General E. L. Bols	1.1.47 – 21.8.47
Major-General H. C. Stockwell	22.8.47 – 7.6.48

Order of Battle

3rd Parachute Brigade— 8th Parachute Battalion
9th Parachute Battalion
1st Canadian Parachute Battalion

5th Parachute Brigade— 7th Parachute Battalion
12th Parachute Battalion
13th Parachute Battalion

6th Air-Landing Brigade—2nd Bn., Oxford & Bucks L.I.
1st Bn., Royal Ulster Rifles
12th Bn., Devonshire Regiment

Plus **Divisional Support Units**

6th Airborne Division

3RD PARACHUTE BRIGADE

Commanding Officers
7th Nov, 1942	Brigadier Sir A. B. G. Stainer, Bart
8th Dec, 1942	Brigadier G. W. Lathbury
25th Apr, 1943	Lt-Colonel S. J. L. Hill *(actg)*
4th May, 1943	Brigadier E. W. C. Flavell
2nd Jun, 1943	Brigadier S. J. L. Hill
20th Dec, 1944	Colonel R. G. Parker *(actg)*
30th Dec, 1944	Brigadier S. J. L. Hill
2nd Jul, 1945	Brigadier G. W. Lathbury

Unit Composition
7th Parachute Battalion	7.11.42 – 8.8.43 *(to 5th P.B.)*
8th Parachute Battalion	7.11.42 – 31.8.45
9th Parachute Battalion	5.12.42 – 31.8.45
1st Canadian Para. Btn.	11.8.43 – 31.5.45
3rd Parachute Battalion	7.8.45 – 31.8.45

The Brigade was formed on the 7th November, 1942, on conversion of the 223rd (Home) Independent Infantry Brigade.

3rd Parachute Brigade—H.Q. some members adopted a dark blue lanyard

8th (Midlands Counties) Parachute Battalion

Commanding Officers
   1943   Lt-Colonel A. S. Pearson, D.S.O., M.C.
   1945   Lt-Colonel G. Hewetson, D.S.O., O.B.E.
   1947   Lt-Colonel J. H. M. Hackett, D.S.O.

Formed in November, 1942 from volunteers from the 13th Bn., Royal Warwickshire Regiment. It fought on D-Day and through to the Baltic Coast in 1945.

It was then sent to Palestine, and on 10th January, 1948 it was amalgamated with the 9th Para. Bn. to form the 8/9th Bn. The Battalion was disbanded in June, 1948.

Insignia note—they wore a green epaulette tab on battledress.

9th (Eastern & Home Counties) Parachute Battalion

Commanding Officers
   1943   Lt-Colonel T. B. H. Otway, D.S.O.
   1945   Lt-Colonel N. Crookenden, D.S.O.
   1946   Lt-Colonel M. A. H. Butler, D.S.O., M.C.
   1947   Lt-Colonel P. C. Hinde, D.S.O.
   1948   Lt-Colonel J. H. M. Hackett, D.S.O. *(as 8/9th Bn.)*

Formed from volunteers from the 10th Bn., Essex Regiment, on conversion of the 223rd Indep. Inf. Bde. With the other two Para. Bns. of the Brigade fought on D-Day to the Baltic Coast, and then onto Palestine. In 1948 it was amalgamated with the 8th Bn., and disbanded in June, on the Division's return to the U.K.

Insignia note—they wore a maroon epaulette tab on battledress, and later a maroon lanyard instead.

1st Canadian Parachute Battalion

Commanding Officers
   1942   Lt-Colonel G. F. P. Bradbrooke *(to 9/44)*
   1944   Lt-Colonel J. A. Nicklin *(K.I.A. 3/45)*
   1945   Lt-Colonel G. F. Eadie

Formed on 1st July, 1942, and was joined by additional officers and men, who passed the parachute course at Ringway, England.

They spent four months at the U.S. Abn. School, Fort Benning, and finally at the new Canadian Para. Training Wing, at Shilo, Manitoba.

They then came to England and joined the Brigade, fighting on D-Day, Ardennes and the Rhine Crossing. In June, 1945 it returned to Canada, and was disbanded in September.

Insignia note—they wore their own beret badge, in silver/gilt for Officers, brass or plastic issues for other ranks. The design was a parachute between two vertical wings, all resting on five maple leaves, and a title scroll "CANADIAN PARACHUTE CORPS".

Their parachute wing worn on the left breast, was also different—large white wings, and parachute, with a yellow Maple leaf at its base on dark green cloth.

They wore their own title above the Pegasus flash.

For more information see "The Badges & Insignia of the Canadian Airborne Forces" by Major Louis Grimshaw, C.D. (1981).

5TH PARACHUTE BRIGADE

Commanding Officers
    1st Jun, 1943   Brigadier E. W. C. Flavell
    5th Jul, 1943   Brigadier J. H. N. Poett

Unit Composition

    12th Parachute Battalion 1.6.43 – 31.8.45
    13th Parachute Battalion 1.6.43 – 31.8.45
    7th Parachute Battalion   9.8.43 – 31.8.45

Formed on 1st June, 1943, the Brigade H.Q. being formed from H.Q. 72nd Indep. Infantry Bde. In July, 1945, the Brigade was formed in a Group and sent to India in readiness to go to Japan. However it flew to Java instead later in the year.

5th Parachute Brigade

7th (Light Infantry) Parachute Battalion

Commanding Officers
- 1943 Lt-Colonel R. G. Pine-Coffin, M.C.
- 1946 Lt-Colonel W. D. H. McCardie
- 1947 Lt-Colonel T. C. H. Pearson, D.S.O.
- 1948 Lt-Colonel P. D. Maud, M.B.E.

Formed from the 10th B. Somerset Light Infantry in November, 1942, on conversion of the 223rd Indep. Inf. Bde. to the 3rd Parachute Bde.

On arrival of the 1st Canadian Para. Bn., the 7th Bn. joined the new 5th Parachute Bde. on 8th August, 1943. After service in Java, the Battalion joined the 6th Abn. Div. in Palestine in the 1st and then 2nd Para. Bdes.

In July, 1948 in Germany, the Battalion reformed as the new 3rd Parachute Battalion, losing its distinctive light infantry green diamond backing to the beret badge, but retaining its light infantry green lanyard. It later adopted a light infantry green Drop-Zone flash on the smock, worn on square.

12th (Yorkshire) Parachute Battalion

Commanding Officers
- 1943 Lt-Colonel R. G. Parker
- 1944 Lt-Colonel Ap. P. Johnson, D.S.O. *(K.I.A. 6/44)*
- 1944 Colonel R. G. Parker *(temp 6/44)*
- 1944 Lt-Colonel W. A. B. Harris, M.C. *(W.D. 8/44)*
- 1944 Lt-Colonel N. G. Stockwell
- 1945 Lt-Colonel K. T. Darling, D.S.O.

Formed from the 10th Bn., Green Howards in June, 1943, and fought with distinction through D-Day being severely depleted. Also took part in the Ardennes & Rhine Crossing. The Battalion was then sent to Java, and on its return in 1946 was disbanded.

Insignia note—wore usual configuration, however for about three months in 1944 they wore an unoffical tab "Yorkshire" in maroon on light blue on the epaulette (BD106). Also a sky blue lanyard was worn.

13th (Lancashire) Parachute Battalion

Commanding Officer
1943   Lt-Colonel P. J. Luard, D.S.O.

Formed from the 2/4th Bn., South Lancashire Regiment in June, 1943, and served in the Brigade throughout its airborne career, with the same C.O.— known unofficially as 13th (Luard's Own). It was disbanded on its return from Java in 1946.

Insignia note—wore a black lanyard.

6TH AIR-LANDING BRIGADE

The Brigade was formed on the 6th May, 1943, as part of the newly raised 6th Airborne Division.

Commanding Officers
14th May, 1943	Col. A. M. Toye *(actg)*
24th May, 1943	Brig. Hon. H. K. M. Kindersley *(W.D. 12.6.44)*
12th Jun, 1944	Col. R. G. Parker
15th Jun, 1944	Brig. E. W. Flavell, D.S.O., M.C.
19th Jan, 1945	Brig. R. H. Bellamy, D.S.O.
21st Oct, 1945	Brig. R. H. Bower, C.B.E.

Unit Composition
2nd Oxford & Bucks.	5.43 – 4.46
1st Ryl. Ulster Rif.	5.43 – 4.46
12th Devons.	7.43 – 6.45
2nd Gordon Highrs.	6.45 – 9.45
1st Argyll & Sthd.	9.45 – 4.46

Theatres of War
United Kingdom	6.5.43 – 6.6.44	
N. W. Europe	6.6.44 – 3.9.44	Normandy
United Kingdom	4.9.44 – 23.12.44	
N. W. Europe	24.12.44 – 24.2.45	Ardennes
United Kingdom	24.2.45 – 24.3.45	
N. W. Europe	24.3.45 – 18.5.45	Rhine to Baltic
United Kingdom	18.5.45 – 29.9.45	
At Sea	2.10.45 – 10.10.45	
Palestine	10.10.45 – 14.4.46	

Reverted to Infantry role—31st Indep. Inf. Bde.
31st Bde. disbanded in November, 1946.
2nd Oxford & Bucks to 3rd Inf. Bde.
1st Ryl. Ulster Rif. to Austria
1st Argyll & Sthd. to 8th Inf. Bde.

6th Air-Landing Brigade

2nd Btn., Oxford & Bucks. Light Infantry

Commanding Officers
1939	Lt-Colonel R. J. Brett, D.S.O.
1940	Lt-Colonel L. W. Giles, M.C.
1942	Lt-Colonel T. G. D. Rowley
1943	Lt-Colonel M. W. Roberts, D.S.O.
1944	Lt-Colonel M. Darrell-Brown, D.S.O.
1946	Lt-Colonel H. H. Van Straubenzee, D.S.O.
1946	Lt-Colonel C. L. C. Ward

Brief History
The Battalion's Airborne career started in December, 1941 when the 31st Independent Infantry Brigade became the 1st Air-Landing Brigade. It remained in the U.K. to form a glider-borne battalion of the new 6th Air-Landing Brigade in May, 1943.

It fought on D-Day, being involved in the capture of the Orne and Caen bridges, and the fighting afterwards. It then returned home in September, 1944 only to be recalled for the heavy fighting in the Ardennes from December to February. In March it was involved in the crossing of the Rhine and the advance to the Baltic coast. It returned to the U.K. on the 18th May, 1945. Then to Palestine.

Insignia
The beret badge consisted of a small silver bugle-horn worn on a circular patch of light infantry green, and worn on the Airborne Red Beret.

At first like quite a few other units, it wore unofficial titles. Between 1941 and 1943 it wore "FIFTY-SECOND" in buff, edged red on a blue field. Then in the spring of 1943, regimental titles were forbidden, and official ones were issued. These were unimaginative and standard white letters on red title was issued to all infantry regiments, save for the Rifles, who retained their own colourings. The Battalion then wore "OXF. & BUCKS." shoulder titles white on red. Some members wore "OXFORD & BUCKS. L.I." yellow on dark green on walking out dress. This pattern was adopted for all Battalions, Regular &

Territorial after the war.

Since they were glider-borne unit they wore the standard Pegasus arm flash, with "AIRBORNE" on a straight tab beneath. Also on the lower right forearm, the glider badge in blue thread on khaki. A L.I. Green lanyard was also worn.

1st Btn., Royal Ulster Rifles

Commanding Officers
    1939   Lt-Colonel G. Brunskill, MC
    1941   Lt-Colonel R. J. R. Campbell
    1943   Lt-Colonel R.J. H. Carson
    1945   Lt-Colonel G. P. Rickcord, DSO
    1946   Lt-Colonel R. J. R. Campbell

Brief History
Like the 2nd Oxf. & Bucks., the Ulsters were part of the 1st Air-Landing Bde., but when the Bde. left for North Africa, it remained to become a Battalion of the 6th Air-Landing Bde.

It was in the second lift on D-Day, and captured Longueval. It fought in the Ardennes, and from the Rhine to the Baltic in May, 1945. Then it went to Palestine.

Insignia
Its beret badge was the white-metal Harp, topped with the King's Crown, and the motto "QUIS SEPARABIT" (Who shall separate us?) below on a rectangle of rifle green. An early pattern worn on a rifle green circular patch was the Harp & K/C with a scroll across the middle "ROYAL ULSTER RIFLES" (BD23), by Officers and N.C.O.'s.

Their shoulder title was dark rifle green, with black lettering "ROYAL ULSTER RIFLES", though for a time in Palestine a light blue on dark blue title was worn, in 1946 by the **2nd Bn.**, which was under control of 6th Abn. Div. Brian Davis shows on Pages 23 & 105, examples possibly of this title, which would date it earlier, and make it an unofficial issue. (Also ABF).

They wore the glider badge on the lower right forearm, and Pegasus arm flashes, with "AIRBORNE" tab beneath on both arms. Epaulette flashes were also worn by Rifle Companies, 'A' Red, 'B' Yellow, 'C' Blue and 'D' Maroon.

12th Btn., Devonshire Regiment

Commanding Officers
    1939   Lt-Colonel R. A. O. Smith, M.C.

1941   Lt-Colonel R. G. Coates
1942   Lt-Colonel D. D. Rutherford, M.C.
1943   Lt-Colonel R. F. B. Hill *(until November)*
1943   Lt-Colonel G.R. Stevens
1944   Lt-Colonel P. Gleadell, D.S.O. *(August-June, 1945)*
1945   Lt-Colonel A. Tilly

Brief History

At the start of the war, it was known as the 50th Battalion, formed from 12th (Holding) Battalion and members from the Depot, and was responsible for the training of recruits to the Regiment.

In the autumn of 1940, it manned the beach defences at Dawlish and then at Budleigh Salterton. Then in September, 1942, as part of the 214th Infantry Brigade, it moved to the Isle of Wight in a similar role. It returned in May of 1943 to Truro with the rest of the Brigade.

In July, it became part of the 6th Air-Landing Brigade and moved to Bulford, where it trained in its new role, becoming officially part of the Brigade in the October.

It fought on D-Day, the Ardennes and finally in the Rhine Crossing in 1945, and returned with the rest of the Brigade to the U.K. on 18th May, 1945. At Bulford, it trained for the invasion of Japan, but this was cancelled, and at the end of the war, the Battalion was disbanded.

Its place in the 6th Air-Landing Brigade being taken by the 1st Battalion, the Argyll & Sutherland Highlanders, on going to Palestine.

Insignia

The beret badge was a w/m castle, (representing Exeter castle), above a straight scroll "SEMPER FIDELIS" (Ever Faithful), inside a brass circle bearing the full title, surmounted by a King's Crown, all upon a w/m eight pointed star.

Their shoulder title was "DEVON" white on red.

They wore the blue glider on a khaki oval, and the usual Pegasus and tab.

A green and red lanyard was purported to have been worn.

6th Airborne Division Support Units

6th Abn. Div. Armd. Recce Regt., R.A.C.

On the 17th August, 1942 the Airborne Light Tank Squadron was formed from volunteers of the Royal Tank Regiment. They trained in the Tetrarch Airborne Tank, carried in the large Hamilcar glider. On the 26th May, 1943, it joined the 6th Airborne Division as the 1st Airborne Light Tank Squadron. On the 14th January, 1944 it became the 6th Abn. Div. Armoured Recce Regiment, its number being increased by volunteers from the 2nd Dragoon Guards, 9th Lancers and 10th Royal Hussars. It landed on D-Day and provided infantry support, though the Tetrarch's were soon put out of action due to battlefield debris. It was present at the Rhine Crossing using the American Locust tanks.

Insignia

It is possible that they wore the beret badge of their particular Regiment, (or the Recce Corps. badge).

The Royal Tank Regiment's badge was a World War 1 tank moving to the wearer's right in a laurel wreath, topped by K/C and the motto "FEAR NAUGHT" at the base all in w/m. This was worn on the Regiment's black beret.

The 2nd Dragoon Guards wore a laurel wreath in the centre of which was the word "BAYS" topped by a K/C in brass.

The 9th Lancers wore a w/m badge of crossed lances topped by a K/C, the numeral "9" at the intersection with "LANCERS" on a scroll at the base.

The 10th Hussars wore the w/m Prince of Wales's feathers and motto, brass coronet above a brass title scroll "10TH ROYAL HUSSARS".

The cavalry wore their badges on the maroon beret and own titles above the Pegasus arm badge, sometimes with Airborne tab.

An unofficial should title was worn in the early days—"Light Tank Squadron" in yellow on khaki.

Royal Regiment of Artillery

Insignia—as for usual Artillery units

2nd Air-Landing Anti-Tank Regiment

Commanding Officers
1945   Lt-Colonel F. E. Allday
1945   Lt-Colonel R. A. Gorle, M.C.

This unit was formed on the 24th February, 1945 and comprised :
3rd Air-Landing Anti-Tank Battery
4th Air-Landing Anti-Tank Battery

On 1st April, 1947, the Regiment was renumbered as 66 Abn. A/Tk. Regt., and comprised numbers 9, 332, 336 and 29 Abn. A/Tk. Batteries.

3rd Air-Landing Anti-Tank Battery
Formed on the 9th July, 1943, and equipped with 6 Pdr. and a few 17 Pdr. anti-tank guns, the latter being carried in Hamilcars on D-Day. It served as Div. Trps. through its career, becoming a Battery of the above Regiment on the 24th February 1945.

4th Air-Landing Anti-Tank Battery
Also formed on the 9th July, 1943, came in by sea on D-Day and served in the other actions in which the Division participated. Becoming part of the 2nd A/Lng. Atk. Regiment in 1945.

53rd Air-Landing Light Regiment

Commanding Officers
1943   Lt-Colonel A. D. M. Teacher
1945   Lt-Colonel R. A. Eden, D.S.O.

The 53rd (Worcestershire Yeo.) Anti-Tank Regiment became Airborne on the 27th October, 1943, taking up its new title on the 3rd November, 1943, when its armament was changed to 75mm Howitzers.
It comprised three batteries – 210, 211 and 212. Its 211 bty. landed by glider on D-Day. The Regiment served in all the principal battles with the Division and went to Palestine in 1945.

2nd Air-Landing Lt. A-A Battery

This unit was raised on the 25th May, 1943, and disbanded on the 20th February, 1944. The battery was commanded by Major W. A. H. Rowatt.

No. 2 Forward Oserver Unit

This unit was formed in August, 1944, near Salisbury, from the Observation Parties, who had returned from France, after ranging the Navy's gun on D-Day.
The observers had been of two types—the F.O.O.'s: Forward Observing

Officers from the 3rd Infantry Div., with parachutist signallers, and the F.O.B.'s: Forward Observers Bombardment which were parachute trained R.A. officers and parachute trained R.N. signallers.

The No. 2 F.O.U. was commanded by Major Rice, its establishment being 120 all ranks, of which about 30 were Captains. Half the unit was from the Canadian Artillery under Captain Orr.

It first went into action in the Ardennes, when it ranged the guns at Bure and then took part in the Rhine Crossing action.

Every O.P. Party had one Artillery Officer, a signaller and armed support, all were trained in Range-Finding and Fire Control and every Parachute and Air-Landing Battalion had an O.P. Party with them.

Corps of Royal Engineers

Insignia—as for usual Engineer units.

3rd Airborne Squadron

Joined the 6th Airborne Division from the 1st Abn. Div. on 7th June, 1943. On the 29th May, 1945 it became an Airborne Squadron and went with the 5th Parachute Brigade to India and Java in the July.

9th Airborne Squadron

Became a unit of the 6th Abn. Div. on the 1st June, 1945 and went to Palestine in 1945.

591st (Antrim) Parachute Squadron

It was formed out of the No. 1 Company, Antrim Fort Engineers and became the 591st Field Company on 12th October, 1940. On 21st May, 1943 it took the above title, and became an Airborne Squadron on 29th May, 1945 and placed in suspended animation on 1st March, 1946. It was reformed as a Field Squadron in 1947, severing its airborne connection.

249th Field Company (Airborne)

Was formed on the 7th June, 1943, and served with the Division until the end of the war, when some of its personnel joined the 286th Abn. Park Sqn.

286th Field Park Squadron (Airborne)

This unit was also formed on the 7th June, 1943, as the 286th (Abn.) Field park company. At the end of the war it was in Palestine with the Division as the 286th Airborne Park Squadron. A detachment left the Company and formed the **5th Indep. Para. Bde. Park Troop** which went to Java.

Royal Corps of Signals

6th Abn. Div. Sigs. was formed on the 7th May, 1943, and supported units at all levels throughout the war and in Palestine.

Insignia—as for the usual Signals units.

Royal Army Service Corps

The Divisional Support units were:
716th Light Composite Company + it s Parachute Platoon
63rd   Composite Company *(Abn.)*
398th Composite Company *(Abn.)*

Insignia—as for usual R.A.S.C. units.

Royal Army Medical Units

224th Parachute Field Ambulance

Commanding Officers
1942   Lt-Colonel D. H. Thompson *(P.O.W. 6/44)*
1944   Lt-Colonel A. D. Young, D.S.O. *(8/44-)*

Formed in December, 1942, on conversion of the 224th Field Ambulance, served in all the campaigns with 6th Abn. Division and went to Palestine with the Division in September, 1945.

Insignia Note—it wore unofficial "PARACHUTE R.A.M.C." in white on maroon for a short while, then adopted usual pattern.

225th Parachute Field Ambulance

Commanding Officers
1943   Lt-Colonel E. I. B. Harvey, D.S.O.
1945   Lt-Colonel N. J. P. Hewlings, D.S.O.
1945   Lt-Colonel J. C. Watts, M.C. *(July on)*

Formed on the 7th July, 1943, at Castle Cary from the 225th Guards Light Field Ambulance, itself having been formed in September, 1940 from the detachment of 128th Field Ambulance at Reading.

It served in all the battles with the Division, and then went with the 5th Para. Bde. to India, Java, and was disbanded in 1946 in Palestine. Its personnel being transferred to the remaining Field Ambulances of the Abn. Div.

Insignia Note—for a short time it wore "AMBULANCE" in light blue on maroon, (Victory Club, Cheltenham), before adopting the normal configuration, with "AIRBORNE" tab.

195th Air-Landing Field Ambulance

Commanding Officers
1943   Lt-Colonel W. M. E. Anderson
1945   Lt-Colonel S. Smith

Formed on 1st October, 1943, on conversion of the 195th Field Ambulance. Served with the 6th Abn. Div. throughout the war and then in Palestine. In May, 1946, on disbandment of the 6th A/Lng. Bde., the A.F.A. was retrained as a Para. Fld. Ambulance, attached to 1st Para. Bde.

Royal Army Ordnance Corps

Basic information as per 1st Abn. Div., though for a short period, the Sections wore a shoulder title "Ordnance Field Park" in yellow on dark blue, before adopting the usual configuration. (A.B.F.).

Royal Electrical & Mechanical Engineers

Insignia—as per 1st Division.

Units
6th Abn. Div. Workshops—in 1948 became 1st-3rd Abn. Wkshps.
A/Lng. Light Aid Detachments, numbered 7-12th. In Palestine joined by 4th (2nd Para. Bde.) and 1st (1st Para. Bde).

Corps of Military Police

Insignia—as per 1st Division

6th Abn. Div. Provost Company.

Royal Army Pay Corps

Insignia—as per 1st Division

16th Field Cash Office (Light)

Intelligence Corps

317th Abn. Field Security Section

Formed in June, 1943 in the U.K. Following service in N.W. Europe and Palestine, it returned home and was disbanded in July, 1948.

Commanding Officers
 1943   Captain D. Loudon *(then to H.Q., 6th Abn. Div.)*
 1944   Captain MacMillan *(W.D. on D-Day)*
 1944   Lieut. Rogers *(8/44 – 5/45)*
 1945   Captain Fraser *(until 7/48)*

Insignia—as per 1st Abn. Division.

Army Physical Training Corps

Army Catering Corps

Insignia—as per 1st Division

Royal Army Chaplains Department

22nd Independent Parachute Company

Formed in October, 1943, on the same lines as its 1st Abn. Div. counterpart. Following action as Pathfinders on D-Day, it was severely depleted, losing virtually all its Officers by 8/44. It returned home to U.K. for retraining and took part in the Rhine Crossings, and then went with 5th Para. Bde. to Java. On its arrival in Palestine, its members were absorbed by the Para. Bns.

Its first C.O. was Major F. G. Lennox-Boyd, Ryl. Scots. Greys who was killed 6.6.44.

In several books it is attributed that shoulder-titles of "PARACHUTE" with "XX11" in light blue on maroon were worn on walking-out battledress,

224

but I have not been able to trace any confirmation that this was so.

Mention must be made of several units connected with Abn. Forces.

Naval Bombardment Personnel

The naval personnel, who became part of the F.O.U.s wore either their Rank badges, or the naval anchor badge on the beret, with "ROYAL NAVY" titles white on dark-blue/black, woven or printed. With parachute wings, and sometimes the "Pegasus" flash.

Auxiliary Territorial Service

This women's unit formed in 1938, provided clerical staff, drivers, etc., and those who served at Training establishments, connected with the Airborne Divisions and S.A.S. Brigade wore the A.T.S. badge—brass wreath, A.T.S. in centre, topped by K/C, on the maroon beret, and "PEGASUS" flashes on both arms. Sometimes a Parachutist Regiment collar badge was worn on the left breast pocket.

Army Film & Photographic Service

All the Airborne Formations had cameramen with them, most having served in ranks as parachutists, and volunteered, and trained as cameramen, serving in every theatre, and capturing dramatic action such as the Normandy landings and Arnhem. The badge of the A.F.P. Units was the letters "A.F.P.U." in red on a black background, with a camera on a tripod in white in the middle (BD202).

Appendix 13/4

Composition of 44th Indian Airborne Division

I decided to include the above Division, since it did include British personnel. Although this reference work deals with the British Army Air Corps and its Support Units, I did not wish to decry the heroic achievements of this Division, and its predecessors—General Orde Wingate's Special Force or Chindits. It is hoped to cover this in a later work.

October, 1941	50th Indian Parachute Brigade formed
December, 1944	Indian parachute Regiment formed
	44th INDIAN AIRBORNE DIVISION starts to form
February, 1945	77th Indian Parachute Brigade formed from volunteers from the Chindit Special Force
November, 1945	44th Indian Airborne Division renumbered 2nd
October, 1946	Indian Parachute Regiment disbanded
November, 1946	British Parachute Battalions disbanded
August, 1947	Partition of India & Pakistan, Division's units split between the two countries.

44th Indian Airborne Division
formed at Secunderabad, under Major-General E. E. Down, C.B.E.

50th Indian Parachute Brigade

151st (British) Para. Bn.—to Africa, 1942, and became 156th Bn.
152nd (Indian) Para. Bn.—became 1st Bn., India Para. Regt.
153rd (Gurkha) Para. Bn.—became 2nd Bn. India Para. Regt.
154th (Gurkha) Para. Bn.—to 77th Bde., raised from 3/7th G. Rifs.
　　　　　　　　　　　　1944—plus new 4th Bn., India Para. Regt.
50th　　　　Para. Bde. Signal Section
411th　　　(Royal Bombay) Para. Section, Indian Engineers
80th　　　　(Indian) Parachute Field Ambulance, I.A.M.C.

77th Indian Parachute Brigade
154th (Gurkha) Para. Bn.—became 3rd Bn., India Para. Regt.
15th (British) Para. Bn.—formed 2/45 from 1st Bn., King's Liverpool Regt. Disbanded 11/46.
16th (British)　Para. Bn.—formed 3/45 from 1st Bn., South Staffordshire Regt. Disbanded 11/46

14th Air-Landing Brigade

2nd	King's Own Regt—11/44 - 4/45	
2nd	Black Watch	
4/6th	Rajputana Rifs.	
6/16th	Punjab Regt.—from 4/45	

44th Airborne Division Recce Regiment, I.A.C.

44th Airborne Division Pathfinder Company— formed from Special Para. Coy., Chindits.

123rd Para. Fld. Regt., R.A.—283, 284, 488 Btys.— formed 1/45 on redesig. of 123 Fld. Regt., disbands in 1946.

159th Para. Lt. Regt., R.A. —553, 554, 555 Btys.— formed 1/45 on redesig. of 159 Fld. Regt. Sent to 6th Abn. Div. in Palestine late 1946, disb. 12/48.

23rd Para. L.A.A./Atk. Regt.—73, 74, 130 Btys.— formed 2/45 on conversion of 23rd L.A.A. Regt. Retitled 158th Para. Fld. Regt., and disbanded 1947.

44th Divisional Engineers—12th Para. Sqn.

44th Divisonal Signals

44th Divisional Supply Sections, R.I.A.S.C.

7th (British) Parachute Field Ambulance

60th (Indian) Parachute Field Ambulance

Field Hygiene Section

44th Divisional Ordnance & I.E.M.E. Workshop Sections

44th Divisional Provost Company

595th Para. Security Section, Int. Corps.—15.5.45 - 11.46, Indian I.C. personnel took over complete control.

Insignia Note

In the main bush-hats seemed to have been worn in combat situations in the normal manner, and the red beret when in camp. When the Indian Parachute Regiment was formed in 1944, an adapted British Parachute Regiment beret badge was worn by **all** four Battalion. The badge was in cast brass with a tablet across the parachute bearing the word "INDIA". The two British Para. Bns. wore the normal w/m beret badge.

The Pegasus with the word "INDIA" in front of the back legs was worn on both arms, in printed format. Woven examples do exist, but are believed to be reproduction. Genuine local examples in heavy maroon felt, with the details picked out in silver wire for walking out dress also exist. These flashes were sewn or had a press-stud on each corner for fixing to the tunic.

The members of the Division had their own style of parachute wing in the standard colours, and worn on the right sleeve of the walking-out uniform —early tropical dress, and above the right breast pocket on the K.D. shirt.

The 153rd Bn. prior to 1944 wore a rectangular patch in sky blue, on which was a white parachute, and two white kukris.

The 154th Bn. prior to 1944 wore a similar badge, but on dark rifle green, and the blades were upswept.

Section 14

Bibliography

There are now, quite a number of books on the Airborne 1940 on, and those listed below I found to be of interest, many of these have their own bibliographies, which can lead to aquiring a large library on Airborne aspects.

G. Chatterton	"The Wings of Pegasus" (G.P.R.)	(MacDonald 1962)
H. N. Cole	"On Wings of Healing"	(Abn. Medics) (Blackwood 1963)
N. Crookenden	"Airborne at War"	(Ian Allan 1978)
V. Dover	"The Silken Canopy"	(Cassell 1979)
J. Fairley	"Remember Arnhem"	(1st A/Lng. Recce. Sqn.) (Pegasus Journal 1978)
G. G. Norton	"The Red Devils"	(Leo Cooper 1971)
R. Kent	"First In—Para Pathfinder Company"	(Batsford 1979)
H. St. G.Saunders	"The Red Beret"	(M. Joseph 1950)
R. Seth	"Lion With Blue Wings"	(G.P.R.) (Gollancz 1955)
R. E. Urquhart	"Arnhem"	(Cassell 1958)
R. D. Wilson	"Cordon & Search—6th Abn. Div. in Palestine"	(Gale & Polden 1949)
	The London Gazette 1940–48	
	HMSO Order of Battle 1939–45	
B. L. Davis	"British Army Uniforms & Insignia of World War Two"	(Arms & Armour 1983)

Hancock, E., 135
Hancock, R. T., 169
Hand, J., 130
Hardie, E., 27
Harding, E. J., 140
Harding, H. T., 49
Harding, P. G., 143
Hardy, J. S. D., 97
Hardy, W., 68
Hargreaves, R. S., 48
Harman, A., 123
Harrington, E., 69
Harris, E., 23
Harris, E. R., 123
Harris, S., 136
Harrison, C. A., 99
Harrison, G. A. V., 169
Hart, S. K., 123
Hartley, A. D., 49
Harvey, E. I. B., 71, 146
Harwood, G., 131
Hawkins, F. C., 123
Hawkins, J. A. S., 51
Hawthorne, R., 130
Haydon, S. J., 50
Hayes, C. W., 102
Hayhow, -., 25
Hayman, L. G., 121
Heaps, L. J., 93
Helingoe, J. E., 108
Hendon, S., 121
Herbert, W. C., 73
Herford, M. E. M., 100
Hetherington, J. P., 24
Hewetson, G., 135, 167
Hewitt, E., 95
Hewitt, E. N., 27
Hewitt, F. G., 170
Hewlings, N. J. P., 141
Hibbert, J. A., 93
Hicks, P. H. W., 97
Hill, S. J. L., 21, 63, 135, 143

Hindley, D. R., 100
Hines, C., 169
Hinman, R., 136
Hobbs, P. A., 131
Hobson, E., 67
Hodge, F. V., 42
Hodgson, W. F., 64
Hogge, A. M. L., 169
Holburn, A. R., 97
Holden, J. S., 121
Holderness, G. E., 50
Hollis, D. J., 136
Holloway, E. J., 96
Holman, M. R., 109
Holmes, G., 101
Holmes, J. A., 65
Holt, B. R., 137
Holt, E., 98
Holt, J., 27
Hooper, C. A., 67
Hooper, I. E., 141
Hooper, J. H., 138
Hope, E., 133
Horrell, E. A., 140
Horton, S. J., 133
Horwood, B. F., 69
Hose, A. J., 136
Houghton, H., 133, 141
Houghton, H. R., 94
Houghton, T. G. W., 68
Howard, J., 121
Howard, R. A., 73
Howard, R. J., 67, 68
Howe, J., 140
Howells, H., 22
Howes, D. J. V., 171
Hoyer-Miller, F. K., 93
Hughes, H., 139
Hughes, J. H., 117
Hughes, J. L., 131
Hughes, O. G., 108
Hughes, S., 65

238

Westripp, W. G. A., 23
Westwood, W., 23
Wethey, A. B., 138
Weymouth, B., 146
Wheatley, P. R., 4
Wheatley, W., 99
Whimster, W. S., 99
White, F. H., 40
White, R. E., 73
White, W. H. J., 41
Wiggs, F. J., 123
Wilkes, J. D., 50
Wilkinson, -., 132
Wilkinson, P. W., 51
Wilkinson, T. H., 24
Willetts, D. W., 118
Williams, J. L., 117, 123
Williams, J. Ll., 92
Williamson, F., 93
Williamson, J. H. H., 123
Willis, M. D., 49
Wilmott, H., 117, 119
Wilson, B. A., 49, 95
Wilson, D. F., 23
Wilson, R. D., 166
Wilson, R. McE., 139
Wilson, S., 136
Wilson, T. F., 42
Wilson, W., 71
Winchester, J. C., 100
Winter, F. A., 168
Wright, F. G., 24
Winter, V. N., 42
Wishart, C., 150
Withers, L., 37
Wood, P. W., 135
Wood, R., 120
Woodgate, J. T., 66
Woodman, E. G., 135
Wright, D., 26, 110
Wright, F., 25, 41
Wright, F. G., 24

Wright, L., 138
Wyss, E. M., 98

Yates, N., 120
Yeldham, E. C., 25
York, G. E., 50
Young, A. D., 71, 170
Young, G., 169
Young, P. A., 11
Young, P. G. F., 166
Young, W. A., 119